Intelligence for Peace

The Role of Intelligence in Times of Peace

Edited by

HESI CARMEL

FRANK CASS
LONDON • PORTLAND, OR

First published in 1999 in Great Britain by
FRANK CASS PUBLISHERS
Newbury House, 900 Eastern Avenue
London, IG2 7HH

and in the United States of America by
FRANK CASS PUBLISHERS
c/o ISBS, 5804 N.E. Hassalo Street
Portland, Oregon, 97213-3644

Website: www.frankcass.com

Copyright of collection © 1999 Frank Cass & Co. Ltd
Copyright of chapters © 1999 contributors

British Library Cataloguing in Publication Data

Intelligence for peace: the role of intelligence in times
of peace. – (Cass series. Studies in intelligence)
1. Israel. Sherut ha-bitahon ha-kelali 2. Intelligence
service 3. Intelligence service – Middle East – History
I. Carmel, Hesi
327.1'2

ISBN 0-7146-4950-3 (cloth) ✓
ISBN 0-7146-8009-5 (paper)
ISSN 1368-9916

Library of Congress Cataloging-in-Publication Data

Intelligence for peace: the role of intelligence in times of peace /
edited by Hesi Carmel.
   p.   cm. – (Cass series. Studies in Intelligence)
   Includes bibliographical references.
   ISBN 0-7146-4950-3 (cloth). – ISBN 0-7146-8009-5 (paper)
   1. Intelligence service. 2. Intelligence service – Israel.
I. Karmel, Ḥazi. II. Series.
JF1525. I6I577 1999
327.12–dc21

99-21115
CIP

Typeset by Vitaset, Paddock Wood, Kent
Printed in Great Britain by
MPG Books Ltd, Bodmin, Cornwall

CASS SERIES: STUDIES IN INTELLIGENCE

(Series Editors: Christopher Andrew, Michael I. Handel, Wesley K. Wark and Richard J. Aldrich)
ISSN: 1368-9916

INTELLIGENCE FOR PEACE

This volume is the fourth in the Reuven Shiloah Series for Intelligence and Security. It appears under the auspices of the Center for Special Studies (CSS). The CSS is a non-profit association of veterans of the Israeli intelligence community.

Also in the Studies in Intelligence series

Contents

Part Three: Intelligence for Peace in Global Strategy

List of Abbreviations and Glossary

CIA	Central Intelligence Agency (United States)
dhimm	Status of non-Muslim in Islamic country
FBI	Federal Bureau of Investigation (United States)
FIS	Front Islamique du Salut
FLN	National Liberation Front (Algerian): the main Algerian resistance organization which fought against the French in Algeria's struggle for independence. After independence it was, for many years, the main and ruling Algerian political party
GSS	General Security Service (Israeli)
Hagannah	Official security arm of the Yishuv
Hamas	Fundamentalist and extremist Muslim organization, originally set up by Israel as a foil against the PLO and now a militant terrorist organization totally opposed to the Peace-Process (based primarily in Gaza)
Histadrut	General Federation of Labour: official employer of Reuven Shiloah
HUMINT	Human Intelligence
IDF	Israel Defence Forces
intifada	Uprising (Arabic): civil disturbance in the West Bank and Gaza that began in 1987
ISLD	Code name of MI9 in the Middle East
IVI	Indicator of Vital Information: the definition of objectives in intelligence work; also EEI – Essential Elements of Information
IZL	(Irgun Zeva'i Leumi) National Military Organization (Israeli): led at one time by Menachem Begin
jihad	Holy War
Knesset	Israeli Parliament
LEHI	(Lohamei Herut Yisrael) Israel Freedom Fighters: extreme right-wing underground organization

MI5	British Internal Security Service
MI6	British Secret Intelligence Service
MI9	Group for escape and evasion within British Military Intelligence
MK	Member of the Knesset
MO3	British staff department in charge of special military units such as Special Air Service (SAS) and others
MO4	Cover name for Special Operations Executive (SOE) of British Intelligence in Cairo
Mossad	(lit. 'institute') Institute for Intelligence and Special Operations (Israeli Secret Intelligence Service – ISIS)
NBC	Nuclear, biological and chemical
NILI	(Netzach Yisrael Lo Yeshakker): Jewish underground organization
NSA	National Security Agency (United States)
OSS	Office of Strategic Services (American)
Palmach	Plugot Mahatz: elite infantry unit of the Hagannah
Palmach Arab Platoon	Intelligence-gathering unit of the Palmach
PLO	Palestine Liberation Organization
POW	Prisoner of War
SAS	Special Air Service (British)
SBR	Russian Foreign Intelligence
SHAI	Sherut Yediot (lit. 'information service'): intelligence service (Israeli)
Shari'a	Sacred law of Islam
SID	The precursor of SISMI (Italian). Since the Second World War the Italian intelligence community underwent very many changes
SigInt	Signals Intelligence
SISMI	(Servicio Informazione e Secureza Militare): the main Italian intelligence and security service
SOE	Special Operations Executive (British)
SOM	Special Operations Mediterranean (British)
SSO	Secret Service (British)
Territories	The abbreviated common-parlance term for the West Bank and Gaza, or 'The Occupied Territories'
ulema	Moslem men of religion
UN	United Nations
Yishuv	Jewish community in Palestine, before the State of Israel came into being
UAV	Unmanned Aerial Vehicle

Introduction

HESI CARMEL

The collapse of the Soviet Empire, the fall of the Berlin Wall, the continuation of the process of conciliation between Israeli and Arabs, and the consistent efforts being made to solve military confrontations by peaceful means in almost every region in the world, raise the issue of intelligence, both tactical and strategic, in times of peace. Is intelligence, like military prowess, something for which the time has passed or, perhaps, as some security and intelligence experts claim, intelligence plays an important role in the peace processes and in the creation of a defensive shield over the peace itself and its makers. The contribution of Israeli Intelligence to the peace process and the peace agreements with Egypt and Jordan, as well as to the secret contacts with Arab leaders, is already indelibly engraved in the chronicles of our time.

Peace, like war, demands a wide-ranging and ongoing intelligence effort, and the term 'Intelligence for Peace' is a clear expression of the contents of this collection, which deals with this topic and with the new areas of responsibility for intelligence at a time of global rapprochement.

This is the first anthology that is being published in the Shiloah Series on Intelligence and Security, a series that bears the name of the first head of the Mossad, Reuven Shiloah, and which will be publishing additional books and research papers on issues relating to intelligence and security.

In this collection, *Intelligence for Peace*, some of the most eminent researchers in the field have come together, experts in intelligence and security, former heads of the Mossad, the GSS (General Security Service), and the IDF Military Intelligence Branch, as well as heads of the CIA, Italian Intelligence, senior IDF officers and intelligence operatives.

This book is divided into three parts. Part One is devoted to the intelligence activities of the first head of the Israeli Mossad, Reuven Shiloah (after whom this series on Intelligence and Security is named). There are four chapters in this section: Reuven Shiloah, a biographical sketch by Haggai Eshed; Reuven Shiloah's contribution to Israeli Intelligence by historian Yoav Gelber, a leading expert in the history of the State of Israel; Shiloah and his contacts with British Intelligence, by researcher Eldad Harouvi; and an analysis of a little-known story which is a classic model of the role intelligence should play in secret contacts for peace: Shiloah's attempt to arrange, with the help of the CIA, a secret meeting between President Nasser of Egypt and Prime Minister Sharett of Israel, as told by Hesi Carmel.

Part Two comprises chapters by intelligence experts who have dealt with the issue of the role of Israeli Intelligence in the Middle East peace process. In an article on this issue, Major-General (retired) Shlomo Gazit, former head of Military Intelligence and the first Coordinator of Israeli activities in the West Bank and Gaza, analyses the actions of Israeli Intelligence in peacetime, from Sadat's visit to Jerusalem in 1977 up until the present day.

Later in this section, Aluf Hareven, a former high-ranking intelligence officer and today a senior researcher on issues relating to strategic processes, deals with the general philosophy of intelligence in peacetime, and its particular adaptation to intelligence activities in Israel. 'Colonel Shmuel', a senior Israeli Intelligence officer, investigates the role of intelligence research in the Israeli–Arab peace process, with numerous examples from various stages of the process itself.

Dr David Kimche, former deputy head of the Mossad, and former Director-General of the Foreign Ministry, who has published many books and research papers on the Israeli–Arab conflict, looks into the extent of covert diplomacy in the Israeli–Arab peace process. The former head of the GSS, Carmi Gillon, analyses the connection between peace at home and peace with our neighbours, and claims, as he states in the title of his paper: that peace at home takes precedence over peace among neighbours.

At a slight remove from the pressing concerns of the peace process, Israel's current head of the Mossad, Efraim Halevy, who was one of the central figures in the peace agreement with Jordan, deals with an issue that has personal connotations for himself: the right of deniability and the obligation to loyalty on the part of the country's leaders *vis-à-vis* intelligence personnel.

In Part Three we have a number of chapters dealing with the role of intelligence in times of world peace. R. James Woolsey, head of the CIA during the last days of the Soviet Union, analyses the agency's tasks in the aftermath of the Cold War, while Admiral Martini, who served as the head of the Italian Military Intelligence Service and coordinator of intelligence activities in Italy, examines the relations between intelligence, security and peace processes. Historian Emmanuel Sivan, an expert on Middle Eastern affairs, deals in his article with intelligence and the monitoring of the enemies of peace, with particular reference to the manifestations of radical Islam and its world-wide influence. A former senior Iranian Government official during the time of the Shah (whose article is published anonymously for obvious reasons) warns of the dangers to world peace emanating from the Islamic Republic of Iran – a warning that should be taken very seriously. A senior Israeli intelligence officer, with many years of experience in dealing with the Soviet Union and Russia, describes the Jewish aspect with respect to Russian intelligence.

Finally, there is a unique and fascinating account – made public here for the first time – by Major-General (retired) Me'ir Amit, former head of the Mossad, of secret contacts established in 1965 between himself and one of Egypt's top intelligence officers – contacts which led to Amit being invited to Cairo for a meeting with Nasser. Was this an opportunity for peace that was lost? Or a predictable blind alley? Whatever the answer, it is one of the most characteristic stories of the role intelligence can play – and indeed has played – in the Israeli–Arab peace process.

Part One

Reuven Shiloah, Pioneer of Secret Contacts

The Man and his Time*

HAGGAI ESHED

Reuven Shiloah was the remarkable product of a distinctive chapter in the history of Israel: a unique period of national regeneration that has vanished, never to return. At no other time in Jewish history, either before or after, could he have achieved what he did or become the man he was. He was *primus inter pares* – first among equals – in a group of 'operations executives', men who were neither policy-makers nor decision-makers, but undoubtedly much more than just 'senior government officials' as they would probably be called today. He was a central figure in the momentous transition from the era of the Jewish Agency, the Hagannah,[1] and the British Mandate – the period of the 'state-in-the-making' – to the era of statehood and a developing administrative and bureaucratic infrastructure. This was a time of difficult and often turbulent growing pains, of innovation, personal initiative and path-finding. It was a period marked by mistakes and mishaps, as well as flights of bold operational imagination. It was in this tumultuous period that the framework of the Israel Defence Forces (the IDF) was created, literally on the battlefield, and the machinery of national government was generated amid the administrative disarray left behind at the end of the British Mandate over Palestine. It was during this time, too, that the foundations were laid for the Jewish state's civilian and military intelligence services, a period of clandestine arms procurement and secret border crossings, of alliances forged despite the hostility of an Arab world still licking its wounds following its defeat in Israel's War of Independence – and refusing to accept the consequences.

It was a period shaped not by institutions but by people. In the absence of a formal administrative structure, every new instrument of government took on the contours of the people who created it, rather than the other way around as is usually the case. Reuven Shiloah was a prime example of this spirit – a man who became an institution in his own time.[2]

---

*From Haggai Eshed, *Reuven Shiloah – The Man Behind the Mossad*, trans. David and Leah Zinder (London: Frank Cass, 1997).

And yet, despite the unique role he played in this crucial era of Israeli history, somehow he was left behind as the bureaucracy of Israeli statehood developed. Most of his contemporaries and colleagues from this time of transition soon became ambassadors and directors-general of ministries – the backbone of the new establishment – while he remained forever the lone rider, galloping ahead of the rest until, ironically, he found himself languishing on his own in the rear. He was one of a band of like-minded men in the history of nations: fiercely devoted, farsighted individualists in the vanguard, ranging far to the fore, only to find themselves eventually choking in the dust of those they thought were behind them. He was the first to identify critical 'blind spots' in Israel's political and intelligence activities, and was equally farsighted in preparing the conceptual and operational tools to close these potentially dangerous gaps. However, his colleagues in the Foreign Ministry and in the Mossad – his own brainchild – proved more adept than he at taking advantage of the tools he developed. The new national leaders and up-and-coming bureaucrats had no compunction about exploiting his considerable abilities and innovative ideas, but neglected to keep him a place in their ranks. In part, of course, it was his own fault: he simply could not find his niche in the new national order. He was not offered an official appointment, and seemed to lack the determination required to take what was his due. These were tragic aspects of his character and destiny which he, in his own unique way, found a way to commute into tireless energy, and an endless, self-generating resourcefulness. He was possessed of a restless, highly creative mind that spawned ideas and sought solutions to problems at all hours of the day and night, even while reading a book or holding a private conversation. It was a non-stop cycle of activity, year-in, year-out, without a pause for either vacations or rest to relieve the tension: a chain of endeavours in the service of the state, that ultimately afforded him no satisfaction whatsoever – with his own achievements, with the extent of his colleagues' cooperation, or with political developments in the country.

Reuven Shiloah was an impressive man of considerable personal charisma. His was a troubling, urgent presence, at once annoying and provocative. Neither he nor his opinions could be easily dismissed by those who worked with him and knew him, and opinions about him were sharply divided between those who thought highly of him and others who made no effort to conceal their dislike for the man. Cloaked in mystery and radiating an aura of power, Shiloah was always deeply immersed in his work, responding to every call, mobilizing others when necessary, and, consequently, not easy to approach or befriend. He was a man who emerged from the shadows surrounding the two pillars of national authority in those days – David Ben Gurion and Moshe Sharett – both of whom shared, unequally, the power to make decisions on all matters of state, foreign affairs, security, and the multitude of other issues facing the Mapai party[3] and the national leadership.

They were the decision-makers, and Reuven Shiloah was constantly at their side. More than almost anyone else in those circles of the Jewish leadership in Palestine, he understood the complex relationship that bound Sharett and Ben Gurion, and knew how to negotiate the hazardous terrain that separated them – or so, at least, most political insiders at the time tended to believe, adding a great deal of clout to Shiloah's already charismatic status. He was the go-between for many of these two leaders' policy decisions and for much of the classified information they had at their disposal. It was generally believed that if there was anything of importance worth knowing, Shiloah knew about it long before anyone else. His well-known tendency to hold his cards close to his chest caused no little discomfort to people who worked with him, particularly those who did not share the secrets he was privy to. On the other hand, the aura of mystery surrounding his persona earned him high marks among foreign friends of Israel – British and American, Jew and non-Jew alike. All of them sought his company, treasured his penchant for long conversations deep into the night, admired his comprehensive grasp of the issues at hand, and deeply appreciated his proven loyalty to those he counted among his friends. British Intelligence reports from Cairo during the Second World War described him as 'Shertok's deputy' (later Sharett), while American friends of Israel at the time cited him as the man closest to Ben Gurion. This was the aura that accompanied him wherever he went.

A small, bespectacled man, Shiloah had grey-blue eyes and a clear, penetrating gaze. In a conversation with Abba Eban,[4] the former President of the State of Israel Haim Herzog once described the experience of coming under Shiloah's gaze 'as though he were examining you by X-ray'. A long diagonal scar on his right cheek, a reminder of shrapnel wounds incurred in the car-bomb explosion at the Jewish Agency building in Jerusalem in 1948, lent his persona a touch of mystery, the shadow of enigma, and a hint of covert missions.

In fact, this was a totally misleading impression. As a youth in the Jerusalem of the 1920s, he had taken classes at a local acting studio. Although he was not a born actor, over the years he learned how to add a measure of theatricality to everything he did. It was as if throughout his life he played a role in a tale of espionage among a cast of fellow actors, spinning a rich web of fanciful legends and tall tales. He became the butt of many jokes, like the one about the man who gets into a taxi and will not tell the driver where to go because his destination is 'Top Secret'. He was also jokingly accused of hiding important information from himself, even when there was nothing of any substance to hide.

Shiloah constantly sought ways of developing intelligence-sharing and strategic cooperation with friendly nations – first with the British and later with the Americans. From the time of the Arab Riots of the 1930s (which later developed into the so-called 'Arab Revolt'), he was among the prime movers behind a concept designed to combine the attainment of political and military power with a realization of the Zionist dream. The concept, which he tried to implement, with some variations, both before and after the establishment of the State, called for the development of operational cooperation with foreign allies on covert intelligence and espionage matters, carrying out 'special operations' deep in enemy territory, and seeking political allies in unexpected places. In this way, with the help of the well-connected Jewish communities around the world, Shiloah believed that the Jewish community of Palestine – and later Israel – could be turned into a major partner in international diplomacy and intelligence, a force that would have to be reckoned with and with whom it would be 'good to do business'. Was there a country in the world, he reasoned, where you couldn't find Israelis and Jews, all closely knit, with privileged access to a veritable treasure trove of information, with the added advantage of holding key public and private positions that enabled them to pull all the right strings? Was there a country in the world where Jews did not wield real or imagined power? If the State of Israel were to use these advantages wisely, Shiloah suggested, it could become a 'strategic asset', or a 'strategic partner' – a player on the field of intelligence with access to highly privileged information, and equipped with an almost limitless potential for gathering more. The Jewish community of Palestine, and later the State of Israel, could become an intelligence asset of the first order, that would be worth dealing with on a 'give and take' basis in this clandestine world, where diplomatic and strategic information is constantly being either discovered or generated virtually out of thin air. This was the world Reuven Shiloah moved in both before and after the State of Israel was created: a world where projections were made into the future alongside attempts to alter its course; a world of intelligence gathering and dissemination, of disinformation and strategic and political gambits played out daily for the greater benefit of the State of Israel.

He was 'Mister Intelligence', the first among the major functionaries of the Zionist movement and the state-in-the-making to declare outright, at the beginning of the Second World War, that the Jewish community in

Palestine and the Jewish state that would come into being in the future needed an intelligence service. Shiloah lost no time practising what he preached by going about setting up the Israeli intelligence apparatus as soon as he was given half a chance – directly after the establishment of the State.

'Intelligence' refers to both information-gathering and espionage, as well as to clandestine, top-secret 'special ops', aimed at pre-empting hostile actions by enemies and opponents, mostly on their own turf; operations for which no one is ever in a hurry to take responsibility, and which exist in the vague overlap between the preservation of law and order on the one hand and self-defence on the other, whenever issues of vital national security are at stake. This was particularly true of the time of 'the state-in-the-making', or when the issue was protecting and looking after the interests of the Jews of the diaspora. Given the development of Israeli history since 1948, it is hard to say whether Israel has not remained 'a state-in-the-making' even after its formal establishment as a national entity, still wrestling with the selfsame problems that Reuven Shiloah dealt with throughout his adult life. What is undoubtedly clear is that this was the case until 1959 – the year of his death.

Every nation has its own intelligence apparatus with its own distinctive mythology. It was the English who coined the term 'intelligence' in the image of their unique national temperament – a lifestyle and code of behaviour that was predominantly cerebral, based on the joining together of intelligence, insight, and a broad knowledge of the facts, and the ability to put all of these elements to discriminating use. Everything in this approach to life favours brain over brawn. To this one must add the romantic aspect of British Intelligence – the concept of a sporting contest or duel, where one mind is pitted against another, one gentleman against another, one professional against another. In these contests, when each side invents its own rules of the game in order to survive and accomplish its mission, victory is determined by the superior resourcefulness and ingenuity of a lone combatant operating in hostile territory. This is the archetypal formula of the myths surrounding British Intelligence, espionage, and counter-espionage, with their tales of the courageous yet despondent, intelligent yet frustrated loner who, more often than not, comes to a tragic end. Beyond this are other aspects of classic British Intelligence tales: the code of personal ethics and discipline, the well-oiled machinery of interdepartmental cooperation and clear-cut divisions of responsibilities and operational areas. It was no accident, however, that beyond this common basis of British Intelligence, different periods of history and different regional activities generated a veritable beehive of special services, each devoted to a different aspect of the intelligence world – to each English gentlemen his own special club.

The British created a vast empire from scratch and defended it almost effortlessly by the judicious application of the 'divide and rule' formula: setting up their enemies one against the other so that the balance of power could be maintained with a minimal use of force.

The Americans, for their part, created an intelligence apparatus that was in fact a massive industry for espionage and 'special ops' – a secret conglomerate serving the State Department and the Pentagon, working for the most part with them but sometimes also against them. However, unlike the English model of individual virtuosity, the American system was founded on the efficiency of the system, the 'Limited Liability Company for the Creation and Marketing of Special Services and Operations' – 'The Company' as the CIA is known. This is an organization that functions virtually as a state-within-a-state, either within the limits imposed on it by the state, or, at times, beyond the pale of the law and in direct opposition to Congressional decisions or to established policies decided upon by various government ministries. The CIA has even been known to operate at times without the President's – or his aides' – knowledge or approval. Senior officials do not always know – or do not know *exactly* – what this enormous, globe-spanning organization is doing for them or in their name. What the professionals of the CIA seem to be saying to the 'amateurs' voted into office by the people is that 'what's good for us is good for America and what's good for America is good for us, therefore you must give us your blind trust'. This is good enough until, from time to time, congressmen or other government officials decide to betray this brand of trust and look into the affairs of the CIA, where they usually uncover peccadilloes committed by one official or another. The official is duly tried and ultimately relieved of his or her duties. But time passes, and invariably someone picks up where his predecessor left off, using more or less the same methods – until his time comes to be caught red-handed and sent packing. And so the system lives on, this state-within-a-state, for-the-state, and even against-the-state, as long as the state is willing to grin and bear it.

During the Soviet regime in Russia, the intelligence apparatus was a 'state-above-the-state' with operational leeway far beyond mere 'intelligence' or 'special ops'. It was a frighteningly powerful, highly centralized and hier-archical organization, dealing in internal and external intelligence of every imaginable kind, zealously devoted to the requirements of 'national security' as it perceived it, and unquestioningly obedient wherever the struggle against so-called 'enemies of the state and the Revolution' was concerned. During the greater part of Russian history – perhaps even to this day – this was a truly limitless power base, overshadowing all other institutions of government and civic power, and deeply feared both inside the country and beyond its borders. It was the moving force behind the Soviets' race for an expanded military capability through the development of science, technology and industry. The pace at which these were developed leads one to believe that a major part of Soviet strength in all these areas could be attributed to their espionage capabilities, which could provide its leaders with virtually any information they needed. Most scientists around the world unwittingly worked for the KGB in one way or another, since the all-powerful organization had no trouble simply lifting the fruits of their labour at will. Espionage was conceivably the most important industry in the former Soviet Union.

Traces of all three of these models of intelligence services can be found in the Israeli machinery of government, from pre-state days to the present. The British influence from Mandatory times, for example, can be found mainly in the area of legal and public administration systems, many of which are still in place in present-day Israeli bureaucracy. The East European influences appear in the area of the administrative and executive government functions which date back to the earliest days of revolutionary socialism – the ideological breeding ground for most of Israel's 'Founding Fathers'. Then there are the pervasive American influences that have become the models – for better or for worse – in every walk of life in Israel. Even though the basic structure of Israeli administration was directly descended from the British formula, all these modes of government left their mark on the Israeli Intelligence community in its early years.

And yet, from its earliest beginnings, Israeli Intelligence possessed a unique character of its own that made all the difference. Part of it evolved out of its earliest beginnings – the voluntary underground movements in Eretz Yisrael[5] and outside it during the period of 'the state-in-the-making', before there was a government, an army, an elected Parliament, or any of the instruments of law and order. Its truly embryonic stages can be found in the efforts of Zionist leaders to protect people and property in the Yishuv[6] in Palestine and in the Jewish communities of the diaspora, in the illegal immigration and blockade-running aimed at circumventing the British ban on Jewish immigration to Palestine,[7] the clandestine arms procurement and manu-facturing under the noses of the Mandatory authorities, or the Hagannah's 'SHAI',[8] an early intelligence operation aimed at gathering information on Arab intentions. At the same time, the institutions of the Jewish community engaged in an ambivalent relationship with the British authorities, on the one hand cooperating with the army and the police on various security matters, while on the other engaging in clandestine operations aimed at enhancing the Yishuv's military capabilities and at trying to do whatever it could to save the remnants of European Jewry during the war and in its aftermath. These were the 'illegal' precursors of the official, legally constituted Israeli intelligence community – including the Mossad.

Reuven Shiloah was an ideas man, a man of stratagems, not an operative in the field, nor an administrator or an organization man. His fertile restless mind was not suited to the methodical routine nature of office work. This was one of the fundamental weaknesses in his character, often exploited by opponents and rivals alike, those efficient 'organization men' of the Foreign Ministry and the intelligence community. Nevertheless, he played such a crucial part in the convoluted, crisis-ridden story of the creation of the Israeli Intelligence service that they were profoundly influenced by the innovative strength of his ideas and operational concepts. He was involved in all the transitional stages from a 'state-in-the-making' to the independent state, from the Hagannah to the IDF, from SHAI to the three distinct branches of Israeli Intelligence: the intelligence branch of the IDF, the GSS (General Security Service), and the 'Political Department' of the Foreign Ministry, which functioned as a state intelligence organization under various names ('Da'at', 'Binah' and others),[9] until its painful and traumatic dismantling by Reuven Shiloah and the establishment of the Mossad in its place. His successor at the Mossad, Isser Harel, reaped the fruits of Shiloah's labours and inherited a properly functioning, solidly based organization, unencumbered by irksome connections to the past,

One of Shiloah's major contributions to Israeli foreign policy was the concept of the 'Peripheral Alliance' that he developed after he made the official move into the area of foreign policy and diplomacy, first as Minister in the Israeli Embassy in Washington, and later at the Foreign Ministry when he returned to Jerusalem. It was part of a more comprehensive security strategy that he developed, tailored to fit the needs of a country under siege and surrounded by deep-seated Arab hostility, which called for creating a 'strategic alliance' with the United States, and Europe, and integrating Israel into the Western front led by the United States. Both of these concepts, initially proposed by Shiloah, eventually became the cornerstones of Israeli foreign policy.

All this was typical of the man and his destiny – to have others adopt his innovative ideas in the area of foreign policy and bring them to their fulfilment after his death. His was the fate of the pathfinders who sow the seeds but never manage to reap the harvest. He suffered many setbacks in his lifetime, but had some important successes as well, which by their very nature were ascribed to the State of Israel as a whole. Israel's status today as a strategic asset in American Middle East foreign policy is virtually taken for granted, as is its standing as a strategic partner with whom the Americans hold regular annual meetings to discuss strategic coordination and other matters of mutual interest. American foreign aid to Israel, which is unique in its scope, is similarly taken for granted. Shiloah embraced this American orientation from the very early years of the State, at a time when the Americans and even most Israelis showed little interest in it. His ultimate goal was what he called a 'comprehensive affirmative plan' by the West for the Middle East, in which Israel would play a central role, thus reducing the possibility of a confrontation between Israeli needs on the one hand and Western interests in the region on the other.

This was by no means an easy task. The Jewish Yishuv and the fledgling State of Israel that followed it, found many potential avenues of development closed off by the powerful influence of Arab hostility and the effectiveness of the Arab boycott on countries trading with Israel. Both before and after the establishment of the State – well into the 1960s and 1970s – one of the main tasks facing the political leaders of the country was to find cracks in this wall of hostility, or to seek ways of getting around it altogether in order to penetrate the sources of international decision-making. To seek out the ways – known only to a select few – to get into the back-rooms where position papers were drawn up or policy proposals that were to be handed to the leaders of the major powers for their approval were hammered out.

Reuven Shiloah was the embodiment of this indirect method of diplomatic penetration. Many of the people he worked with at the time remember his uncanny ability to open any door in the corridors of power – with or without an invitation – the moment he became convinced of its importance to the cause. His style of diplomatic penetration of this sort, always oblique, achieved seemingly by accident or through simple tenacity, was honed by him into a veritable technique: first get your head in, then a foot, and you're in. The latter ploy was his last resort, used only when there was no other way available, no other way of bypassing whatever bureaucratic or personal obstacles may have been placed in the way of his desire to be 'the right man at the right time'.

Shiloah was the son of a well-known Jerusalem rabbi, Rabbi Aharon Zaslansky, author of many religious tracts on questions of *mitzvoth*[10] relating to the Land of Israel, and later in his life honoured by the title of Distinguished Citizen of Jerusalem. Over the years the elder Zaslansky changed his political orientation from the well-entrenched traditional orthodoxy, which was for the most part opposed to the Zionist movement, to the Zionistoriented Mizrahi party. His son, Reuven Zaslansky,[11] completed the shift begun by his father, moving from the milieu of his maternal and paternal grandparents in the ultra-orthodox Jerusalem neighbourhood of Meah She'arim, to the liberal, secular world of the Jewish labour movement in Palestine of the 1920s. This became his new spiritual home, the adopted family with which he felt thoroughly at home yet where he still remained an outsider, and where the central qualities of his character came to light – his utter devotion, zealous motivation and total belief in the aims of the Zionist endeavour. These qualities, as we shall see, were a significant part of the private and public story of Reuven Shiloah.

The art of acting, which he studied briefly as a youth, helped him fashion the persona of a man of power and influence capable of pulling many strings behind the scenes. In his early years of public service this aura served him well, but in the later years – when he tried to come out of the shadows and take centre stage, to claim the limelight not as a go-between for other people or issues, but as a political personality in his own right – this persona he had created became a drawback. The real political authority he wielded was always unofficial, implicit, based on his important behind-the-scenes activities, and the power, real or imagined, that they gave him. His status as a close confidant of the nation's leaders lent a great deal of weight to his reputation in the eyes of all those who dealt with him professionally. Nevertheless, towards the untimely end of his career, what he truly desired was the official sanction of formal authority that goes with political and diplomatic appointments.

Many of those who knew the man and talked about his achievements, among them even some of his former opponents, repeatedly, and with genuine pain and regret, raised the question of how a man like Reuven Shiloah was never given even an ambassadorial posting – particularly when they compared him to some of the other ambassadorial appointments made by the Foreign Ministry after 1948. Former Israeli ambassador to Germany Asher (Arthur) Ben Nathan, who strongly opposed Shiloah's move to dismantle the Political Department of the Foreign Ministry and create the Mossad in its stead, claims that Shiloah was a giant compared to many of those given important diplomatic posts. The most frequently voiced excuse – that Shiloah was 'not suited' for diplomacy, that he was most effective in private dealings and was not cut out for public appearances – is facile and unsatisfactory.

Many people who were asked about this after his death, among them some of the public figures who were instrumental in one way or another in blocking his way, were hard put to find a suitable explanation. One of the most prominent of these was Moshe Shertok (later Sharett), with whom he worked very closely for many years, and who used to call him – with a mixture of admiration and bemusement – 'a one-man reconnaissance unit'. But there were many others, including David Ben Gurion and Golda Me'ir, who had difficulty finding an answer to a question they never fully articulated in their own minds: what was it about Reuven Shiloah's character and *modus operandi* that prevented him from sticking to the straight and narrow or playing according to the rules of the political game – even at the highest levels of power?

Certain characteristic elements of Reuven Shiloah's life-story followed him even beyond the grave. At a memorial service held in June of 1959, 30 days after his death,[12] Teddy Kollek (the long-time mayor of Jerusalem who was then Director-General of the Prime Minister's office) announced the establishment of a research institute for contemporary Middle Eastern studies to be named after Reuven Shiloah. Kollek told all those gathered at the ceremony that it was Shiloah himself who had originally conceived of such an institute, and in the last few months before his untimely death had actively sought support for the idea. Indeed, in what was to be his last official letter, written on 28 April 1959, less than two weeks before he died, he discussed the subject with the President of the Hebrew University in Jerusalem, Professor Benjamin Mazar. Its timing turned its contents into a part of his last will and testament.

As Teddy Kollek described it, the aim of the institute would be to promote scientific investigation into contemporary Middle Eastern issues, and develop a deeper understanding of present-day regional problems. Research in the institute would concentrate initially on the Arab countries, and later include Africa and Asia as well. The institute would also seek the dissemination of Israeli viewpoints on regional problems in various international forums, publish academic research in journal and book form, and cooperate with other institutes for Near Eastern studies around the world. The institute, an independent body, headed by a Board of Governors and an Academic Committee, was to be established in Tel Aviv as a joint project of the IDF, the Foreign Ministry, the Defence Ministry, the Hebrew University and the Israeli Oriental Society. Plans for its future development included incorporating the institute as the backbone of a central Institute for Foreign Relations which was being planned at that time.

The Shiloah Institute was duly established at Tel Aviv University, and within a few years gained international recognition as one of the more important institutes of Middle Eastern studies in the world. It was entirely in keeping with Shiloah's life-story that the institute bearing his name did not manage – or perhaps did not even try – to produce a single research paper in his memory devoted to his life and achievements. Reuven Shiloah's activities in the service of the nation during three critical decades of Arab–Israeli relations, or his contributions to the enhancement of Israel's status in the area, to the peace efforts and to negotiations with the Arab countries, in which he unquestionably played a very prominent role, were never the subject of any scientific or historical research. Within a short time, the name 'Shiloah' became simply the name of an institute, and few people involved in its work really knew or cared about the man behind the name. The final irony was even more bizarre: a donor appeared on the scene, seeking a way to commemorate Moshe Dayan, and insisted that the memorial tribute be situated at Tel Aviv University. The result was the creation of the 'Dayan Centre' into which the Shiloah Institute disappeared without a trace. It would seem that no man can truly escape his destiny – either in his lifetime or after his death.

NOTES

1. The Jewish Agency was established in 1920 as part of the British Mandate, with the aim of representing the Jewish nation before the Mandatory Government and cooperating with it in creating the 'Jewish national home'. As it developed it became the executive arm of the World Zionist Federation. After the creation of the State, immigration and contacts with the Jewish communities of the diaspora became its primary responsibility.

   The Hagannah was the 'official' military self-defence organization of the Jewish community in Palestine before the establishment of the State, and the military formation that fought Israel's War of Independence. There were a number of rival, so-called 'underground' organizations that operated mainly against the British at that time.

2. There is an untranslatable pun here: the Hebrew word for 'institution' is 'Mossad', which is the name that was given to the widely-known Israeli Intelligence service.

3. Mapai – an acronym for Mifleget Po'alei Eretz Yisrael, the Workers' Party of Palestine, a Zionist–Socialist party founded in 1930 that played a central role in all the Jewish institutions in Palestine before the establishment of the State, and was the ruling political party in the State of Israel from 1948 to 1977.

4. Former Israeli Ambassador to the UN, and later Foreign Minister.

5. 'The Land of Israel' – the name used by the Jewish community of Palestine to designate the country before the establishment of the State. On all official documents in Hebrew the country was known as 'Eretz-Yisrael–Palestine'.

6. Yishuv literally means 'settlement', but by extension it became the name for the Jewish community in Palestine as a whole.

7. At various times during the Mandate (1922, 1930 and 1939) the British Government published White Papers that limited, in one way or the other, Jewish immigration to Palestine. The most painful of these, as far as the Jewish people were concerned, was the last one which made it virtually impossible for the remnants of the Jewish communities of Europe fleeing the Holocaust to enter into Palestine. The Yishuv fought these edicts officially by trying to bring pressure on the British Government, and illegally by bringing in thousands of refugees through the British blockade of Palestinian waters.

8. Abbreviation of the Hebrew 'Sherut Yedi'ot' – Information Service.

9. 'Da'at' in Hebrew means 'knowledge' and 'Binah' means 'wisdom'.
10. The Hebrew word for religious duties. According to rabbinical tradition there are 613 such duties in the Bible.
11. During all the pre-State period, Reuven Shiloah was known as 'Zaslany', a variation on his original family name – 'Zaslansky'. After the establishment of the State, he officially changed his name to his intelligence code-name: 'Shiloah'.
12. According to Jewish tradition, on the 30th day after a death – known as the '*shloshim*' (30 in Hebrew) – the members of the family go up to the cemetery to unveil the tombstone and hold a memorial service.

2

Reuven Shiloah's Contribution to the Development of Israeli Intelligence*

YOAV GELBER

Apart from a few short-lived episodes just after the First World War, the history of Israeli Intelligence really began in the early 1930s. In the wake of the Arab Riots of August–September 1929, it developed two principal areas of operation: dealing with the threat to the Yishuv (the Jewish community in Palestine), and finding ways to overcome it by studying and penetrating the neighbouring Arab countries. The first of these tasks evolved directly from lessons learned in the riots, and the second from the policies instituted by Haim Arlosoroff after he assumed the position of head of the Jewish Agency's Political Department in the summer of 1931.

It was Arlosoroff who recruited Reuven Zaslany (later, Shiloah), who at that time was a student in the Department of Oriental Studies at the Hebrew University in Jerusalem. Shiloah's first assignment brought him to Iraq, the first Arab state to achieve independence after ten years under British Mandatory rule. Under the cover identity of a Hebrew teacher assigned to the local Jewish community, Shiloah established ties with Jews, Arabs and Britons in Baghdad. He reported to Jerusalem regularly on the emerging political situation in the new state, on British–Iraqi relations, on the situation of the Jews in Iraq, and on early manifestations of Communist subversion in that country.

Shiloah's stay in Iraq was brief. The local authorities uncovered his

---

*From Haggai Eshed, *Reuven Shiloah – The Man Behind the Mossad*, trans. David and Leah Zinder (London: Frank Cass, 1997).

Author's Note: This article is based on the extensive research that I have been conducting on the history of the Jewish Yishuv in Palestine, and on Israel's intelligence services from 1918 to 1953. Parts of this research have been published, parts are about to be published, and other parts are still being worked on. See Gelber: *Growing an Iris* [the symbol of Israel's Military Intelligence]: *The Intelligence Services of the Jewish Yishuv in Eretz Yisrael, 1918–1947* (Tel Aviv: Ministry of Defence, 1992) and *Israel's Intelligence in the War of Independence, 1947–49*, 2 vols (Tel Aviv: Ministry of Defence, forthcoming).

clandestine activities, and he was forced to leave the country. Back in Palestine, he switched to the second task of Yishuv intelligence: providing advance warning of any potential Arab threat to the Jewish community. Officially he was employed by the Histadrut,[1] and it was within that organization that Shiloah coordinated the Hagannah's[2] first countrywide spy network. These were local informers who volunteered to utilize their connections with Arabs in their vicinity for intelligence purposes. They reported to Shiloah on the prevailing mood in their areas, and on developments or rumours, or special occurrences when and if they took place. Shiloah collated these reports, edited them, and then sent them out in the form of intelligence bulletins to Hagannah commanders throughout the country. In this way, he added to his field experiences in Iraq, experience in research and information assessment.

The third chapter of Shiloah's intelligence career began with the outbreak of the Arab Revolt of 1936. At that time he was transferred from Histadrut headquarters in Tel Aviv to the Jewish Agency's Political Department in Jerusalem, where he began his career as assistant to Colonel Frederick H. Kisch (who was head of the Political Department before Arlosoroff, and volunteered to come back from retirement to help in the crisis), chief liaison officer with the British security services. When the revolt came to an end in October 1936, Kisch returned to private business, and Shiloah succeeded him.

In his capacity as liaison officer to the British Army, police and secret service (SSO), Shiloah initiated an important new field of intelligence work: the exchange of information with foreign intelligence services. No intelligence service is capable of gathering on its own all the information it requires. Therefore, over the years, the exchange of knowledge with colleagues in sister services became one of the most important means of information-gathering. Although occasional contacts between the Jewish Agency and the SSO had taken place prior to the Arab Revolt, Shiloah extended them to other services, and made these exchanges operational and systematic, and a permanent feature of his work.

Shiloah's contacts with British police and army officers, and particularly with the head of the SSO, Patrick Domville, were an important source of information for the Hagannah. However, his role as the recipient of intelligence information from the various British services, was no less crucial than his role as a provider of information to these same services. There was a huge gap between the information that the Jewish Agency was able to collect in the field and its translation into action, since the Hagannah, at that time was still incapable of mounting independent offensive action against rebel gangs or Arab terrorists. Such actions were the responsibility of the police and the army, and the usefulness of any information given to these bodies depended very much on the military's readiness to accept it and act upon it.

The Jewish Agency's sources were, for the most part, Arab informers handled by the Political Department's Arab Bureau and its Jewish agents throughout the country. The Bureau's officials, most of whom did not speak English and were unknown to the British, were not suited to the task of convincing the British authorities of the value and authenticity of their intelligence. It fell to Shiloah, then, to collate the information, present it to his acquaintances in the British security services, and persuade them of its value. This necessitated separating facts from rumours, verifying details, and on occasion, preparing background papers in the form of more comprehensive evaluations of the situation. In other words, it marked the modest beginnings of Shiloah's training in assimilating and analysing intelligence data.

Through his links with Domville, Shiloah introduced some of the Jewish Agency's regional agents to their opposite numbers in the SSO. This, in turn, cleared the way for British–Jewish cooperation against the Arab terrorist gangs at the field level. Emmanuel Vilensky (later, Yelan) in Haifa and Ezra Danin in Samaria, for example, were provided by the British with funds for the purpose of engaging Arab and Jewish spies in their areas. Their reports were submitted simultaneously to the district SSO, to expedite the army's operational response, and to Shiloah in Jerusalem, who kept records of the overall intelligence picture.

Apart from his one-man research operation, and his liaison activities with the British, Shiloah embarked on a number of intelligence-gathering activities in Syria and Lebanon, together with his colleagues Eliyahu (Elias) Sasson and Eliyahu Epstein (later, Eilat), both of whom were members of the Jewish Agency's Arab Bureau. These field operations were also financed by the British secret services, and usually involved coordination with local British representatives, such as Gilbert McKereth, the British Consul-General in Damascus.

Shiloah's multiple functions as liaison officer and coordinator, as well as his gathering, analysis and dissemination of intelligence information, eventually brought him into close working relationships first with Shertok (later, Sharett), and subsequently with Ben Gurion, both of whom made him their adviser on intelligence affairs. Although both men were in the habit of making their own, independent, evaluations of the information that reached their desks, they soon learned to appreciate Shiloah's special knowledge and use it to their advantage.

After the suppression of the Arab Revolt and the publication of the White Paper in May 1939,[3] cooperation with the British security services dwindled.

Close mutual relations resumed with the outbreak of the Second World War, and expanded considerably during the course of the war itself. Shiloah continued to be responsible for liaison with the British secret services, and soon developed contacts throughout the Middle East, as a number of his acquaintances on the British side were transferred from Palestine to Egypt and Iraq.

This newly revived cooperation concentrated mainly on issues relating to counter-intelligence and internal security measures. MI5 turned to Shiloah to request the Jewish Agency's assistance in screening immigrants arriving in Palestine from Germany, since they feared that the Germans had somehow managed to insert agents into Palestine through the illegal immigration operations of the Yishuv. On occasion, the British also needed help in tracing and identifying suspected German spies in neighbouring Arab countries. While the immigrants from Germany and other European countries did constitute a real security risk, they also served as an important source of basic information about German infrastructure such as the economy, transportation, industrial plants and other strategic installations in their countries of origin. The screening process of the immigrants was soon turned into a method of gaining first-hand information in all these areas.

Within a short time, the British had widened the scope of their requests for assistance into new areas of cooperation. The Jewish Agency helped 'the Friends' – as the British were known – in almost every area of clandestine warfare. The Agency's local Arab and Jewish agents gathered military and political information, and disseminated disinformation propaganda in Syria, Lebanon, Turkey, Iran, and even as far afield as the Caucasus and Yemen. In Haifa, a special team widened the net of interrogation so that not only immigrants but all travellers, refugees and escaped POWs who arrived in Palestine from Europe were included in the questioning about strategic targets, economic conditions, and the political atmosphere behind the German lines. Powerful radio stations were set up in Haifa and Jerusalem to broadcast propaganda to Syria and the Balkans.

Jewish agents from Palestine were dispatched to Romania to enlist local Jewish youth to help sabotage the Ploesti oil-fields. Another sabotage alternative that was considered at the time was sinking a vessel in the Iron Gates of the Danube to block the delivery of petrol from Romania to Germany. Yet another task assigned by 'the Friends' was the establishment of a wireless transmitting station in Salonica to facilitate wireless communication between Egypt and northern Yugoslavia. Not all of these missions were in place by the time the Germans occupied the Balkans. In the spring of 1941, the focus of the 'clandestine cooperation' between the Yishuv and the British, reverted from the European theatre of operations back to the Middle East.

Jewish agents posing as Arabs infiltrated Syria, and established an underground network for sabotage and espionage. Others served as reconnaissance guides for the Australian forces that took part in the invasion of Syria. In Palestine, the SOE (Special Operations Executive), trained members of the Hagannah to form a cadre of saboteurs, wireless operators, reconnaissance and intelligence agents. They were meant to form the nucleus of an underground resistance movement in the event of Axis occupation of the country. And all of these joint activities were, in fact, merely a prelude to what turned out to be, historically speaking, the most significant operation that took place under the aegis of the 'clandestine cooperation' – the 'parachutists' mission' into occupied Europe during the years 1943–45.[4]

In his capacity as liaison officer between the Jewish Agency and the British secret services, Shiloah was deeply involved in all of these activities – some of which he himself initiated. His duties brought him frequently to Egypt, and later, to Italy, where his task was to encourage, coordinate and monitor the execution of operations in the field. During this time he became familiar with a wide variety of clandestine organizations operating in the Middle East and the Mediterranean theatres of war, their functions and *modus operandi*. Among these were the office of Brigadier Iltyd Clayton, the British Army's political officer in the Middle East GHQ in Cairo, and his intelligence department – Political Intelligence Centre Middle East (PICME); Security Intelligence Middle East (SIME), the regional offspring of MI5; MI6 (the secret service); Special Operations Executive (SOE), in charge of activating resistance organizations in enemy-occupied countries; MI9, responsible – among other things – for rescuing allied POWs from enemy territory; and the staff branches of MO3 (British staff department in charge of special military units such as Special Air Service (SAS) and others) and MO4 (cover name for Special Operations Executive (SOE) of British Intelligence in Cairo), who were responsible for coordinating and conducting special operations.

The contacts with all these bodies broadened Shiloah's professional experience, and enriched his comprehension of intelligence and clandestine operations. He adopted a maximalist understanding of the concept of 'intelligence', which, as he saw it, included not only handling information, but also subversion, sabotage, psychological warfare and propaganda, political warfare, internal and field security, and activating fifth columns.

Shiloah was convinced that intelligence, subversion and other clandestine activities were likely to play a major role in modern warfare and diplomacy in the post-war period. It was his belief that the state-in-the-making should prepare the nucleus of its personnel in advance for their effective employment in time of need.

Several times throughout the Second World War, Shiloah displayed truly remarkable foresight. As early as the summer of 1941 he pointed out the Yishuv's unique potential for providing suitable candidates for subversive activities in occupied Europe, in cooperation with local Jewish underground movements. This was the first time anyone had suggested this possibility, which later became the basis for the parachutists' mission to Europe. Two years later, in 1943, Shiloah, together with Tony Simmonds of MI9, began implementing this concept of inserting Jewish agents into Romania.

Shiloah was anxious to develop contacts with the American Office of Strategic Services (OSS), the forerunner of the CIA, which appeared on the Middle Eastern scene in 1943. When the parachutists' mission ended, early in 1945, and in anticipation of the emergence of the United States as the dominant power of the post-war world, Shiloah asked to be dispatched to Washington. His purpose was to learn the American scene, to make acquaintance with the chiefs of intelligence there, and to prepare the ground for future cooperation between the Jewish Agency and the American secret services.

In the summer of 1946 Shiloah returned to Palestine, to his post as liaison officer to the British services, this time under very different circumstances, with relations between the Yishuv and the Mandatory government severely strained. Shiloah managed to preserve some open channels of communication, but cooperation between the two sides was limited mainly to exposing pro-Nazi underground networks, and tracing subversive Communist activities throughout the Middle East. Nevertheless, these few channels that he did manage to maintain, and his connections with the American Consulate in Jerusalem, enabled Shiloah, in July 1947, to give the first warnings of the Mufti's[5] preparations for riots in the event of a UN decision on the fate of Palestine that would be unacceptable to the Palestinians.

At the start of the disturbances that marked the beginning of Israel's War of Independence, in December 1947, Shiloah was summoned from Jerusalem to Tel Aviv to act as Ben Gurion's assistant for intelligence affairs. Considering his experience and record in intelligence matters, this was a natural choice. Like many other official positions created in the transition from the mostly voluntary Yishuv society to the mechanisms of statehood and sovereignty, Shiloah's new status was never clearly defined. He had no formal authority over the various organizations that constituted the fledgeling Israeli intelligence community – SHAI,[6] the Jewish Agency Section, the Political Department's agents abroad, the Hagannah's early version of the IDF's Military Intelligence, and the Palmach's[7] Arab Platoon. Nevertheless, he soon set up mechanisms to ensure the flow of information and evaluation from their agents and officers in the field to his desk. At the same time, the chiefs of all these organizations also had direct access to Ben Gurion himself, with the result that Shiloah was only partially successful in establishing himself as the principal intermediary between these services and Ben Gurion.

Instead of involving himself in the internecine rivalries over authority within the existing intelligence community, Shiloah preferred to concentrate on expanding this community into new areas where he encountered no opposition. He foresaw the eventual paralysis of the Jewish Agency's pre-war networks and agents in the Arab countries, and to meet this contingency, he established new branches in Cyprus and Europe that were supposed to serve as bases for future penetration into the Arab world. He encouraged the recruitment of new agents for missions to the Arab countries, and promoted professional exchanges with foreign intelligence services, particularly the French, in both Europe and the Middle East.

Shiloah did not want to position himself within the semi-formal and still amorphous hierarchy of the Israeli intelligence community. He avoided administrative responsibilities, preferring, rather, to act as an adviser, aide or special emissary. In February 1948, he set out on a three-week mission to London, in an attempt to uncover Britain's real intentions in Palestine. This was an issue that troubled Ben Gurion, who feared a possible conspiracy on the part of the British policy-makers to avoid the implementation of the Partition Plan,[8] and delay or put off altogether the withdrawal of British forces from the country. In his search for information on this issue, Ben Gurion was disappointed by the SHAI and the Political Department's assessments, since they were based on poor and, for the most part, secondary sources, and their professional judgements were influenced by the prevailing anti-British bias in the Yishuv. Without reliable information, and faced with a number of political moves made by the British which he found inconsistent, Ben Gurion found it difficult to form his own appreciation of the situation. However, Shiloah's mission failed to solve the riddle of Britain's future plans for Palestine. Although he managed to calm Ben Gurion's apprehensions concerning any possible direct action by the British against the Yishuv, he did not grasp the full meaning of the British–Jordanian understanding about the annexation to Jordan of the predominantly Arab-populated parts of Palestine, and the possible repercussions that might ensue from such an action. Shiloah's erroneous conclusions concerning Britain's plans for the region after the dissolution of the Mandate further confused Ben Gurion's understanding of the situation at that time.

The invasion of Palestine by the Arab armies on 15 May 1948, and the outcome of the subsequent military campaigns, proved the inadequacy of the intelligence community of the state-in-the-making in these new circum-stances. They had focused on the Arabs of Palestine, and failed to deploy in time against the new enemies – the neighbouring Arab states – and adjust to the different nature and exigencies of all-out war. For several weeks after the outbreak of the war, the Israeli leadership was in the dark about the intentions of the Arab states and Britain, and about the combined Arab armies' capabilities and their movements. Information was scanty at best, and whatever was available was often misinterpreted. At that point, Ben Gurion decided to go ahead with the necessary reforms, and on 30 May appointed Shiloah as head of a military and political intelligence wing in the Foreign Ministry, which was to be directly subordinate to Ben Gurion himself in his capacity as Minister of Defence.

This was primarily a personal gesture made by Ben Gurion for Shiloah's benefit. There was no 'Intelligence Wing', and no Ministry of Defence to speak of. At the same time, Ben Gurion did regard this appointment as a first step toward the reorganization of Israel's intelligence community. The reform was meant to enable it to function properly in wartime, and grant the Foreign Ministry a leading role in the intelligence community, along the lines of the British model that was introduced prior to the Second World War.

Ben Gurion took the next step in this reorganization in early June, 1948, when, in consultation with Shiloah and the head of SHAI, Isser Be'eri, he decided on the future structure of the community. Three elements were to replace SHAI and the Jewish Agency's Political Department: (a) a Military Intelligence branch under the IDF General Staff; (b) a domestic security service that was to deal with subversion inside the country: the General Security Service (GSS); (c) Political Intelligence which would be responsible for information-gathering abroad. The last of these was to be headed by Shiloah who, at the same time, would retain his position as intelligence adviser to Ben Gurion. After further consultations, the new order was launched and, during the month of July of that year, the old structure was gradually phased out.

Upon assuming his post, Shiloah immediately embarked on the project of setting up the new 'Political Department' of the Foreign Ministry and its offices in Cyprus, Europe and the United States. Simultaneously, he helped Ben Gurion impose the new military intelligence apparatus on a reluctant General Staff, and divide the SHAI and the Jewish Agency's physical legacy – records, files, indexes, etc. – among their successors. He also strove, already at this early stage, to create a permanent committee to coordinate the activities of the new Israeli intelligence community. Be'eri, who was appointed as head of Military Intelligence, opposed this concept, and Ben Gurion, who supported it in principle, postponed his final decision on the issue.

Shiloah's close relations with both Ben Gurion and Shertok (later Sharett) made him a natural intermediary between the military and the diplomats of

the Foreign Ministry. He supervised joint operations, such as the establishment of the IDF's Druse unit,[9] and its deployment by the Political
Department for irregular warfare and subversive missions. His main function
was to present to the General Staff the Government's foreign policy
considerations and viewpoints, and vice versa – to transmit the military point
of view on the issues at hand to Foreign Ministry officials. This status,
however, rendered him an outsider on both ends, and provided him with no
administrative/organizational power base in either one.

Ben Gurion entrusted Shiloah with a number of sensitive diplomatic
missions, preferring him over Eliyahu (Elias) Sasson, whom he regarded as
too soft on Arab demands. Shiloah played a major role in the secret negotiations that led to the ceasefire agreement with Jordan in Jerusalem. At the
beginning of 1949, Shiloah also participated, together with Moshe Dayan,
in talks with King Abdullah of Jordan, that culminated in the Shuneh Agreement, and opened the way to the signing of the armistice agreement in
Rhodes. The Dayan–Shiloah team also conducted most of the ultimately futile
peace negotiations with King Abdullah, which were resumed at the end of
1949, and continued intermittently until their final breakdown in May 1951.

Immediately after the War of Independence, Shiloah went to the United
States to organize the Political Department's activities there, and to
coordinate its activities with other official Israeli bodies – the embassy in
Washington, the United Nations delegation in New York, the military and
scientific attachés, and the Ministry of Defence's arms acquisition mission.
However, his principal activities during this time concentrated on setting up
cooperation with the various American intelligence agencies. The FBI soon
became suspicious when an Israeli official who had come to the United States
ostensibly to supervise the logistics of the Israeli Foreign Ministry in the
United States, asked to meet with top-ranking officials of the American
intelligence community. Despite the fact that his visit did not yield any
immediate results, it did contribute to the creation of cooperative relations
between the two countries on intelligence matters a few years later, when
Shiloah returned to the United States, this time as Minister at the embassy
in Washington.

Upon Shiloah's return from America, Ben Gurion sent him out on another
important diplomatic mission: heading the Israeli delegation to the Lausanne
Conference, which was held under the auspices of the Palestine Conciliation
Committee.[10] Ben Gurion was aware of the conflicts inherent in Shiloah's
many overlapping assignments, but he decided that the talks in Lausanne
were more important than the completion of the reorganization of the
intelligence services. As far as Ben Gurion was concerned, Shiloah was the
most trustworthy diplomat in Shertok's Foreign Ministry, and he was

therefore loath to forego his presence at the conference, or his reports and analyses of developments on Israel's principal political front.

Throughout 1949 Shiloah found himself drawn more and more into matters of high government policy. His frequent trips abroad in his capacity as 'Adviser on Special Affairs' to Ben Gurion, interrupted the methodical rebuilding of the intelligence community. In his absence, the services competed among themselves for authority and areas of responsibility – which translated directly into status and resources. With Shiloah absent and Ben Gurion frequently inaccessible, the services learned – through this fraternal squabbling – how to get along with each other, without requiring the intervention of any higher authority.

A 'Supreme Coordination Committee', composed of all the heads of services and chaired by Shiloah, was officially appointed in May 1949. Its Mandate was not made clear, however, until the end of that year, and, in Shiloah's absence, the Committee could not function effectively. Consequently, most of its meetings were devoted to minor issues relating to internal security and inconsequential bureaucratic problems.

Before his departure for Lausanne, Shiloah presented Ben Gurion with an outline for the creation of a central organization for intelligence and security in the Prime Minister's own office. This body was supposed to serve as an overall framework for the intelligence community, and to supervise all their activities. Chaim Herzog, head of Military Intelligence (later, President of Israel), and Isser Halpern (later, Harel), head of the GSS, vehemently opposed the idea. As a result, Ben Gurion decided to postpone any decision on the community's structure and mandate until Shiloah's return.

After Shiloah's return from Lausanne, Ben Gurion called a meeting with Shiloah and Shertok (who changed his name to 'Sharett'), to discuss the future of the intelligence community – its structure, methods of action, coordination among its various components, and Shiloah's own status and the measure of his authority over the services. At this meeting, Sharett agreed to release Shiloah from all other duties for a period of six months, in order to give him time to devote all his attention to the restructuring of the intelligence community.

In November 1949, Shiloah reactivated the Supreme Coordination Committee. The following month, Ben Gurion agreed to replace this committee with a central body (the Mossad) for coordinating the state's intelligence and security services. Ben Gurion asked Shiloah to set up this new body within the Foreign Ministry, but to make it directly responsible to the Prime Minister himself.

In his capacity as head of the new institute ('mossad' in Hebrew means 'institute' or 'institution'), Shiloah set out to put into effect the reorganization of Israel's intelligence community. Early in 1950, he transferred all the local activities of the Political Department and three district offices to the GSS. The Political Department retained its responsibility for political intelligence and operations abroad. Shiloah abolished the special section within the Political Department, known as Hekker Bet,[11] which had been responsible for monitoring Arab arms purchases, and dealt with deception and sabotage as well as intelligence. He also set up routines for handling information, and distributing it among the various services.

Shiloah guided the community's developing research work by deciding on the issues that were to be researched and determining priorities, but refrained from interfering directly in the day-to-day work of the services. His control over the Political Department and its activities was hampered by his frequent trips abroad on political missions, particularly the negotiations with Jordan. The various service chiefs complained of delays and even outright disruptions of operations caused by his many periods of absence.

Shiloah soon became aware of the principal shortcoming of the community's structure as he himself had shaped it after 1948: the direct correlation between political intelligence and information-gathering outside Israel. This was the pre-war British format that had served them well in peacetime, but now proved incompatible with the prevailing conditions in Israel and the Middle East. The ever-present potential state of war, and the repeated Arab threat of a 'Second Round', gave the IDF's Military Intelligence the leading role as the service chiefly responsible for early warning of any hostile military move. The Foreign Ministry, which controlled both political intelligence and operations abroad, followed an agenda based on its own priorities, with the result that it could not meet the IDF's requirements for vital information. Military Intelligence 'retaliated' by barring the Political Department from access to any SigInt (Signals Intelligence) material, which was totally within the purview of the army. Teaming up with the GSS, Military Intelligence embarked on independent intelligence-gathering operations in the Arab countries and in Europe in order to satisfy its own intelligence needs.

Throughout 1950 several attempts were made to solve the problems through direct discussions between Military Intelligence and the Political Department, but to no avail. Shiloah, too, failed in his attempts to establish proper routines of cooperation and division of responsibilities between the two services. Faced with this difficulty and its far-reaching implications, he suggested establishing a new central authority that would be responsible for all intelligence operations outside Israel's borders. The idea was that this authority would be independent of the Foreign Ministry, and committed to providing political, military, security, technological, economic and scientific information equally to all branches of the intelligence community. This proposal sparked a battle royal between Shiloah and the heads of the Political Department, Boris Guriel and Asher (Arthur) Ben Nathan, eventually leading to Ben Nathan's dismissal by Shiloah. This, in turn, ignited what became known as 'The Spies Revolt', when most of the Political Department's operatives abroad sided with Ben Nathan against Shiloah.

At that point, Ben Gurion intervened and endorsed Shiloah's proposed reforms. He approved the dismantling of the Political Department, and the separation between intelligence activities abroad, political intelligence and the Foreign Ministry. The Political Department's networks abroad were to be disbanded and replaced by an 'Intelligence Authority' ('Ha-rashut') under the direction of Haim Waldner (later, Ya'ari), a senior army officer, head of the intelligence community's Technical and Scientific Unit, who had served as a paratrooper in the Second World War. The new body was directly subordinate to the Prime Minister's Office, had exclusive responsibility for all operations abroad, and was meant to provide all the services' needs in its sphere of operations. The remainder of the Political Department was turned into the Foreign Ministry's research unit.

In terms of governmental hierarchy, the Intelligence Authority and the Research Department of the Foreign Ministry were under the Mossad – the 'Institute for Coordination and Special Duties', which belonged to the Prime Minister's office and was headed by Shiloah and his deputy, Izzy Dorot. This was a new version of the 'Institute for Coordinating the Actions of State Intelligence Services', which had been established in December of 1949, but failed to develop into a viable organization. Shiloah's new institute coordinated the activities of the secret services in those fields in which there was an overlap, and allocated their information-gathering and research tasks.

The new structure embodied two significant principles: coordinated action abroad, and stricter supervision of the services by the political echelon, namely Ben Gurion through Shiloah. The first principle stemmed from the Israeli Yishuv's absolute dependence, in those early years, on the services of Jews living in Arab countries, in eastern Western Europe, and in the United States. This latter point constituted both an advantage and a potential danger. Shiloah understood the importance of the willingness of young Jews abroad to undertake personal risks in order to serve in clandestine capacities of various kinds, and he was fully aware of the sensitivity of this issue. At the same time, he was no less aware of the potential danger to the services and the possible impact on them should these activities be exposed. Ben Gurion and Shiloah were determined to avoid unnecessary exploits, such as the one that brought about the demise of the intelligence ring in Iraq in the summer of 1951 as a result of a lack of coordination, to say nothing of outright competition between the Israeli Intelligence services.

The second principle was a reaction to the Yishuv's tradition of volunteerism and a multiplicity of authorities which led, in effect, to a total lack of any clear chain of authority. Shiloah's knowledge of the experience gained by other countries, gave him reason to fear the possible results of endowing the services with an excess of autonomy, which might lead to the use of undemocratic practices. Hence he suggested, and Ben Gurion insisted upon, the creation of a centralized structure that could exert proper authority over their actions and supervise their operations.

This structural improvement was the last step in the shaping of Israeli Intelligence in the early years of the State. Apart from the change in the status of Military Intelligence introduced in 1953 – turning it from a 'G' department into an independent branch of the General Staff – the structure of Israel's intelligence community has remained virtually the same to this day. This reform also brought to an end the close correlation that had existed until then between that era of Israeli history and Shiloah the man. The time for laying foundations, which required qualities such as creativity and imagination, was over. An era of consolidation and professional expertise had begun. Leadership, teamwork and management skills overshadowed such qualities as conceptual and organizational vision, personal charm, the ability to identify needs and create contacts. The reform was Shiloah's last major contribution to Israeli Intelligence. The following year, 1952, Reuven Shiloah resigned from his position as head of the Mossad, leaving the ultimate consolidation of the structure he had established, to his successors.

NOTES

1. The General Federation of Labour.
2. The Hagannah was the official security arm of the Yishuv, and the core of Israel's army in the War of Independence.
3. Among its many proposals for restrictions on the Jewish community in Palestine, the most inflammatory one in this official British Government document was the restriction it set on the number of Jews who would be allowed to enter Palestine.
4. A joint British–Yishuv operation that involved British training of Jewish agents to drop into occupied European countries, and set up local resistance cells among the Jewish population, as well as to help the British to rescue escaped POWs and downed air crews.
5. Haj Amin el-Husseini, religious and political leader of the Arab population in Palestine.
6. Acronym for Sherut Yedi'ot – information service.
7. Acronym for Plugot Mahatz – Storm Companies – the elite infantry unit of the Hagannah and the Israel Defence Forces during the War of Independence, which was disbanded immediately after the war.

8. Agreed on by the United Nations General Assembly at Lake Success in 1947, calling for the partition of mandatory Palestine into two sovereign states, one Arab and one Jewish.
9. The Druse are a religious sect, based mainly in Israel and in Syria, whose religion derives from Muslim, Christian and Persian sources. They are the only non-Jewish ethnic group in Israel whose youngsters do obligatory National Service in the army, some of whom have reached very senior officer's rank.
10. Convened following a UN General Assembly resolution of 11 December 1948, and involving Israel and her four neighbouring Arab countries. The Conference proceeded in two stages that lasted for a total of four months. The first stage took place between April and June, and the second between July and September 1949, and ultimately yielded no significant resolutions of the outstanding problems between Israel and the Arab states.
11. Literally: 'Investigation B' or 'Research B'.

3

Reuven Zaslany (Shiloah) and the Covert Cooperation with British Intelligence during the Second World War*

ELDAD HAROUVI

The Second World War marks an important milestone in the annals of British Intelligence. For some elements within the service, this period was a watershed, as several well-entrenched modes of operation were recognized as outdated and were completely overhauled in the course of the war. Recognition of the importance of the changes that occurred in British Intelligence will bring us to our subject: the covert cooperation on intelligence matters between elements of British Intelligence and the Jewish Yishuv[1] during the Second World War. Among the leading figures in this cooperation was the late Reuven Shiloah (Zaslany). His productive and wide-ranging activities are the subject of this study.

To begin with, let us examine the structure and functions of the various branches of British Intelligence at the outbreak of the war. During the years following the First World War, some of these units had partially atrophied and had been swallowed up by larger frameworks in the Foreign Office and the War Office. The British had enjoyed a number of impressive successes in information-gathering during the First World War, but their glow soon dimmed in the general atmosphere of despair that settled over Great Britain after the war. This was a war which had cost the lives of hundreds of thousands of soldiers, many of them from the upper classes of British society. The severe economic crisis that developed after the war prevented the growth of the British economy in any significant way, and led in many cases to an uncomfortable dependence on the American economy – all of which added to the general malaise of the times.

---

*This article is primarily based on Eldad Harouvi's MA thesis, trans. David Zinder. All quotes not otherwise noted are from this source.

Britain's intelligence units had not weathered the war unscathed. The Secret Service (SIS) was forced to rely on the Imperial diplomatic services for financing and logistics. Its intelligence operatives worked as clerks in British embassies around the world, performing bureaucratic tasks such as issuing and examining passports. Even their salaries were paid by the Foreign Office. The Internal Security Service (MI5) dealt with issues of internal security such as the uprising in Ireland, and events in India. Military Intelligence units dealing with wireless interception and aerial reconnaissance were still in their infancy. The field intelligence operatives were co-opted into the Operations Branch in the army and, between 1918 and 1939, many of them were shunted aside.

Hitler's rise to power and the ensuing political and military upheavals caught the British off guard, unprepared and, most significantly, wholly unequipped to deal with the new situation in Europe. British Intelligence coverage of Europe was very poor, relying mostly on Secret Service officers in the embassies. Major breakdowns in the system were not long in coming. The kidnapping by the Germans of the heads of the Secret Service station in The Hague in November 1939 was a case in point which highlighted the organizational muddle that was so characteristic of the Secret Service at that time.

British Intelligence was taken by surprise time and again. The German army's actual military potential was unknown, and the invasion of Poland stunned the intelligence services as well as Britain's political and military leaders. The total lack of any prior intelligence on the convoy of German warships that set sail for the conquest of Scandinavia at the beginning of 1940 was a stinging setback for British Intelligence. Two events – the German conquest of France and Winston Churchill's election as Prime Minister in May 1940 – were highly instrumental in initiating far-reaching changes in this sorry state of affairs.

The changes manifested themselves in several areas. First of all, new intelligence organizations were set up, and, secondly, the attitude of both political and military leaders underwent a major shift in relation to almost every aspect of intelligence work – information-gathering, interpretation, dissemination to relevant consumers, and the sheer need for acquiring as much information on the enemy as possible.

Two new intelligence organizations were created during the first year of the war. MI9 was established within Military Intelligence, with the aim of planning and carrying out escape plans for British soldiers in German POW camps, and organizing and leading groups of escapees from the occupied countries to safe havens. This new group was responsible for contacts with Allied POW camps in Europe and elsewhere, as well as for the interrogation of enemy POWs.

The second new unit was the 'Special Operations Executive' (SOE), which was set up in July 1940. Its principal function was to use any means at all – subversion, sabotage, and/or psychological and economic warfare – to carry the fight to the enemy. For internal political reasons the new unit was placed in the Ministry for Economic Warfare, rather than the War Office or the Foreign Office.

The establishment of these new units, and the escalation of the war into a world-wide conflagration, required the recruitment of a large number of civilians to fill the ranks. Many of these recruits came from the British business world, people from the City of London: bankers, brokers, traders, lawyers. Many in the field of education, teachers and headmasters, were recruited as well. These new recruits, some of whom would rise through the ranks of British Intelligence to very high positions, brought with them into the service a vitality, a flair for innovation, an open-mindedness and a burning desire to do whatever might be necessary to defeat the enemy.

The creation of new intelligence frameworks, the expansion of existing ones, the state of war and the desperate need to obtain information – all these became a fertile breeding ground for enhanced cooperation between British Intelligence and the Jewish Yishuv during the Second World War. The first attempts at this kind of cooperation were made during the First World War, when Jewish volunteers from Palestine were drafted into the British Army to help fight the armies of the Ottoman Empire. The members of the underground NILI organization[2] were the first to pave the way. Cooperation in this vein continued during the early years of the Mandatory government in Palestine, and intensified during the Arab Revolt of 1936–39. As the riots tapered off, so too did the measure of cooperation between the Yishuv and the British authorities, particularly after the publication of the White Paper of May 1939.[3]

Reuven Zaslany was born in Jerusalem in December 1909, and began his career in intelligence in 1931, when he was sent to Baghdad as a teacher and counsellor for the Jewish community there. Prior to that he worked in the Political Department of the Jewish Agency: among other things, writing up summaries and reports from the Arabic press for the head of the department, Dr Haim Arlosoroff. Zaslany, who at that time was a young student in the Department of Oriental Studies at the Hebrew University, studied Arabic diligently. In the course of his career he would make extensive use of his knowledge of the language.[4]

Upon his return from Iraq, he went back to the Political Department and became acquainted with the heads of the Yishuv at that time: Yitzhak Ben-Zvi, David Ben Gurion, Moshe Shertok, Dov Hos, Shaul Meirov and others. From the very early stages of his work in the Jewish Agency, Reuven Zaslany made efforts to establish special relations with members of British Intelligence units serving in Palestine. The first among these was Patrick Domville, commander of RAF Intelligence in Palestine at the beginning of the 1930s. Zaslany was appointed as his aide in Jerusalem, serving as interpreter, and as liaison officer to the Political Department and to the leaders of the Yishuv.[5]

One result of these relations was that Zaslany was a frequent visitor to the headquarters of British Intelligence and the army, the police and the CID.[6] The importance of his activities and his strong ties with the British military establishment would come into full bloom later during the Second World War. When the Arab Revolt erupted in April 1936, Colonel Kisch was appointed chief liaison officer between the British Army and the Jewish Agency Executive. Zaslany became his assistant and continued to nurture his ties with the heads of British Intelligence in the country.[7]

In September 1937 Reuven Zaslany was appointed liaison officer for intelligence and security affairs between the Political Department of the Jewish Agency and the political–military intelligence arm of the RAF and the CID.[8] In this capacity, Zaslany played a key role as the main conduit for contacts between operatives in the field and the Jewish leadership. The heads of the Jewish Agency, David Ben Gurion and Moshe Shertok, were abroad at that time, and Zaslany and his colleague, Eliyahu Sasson, filled the gap. It was at that point, according to Zaslany's biographer, the late Haggai Eshed, that Reuven began collecting important intelligence material and reporting on his findings to the Jewish leadership. Soon afterwards he became an adviser to the heads of the Yishuv, and not long after that a major participant in high-level decision-making and in actual operations.

The period of the Arab Revolt, from about September 1937, proved an excellent training ground for Zaslany, who used the events to fine-tune his *modus operandi* regarding the leaders of the Yishuv on the one hand, and the Mandatory authorities and members of British Intelligence, on the other. At the same time, Zaslany and Sasson served as chief negotiators on behalf of the Yishuv with moderate factions from among the Palestinian Arabs, which were seeking to depose the Mufti (Haj Amin el Husseini, head of the Arab community in Palestine) and his henchmen. It was in pursuit of these aims that Zaslany and Sasson went to Damascus and met, among others, with the British Consul in Iraq and the so-called 'Peace Gangs'.[9]

During the Arab Revolt, Reuven Zaslany collected and sifted through much of the information sent to the Political and the Arab Departments of the Jewish Agency. He checked through the information and then sent it on to the British. Right from the outset, contacts with the British were on a 'give and take' basis, with each side delivering its 'goods' to the other according to its abilities and in line with accepted policies of the time. The Jewish side mainly provided information from the field, gathered with the help of Jewish and Arab operatives and informers whose great advantage was their intimate acquaintance with the area and the local population.

The British side returned the favour, so to speak, within its own limitations, at times providing logistical support to bolster Jewish defence capabilities, and at others turning a blind eye to illegal activities carried out by the Hagannah. Within this uneasy balance, there were also times when the British behaved like sworn enemies of the Jewish Yishuv. From its inception, then, the cooperation was never totally symmetrical. What is more, the patterns of this cooperation established during the Arab Revolt were more or less repeated at various stages of the Second World War.

Following the publication, on the eve of the war, of the White Paper's harsh land and immigration restrictions – which threatened the very existence of the Zionist endeavour in Palestine – frustration, bitterness, unrest and dissatisfaction replaced visionary hope in the Yishuv. It was David Ben Gurion who, at the beginning of September 1939, coined the phrase that set the tone for continued cooperation with the British: 'We must help the British as though there were no White Paper, and fight the White Paper as though there were no war.'

Official British policies were governed by the empire's strategic considerations – which meant that as long as all-out war against the Germans in Europe continued, every effort had to be made to keep the Arabs on the Allied side. The overall effect of the Arab Revolt was still fresh in British memory, as was the need to transfer two fully-equipped divisions from active duty elsewhere, to Palestine, in order to suppress the disturbances. This was not a matter that the British could take lightly, and the result was that the Jewish community was sacrificed, as it were, on the altar of Britain's good relations with the Arab countries. Palestine's strategic location, and its importance in the Middle East theatre of operations, obliged the British to seek ways to placate the Arabs, while overlooking their notorious and openly nationalist fascist leanings.

The periods of close cooperation between Britain and the Yishuv followed a cyclical pattern, rising or falling in direct relation to fluctuations in British policies toward their Jewish partners in Palestine or toward broader Zionist interests world-wide. Whenever Britain needed intelligence on a given objective, or required new field agents or other forms of assistance, cooperation intensified and official policies were temporarily laid aside. On the other hand, when the fortunes of war changed in their favour and the

front lines of combat moved further away from the region – British willingness to cooperate with the Yishuv waned accordingly, and the relationship
between the Mandatory authorities and the Yishuv were again marked by
strict adherence to official policies. As coordinator of both the open and
the covert ties with the British, Reuven Zaslany experienced at first-hand
this seesaw diplomacy which, at least as far as the British were concerned,
naturally tended more toward the official policy and less toward the covert,
more flexible relationship.

The outbreak of hostilities in Europe forced the British to take desperate
steps to keep up with rapid developments on the fields of battle and
diplomacy. At this particular point in time, the interests and needs of British
Intelligence converged with those of the Jewish–Zionist cause. At the
beginning of September 1939, contacts were renewed in London by Dr
Chaim Weizman and Major Grant, head of D Division in the Secret Service.
The two men agreed on cooperation between the two sides, with the British
acceding to a number of Jewish Agency requests, such as access to the Secret
Service's communications network between London, Jerusalem and New
York, preparation of *laissez-passez* documents to facilitate travel for Jewish
operatives between Britain and various European countries, and – following
the suspension of commercial air traffic in the region because of the war –
priority in the use of British military aircraft.

For his part, Dr Weizman promised the British assistance through the
extensive network of Jewish contacts throughout Europe and the Middle
East. He also informed Major Grant that Moshe Shertok would be his
representative in the Middle East. Thus the first seeds were planted for
cooperation at the highest level.[10]

The success of the covert cooperation between British Intelligence and
the Yishuv on intelligence matters required a high degree of secrecy, strict
compartmentalization, and careful screening of personnel to find the most
highly qualified and trustworthy people. The enemy was not only Nazi
Germany, fascist Italy or Vichy France, but rather – and often more
vehemently – enemies from within the Jewish Yishuv, and the official policies
of the Mandatory government. The basic form of cooperation was hammered
out by David HaCohen, who was chosen as official liaison on behalf of the
Yishuv, and a Secret Service officer, George Taylor, an Australian merchant
who had joined the Service and was responsible for D Division's activities
in the Balkans. There were a number of reasons for the shift that occurred
in the attitude of British Intelligence personnel toward the Jews. First and
foremost, there was the operational–professional aspect, according to which
– categorically – every means possible had to be exploited to achieve the
overall goal of defeating the enemy. Secondly, there was the personal aspect:
as we noted above, many of the people in British Intelligence during the war

were not hardened military professionals, but civilians pressed into service because of the war, who were somewhat more pragmatic and open to discussion – depending on their civilian calling prior to their mobilization. Last but not least among the reasons for this shift in attitude, there was also the favourable impression the Jewish liaisons made on the British, who soon realized that they were good partners to do business with.

Reuven Zaslany and Eliyahu Sasson both helped to strengthen ties with the British on Arab affairs, while Zaslany also worked with David HaCohen on issues relating to anti-German activities. From the outset, the two men made it clear to the British side that they represented the Yishuv institutions, were working strictly on their behalf, and were unwilling to accept a salary for their pains. They also refused to be drafted into the army and receive officer rank although this was accepted practice in wartime. They retained their status as civilians, and as such were not subordinate to officers of the British Army.

After the fall of France, D Division changed its deployment in the Balkans and moved its headquarters to Cairo. From the summer of 1940 on, Cairo became the centre for the covert contacts between the Yishuv and British Intelligence. The sheer distance from London gave the intelligence people in Cairo leeway to respond to ongoing developments in the field.

The establishment of the SOE, and the transfer of D Division to its command, created endless friction between the Secret Service and the SOE, particularly in the East European theatre. This friction was much less apparent in the Middle East, due to a great extent to the people involved – a fact which made it easier for the British officers to cement their contacts with the Yishuv.

Slowly but surely, Reuven Zaslany assumed the lead role in the web of special relations being spun between various British Intelligence bodies and the Yishuv. It is important to point out that Zaslany was the Jewish Agency's official liaison with the British, and operated openly in this capacity in all his contacts with the civilian authorities, the army, the police and the CID in Palestine. He was the official and legal representative of the governing bodies of the Yishuv, and it was to him that private citizens or public institutions applied when they wanted to contact the British authorities on various matters, from commercial ties to requests to visit relatives detained at the Latrun police station. In other words, Zaslany combined – even juggled – official and covert activities in all his contacts with various British officials.

Under the circumstances, discretion was of paramount importance, and in order to create a solid basis for contacts with the SOE, a covert channel of communication was established. All the traffic on this channel was transmitted in English, using specially devised code names. It was impossible to maintain covert operational relationships with representatives of a government officially opposed to any form of cooperation with institutions of the Yishuv – beyond the necessary ruler–subject relationship – unless one took great precautions.

Reuven Zaslany's nature, manner and working methods, and particularly his ability to forge close ties with officials in British Intelligence – all these were to a great extent responsible for the success of the covert cooperation between British Intelligence and the Yishuv during the Second World War. Zaslany, an honest, dedicated, hardworking, well-organized and naturally wary man, maintained well-compartmentalized working relations with various intelligence bodies, each serving his needs in a particular matter. The ability he displayed during the Arab Revolt to gather intelligence information, analyse and disseminate it to the appropriate authorities, now made it possible for him to participate as an equal in meetings with the British, some of whom were new to the region, others people with whom he had worked previously and counted among his personal friends.

In all the secret communications between the two sides, and in the written reports on joint operations, Zaslany and HaCohen used various code names: co-workers on the Jewish side were known as 'Friends' (F), and their British opposite numbers were 'D' (for D Division); Moshe Shertok was F/S, F/BK; David HaCohen, F/D; Reuven Zaslany, F/Z; Yehuda Arazi, F/J; David Ben Gurion, F/BG, and so on. On the British side: George Taylor was A/D, D/H; George Pollock, head of the SOE in Cairo from 1940–41, D/HP, etc.[11] Zaslany himself used a number of code names in his contacts with the Yishuv: 'Raphael', 'Shiloah' or 'Raz'. The last of these, comprising the initials of his name in Hebrew, was particularly apt since it not only included his name but also alluded to his activities – 'raz' in Hebrew means 'secret' or 'mystery'.

The parameters and specific nature of each instance of cooperation were determined initially by an agreement on general principles, and then on the basis of specific operational circumstances relating to the task at hand. In the meetings between the two sides, the espionage agents set out their operational requirements which ranged from the recruiting of candidates for undercover missions, through requests for specialized communications equipment and operatives for sabotage operations behind enemy lines, and finally – the pinnacle of the cooperation – recruiting and dispatching volunteer parachutists from the Yishuv into occupied Europe. For his part, Zaslany had much to offer: trained men and women, a proven ability to set up espionage rings, an enormous amount of goodwill and high motivation, and at times even unique possibilities, such as the establishment of the interrogation centre in Haifa headed by Emmanuel Vilensky (Yelan), or the creation of custom-built communications equipment by the men of the Hagannah's Communications Service – Moshe Bassin, Mounya and Mischa Gordin.

More than once, the cooperation and the various operations that ensued produced a conflict of political and diplomatic interests between the official British Government policy line to the tacit operational-covert policy line. To a large extent, it was Reuven Zaslany's ability to act wisely, tread cautiously, and display a great flair for manoeuvring, that made these operations possible.

It is impossible within the limited scope of this article to describe in detail the many and diverse activities undertaken by Reuven Zaslany and his people during the war. We shall therefore note the most important of them, and concentrate on one particular framework of cooperation in which Zaslany played the lead role.

Active cooperation began in the spring of 1940, when attempts were made to assist the Secret Service D Division in carrying out sabotage and blockade missions on shipping lines in the Danube. Their aim was to prevent shipments of petrol from the oil-fields of Romania into Germany. These operations were not successful, but they did create a framework for co-operation that would become more effective in subsequent joint ventures.

At a meeting that took place in the summer of 1940 between Reuven Zaslany, David HaCohen and Arthur Goodwill, details were concluded for future cooperation between the two sides. These now included a British request for custom-built communications equipment for agents about to be sent behind enemy lines. The Jews were also asked to provide the SOE with explosives and detonators. The financial arrangements involved in these transactions were also agreed upon at this meeting, to the mutual satisfaction of the two sides.

Operational cooperation continued with the creation of the 'Fake Arabs' unit[12] in Syria, under the command of the Syrian Platoon of the Hagannah. The platoon, commanded first by Aharonchik Leshem and later by Yigal Allon, carried out missions up until the beginning of 1943. Information gathered by its operatives was transmitted to Zaslany in Palestine, and he in turn handed it over to the British. The experience gained by the members of this platoon during these missions provided a solid basis for the development of the 'Fake-Arab' concept in the Palmach itself, and later for the activities of the Mossad in Arab countries.[13]

Another mission was carried out in Syria by Yohanan Ratner and a group of professionals from the Hagannah, as the Secret Service looked for ways to check out and mark strategic objectives throughout Syria and Lebanon: bridges, water conduits, high ground, etc. This kind of pre-operation intelligence-gathering was carried out as part of the cooperative actions undertaken in preparation for a possible British invasion into the Levant, or, alternately a German conquest of the region.

The failure of a team of 23 men from the Hagannah, secretly trained and outfitted by the SOE, to complete a sabotage mission to the oil refineries in Tripoli, Lebanon,[14] cast a pall over the cooperation, and was deeply distressing for everyone involved. The Allied invasion of Syria was imminent, and pressures to continue the joint operations intensified. Ya'akov Dostrovsky (Dori), the Hagannah's Chief-of-Staff, who coordinated British operational demands from the Hagannah in advance of the invasion, asked Reuven Zaslany to slow down the pace of the cooperation, and particularly to look after the people who had been involved in the operational missions. In the final analysis, members of the Palmach, the Hagannah, and local collaborators provided assistance to the British forces in transportation, sabotage and intelligence during the invasion of Syria.

In the summer of 1940, a special interrogation office, run by Emmanuel Vilensky, began operating in Haifa under the direct supervision of the ISLD (MI9's code name in the Middle East), and its commander John Teague, who maintained headquarters in Jerusalem. The interrogation office, which operated very successfully until July 1944, was an excellent example of the unique forms of assistance the Yishuv could offer the British. The office interrogated and interviewed thousands of Jewish and foreign refugees about their countries of origin, and Reuven Zaslany saw to it that the data from these investigations were transmitted to the British.

During the course of 1941, and up to the spring of 1942, anxiety about the fate of the Suez Canal Zone and Palestine increased among the British forces in the Middle East, as the Germans continued their eastward push in North Africa. Ultimately, Rommel's forces, advancing along the Libyan coastline toward the Egyptian border, were stopped only at el-Alamein. In preparation for these potentially dangerous developments, the SOE proposed setting up guerrilla and intelligence forces in Palestine that would be able to operate behind the German lines in case of an invasion. These units were to undergo special training to prepare them for this kind of warfare. Reuven Zaslany took it upon himself to organize the required forces, in cooperation with Palmach commander Yitzhak Sadeh, and others. In 1942, under a heavy cloak of secrecy, a training programme was launched in the forests near Kibbutz Mishmar Ha-emek. Palmach volunteers chosen for this mission underwent training in fieldcraft, sharpshooting, sabotage and guerrilla warfare under the watchful eye of British instructors. During these training sessions, Palmach commanders managed to impart to their soldiers various elements of military theory, and most importantly, with British financial assistance, managed to train entire companies for extended periods of time.

During these preparations for the defence plan, which became known as 'The Palestine Scheme', a number of new platoons were set up in the Palmach: the 'German' Platoon, the 'Arab' Platoon (also known as the 'Dawn' Platoon), and, later, the 'Balkan' Platoon. The men of these units underwent special training, and were supposed to take an active part in British military operations, should hostile elements overrun the country. At the same time, Zaslany was busy trying to set up a secret wireless network, and managed to persuade Moshe Dayan, who was recuperating from the loss of his eye during the invasion of Syria, to lend a helping hand. Some of the men who belonged to what became known as 'Moshe Dayan's Personal Network', later participated in the parachuting operations in the Balkans. In fact, it could be said that the establishment of this network was the basis for the parachutists' operation.

Army personnel and civilians throughout the Middle East breathed a sigh of relief when Field Marshal Montgomery managed to stop Rommel's Afrika Korps at the battle of el-Alamein in October 1942, thus removing the immediate threat of a German invasion. These events marked a turning point in the web of relationships that comprised the covert cooperation. As the main thrust of the war moved from the Middle East back into North Africa and then to Europe, so relations between British Intelligence and the Jewish Agency cooled. Earlier, in 1940, the SOE had been grievously offended by a Palmach raid on the arsenal of its commando school in the Carmel mountains. The school was one of the most successful and practically-oriented of the cooperation projects, and Reuven Shiloah had hoped to use it as a lever for expanding the framework of cooperation. He had envisioned bringing large numbers of Jewish volunteers from Palestine to train there, and, with their help, to pave the way to independence. However, as a direct consequence of the arms raid, the British announced their intention of shutting down the school. For hard-line SOE opponents of the cooperation, the raid was as good a reason as any to sever relations with the Yishuv, and they backed their demand with a call to adhere to the official anti-Zionist policy of the Government in London.

Thus during the early months of 1943 relations between British Intelligence and the Jewish Agency had cooled considerably – the Fake-Arabs unit in Syria had suspended all its activities on behalf of the British, and all cooperation with the SOE had ceased. Vilensky's interrogation office continued to function, but part of its work was diverted to a regional prisoner-interrogation centre which had been set up in Cairo.

At the same time, the plight of the Jews in Europe had become desperate. The reports, eye-witness accounts, and rumours concerning the bitter fate of European Jewry – which had begun filtering into Palestine toward the end of 1942 – placed the question of trying to extend help from the Yishuv to the Jews in Europe, in sharp focus. Reuven Zaslany and his colleagues from the Political Department in the Jewish Agency were faced with an agonizing dilemma: how were they to provide help for the Jews of Europe and, at the same time, maintain the vital covert cooperation with the British?

Reuven Zaslany and Eliyahu Epstein had, on various occasions, suggested the possibility of including the Jewish diaspora in the Allied war effort. Epstein did so from Istanbul in 1941, during the German invasion of Russia, and Zaslany expressed his support for this concept some time later. Dr Chaim Weizman preceded both of them when, in his first meeting with Major Grant, he raised the possibility of working with the Jews of Europe in the war against the Nazis. David HaCohen continued this line in his meetings with George Taylor in the winter of 1940.

Zaslany understood that a new period had begun, and that, as the main theatre of war operations moved to Europe, the elements of cooperation with the British must be moved into that area as well. Naturally, the actual participants in these operations at the beginning of 1943 were the same as they had been in the past, and Secret Service and SOE agents, who now had to concentrate all their intelligence efforts in the Balkans, often initiated contacts with private individuals in the Yishuv and with Zaslany, in order to seek candidates for intelligence work in Europe. SOE representatives were asked to come from Cairo to Jerusalem at the beginning of January 1943, to interview potential candidates for their operations. As noted above, however, all contacts with them were suspended in March of that year.

As usual, Reuven Zaslany was indefatigable, and at the beginning of February 1943 officers of the ISLD came to Jerusalem to screen the candidates. Fourteen people were chosen and taken to Egypt to undergo intensive professional and operational training. There were three Palestinian Jews who worked with the ISLD in Egypt as communications instructors: Peretz Rosenberg, Rehav'am Amir and Ya'akov Shapira. It was through their work that contact with the ISLD was maintained, and their activities may be seen as the basis for the parachutists' operation that was to follow. In May of 1943 Peretz Rosenberg joined a British mission to Tito's headquarters in Yugoslavia, thus becoming the first member of the group to be sent on an SOE mission.

The poor results of the cooperation with the SOE and the ISLD up to that point prompted Zaslany to turn to his old friend Lieutenant-Colonel Anthony (Tony) Simmonds, who had been posted to Cairo. During the Arab Revolt, Tony Simmonds had served as an Army Intelligence officer, and lived in Jerusalem, not far from Reuven Zaslany. At the beginning of 1941 Simmonds was transferred to a new unit set up in the region under the command of Brigadier Dudley Clark. This new unit was named the 'A Force', and dealt with subterfuge and deception. Simmonds was brought in to take command of the Middle East arena of MI9, the unit in charge of helping downed airmen and POWs to reach Allied lines.

At the beginning of 1943 Simmonds was approached by his old friend Reuven Zaslany in an attempt to organize some form of cooperation between Simmonds' MI9 and the Jewish Agency. Each side promised to deliver whatever it could to the other. The Jewish side, represented by Zaslany, undertook to include the rescue of British POWs in operations mounted to rescue Jews from the Balkans. The British, for their part, promised that as part of their assistance to their own MI9 agents, they would help insert agents from the Aliya Bet Institution[15] into the Balkans in order to set up rescue operations for Jews. The so-called Tony–Danny Agreement was signed on 15 January 1943 between Tony Simmonds and Ze'ev Shind (code-named 'Danny'), with Reuven Zaslany as the third party. At the time, there was no direct operational need for implementing this agreement, but the collapse of the contacts with the SOE and the ISLD in the spring of 1943 made it necessary for Zaslany and Simmonds to revive their negotiations.

In their wisdom, both men understood the potential advantages to both sides from their cooperation in the Balkans. Simmonds, who was well versed in the geographic–ethnic and political–military situation in the Balkans, had come to the conclusion that Jewish agents, who were born in Eastern European countries, spoke the languages and were intimately acquainted with the areas of operation, would be the best and most trustworthy agents for his missions, and, of no less importance, they were trained and immediately available.

The different aims of the two sides converged therefore at this point in time and space. The Jews were trying in any way possible to help their beleaguered brethren, while the British were desperately seeking agents to provide aid and assistance to downed airmen, POWs, and escapees in the Balkans, whose numbers had been rising steadily since the summer of 1943.

With Simmonds' blessings, the parachutists' operation got under way. There were three people involved on the Jewish side: Reuven Zaslany, Enzo Sireni and Zvi Yehi'elli. Zaslany, the most senior in political rank and position, was the driving force behind the entire operation. He cajoled, encouraged, monitored and supported all the people involved, particularly the agents who had been chosen and trained for the mission. Zaslany came to Cairo to be with them prior to their departure, and kept in constant touch with Tony Simmonds and his men in order to prevent any possible friction of the kind that had been known to occur between Jewish Agency officials and representatives of the SOE and the ISLD.

Despite the failure of the talks with the SOE and the ISLD in spring 1943, Zaslany persevered, and toward September of 1943, negotiations were resumed. The fact that the headquarters of the SOM (Special Operations – Mediterranean) had moved to Bari, and that all the operational intelligence elements in the region had been consolidated under one joint command, facilitated the renewal of these contacts. In all his meetings with the intelligence people, Reuven Zaslany emphasized the double function his men were to fulfil: 'It was agreed that these operatives, apart from serving the British authorities on the information side, would also serve as emissaries of the Zionist movement and the Yishuv in Palestine to the Jews of the occupied countries.'[16]

The British espionage people requested candidates who could serve as wireless operators and instructors at partisan headquarters in Yugoslavia and neighbouring countries. As a direct result of these developments, the Jewish Agency ran a number of courses in the relevant disciplines: a course in wireless operation at Kibbutz Ramat Ha-Kovesh; courses in parachuting at the Ramat David airfield; and a special course for infiltrating agents at Kibbutz Ha-Zorea. The candidates participating in these courses were selected and screened by the Jewish Agency and by the British.

The 37 parachutists who eventually set out on the operational mission as part of the overall British Intelligence effort in Europe to a great extent symbolized Reuven Zaslany's burning ambition and the measure of his success in his secret contacts with his British colleagues. The significance of the covert negotiations, at a time when official British policy was anti-Zionist, hostile, tough, and uncompromising, and totally oblivious to the fate of European Jewry, was highlighted by the success of the parachutists' mission which was, undoubtedly, the climax of the covert cooperation between the two sides. The missions themselves were only partially successful, but the very fact that emissaries from the Yishuv landed on European soil was of supreme importance to the status of the Jewish people in the eyes of the nations of the world during and after the war.

Moshe Shertok and his faithful right-hand man, Reuven Zaslany, did not pause to rest on their laurels. As they were putting the finishing touches to the parachutists' operation, they were also hard at work preparing an ambitious plan – which many thought was too grandiose – to save the Jews of Hungary. The 'Resistance Plan' or the 'Europe Plan' was first suggested at the outset of the war. The idea was to recruit, train and dispatch a group of volunteer soldiers from Palestine to operate in occupied Europe. Unlike the parachutists' operation, this plan involved an independent unit that would function autonomously in the area with support from nearby Allied forces.

The theoretical concept turned into an operational plan at the beginning of 1944, after it transpired that it would be impossible to carry out such an operation in Poland. Attention was turned to the Balkans, and in particular to the Jews of Hungary. Moshe Shertok prepared a memorandum on the subject and Reuven Zaslany immersed himself in the details, in the hope of pursuing the plan and bringing it to fruition. Given the circumstances, time was of the essence, so Zaslany concentrated all his efforts on contacts in Jerusalem, Cairo and Bari. Shertok handled all the diplomatic aspects of the enterprise in Cairo and in London. Everything relating to the plan was designated as Top Secret and marked with a secret code letter – 'T'. All the documents pertaining to this plan bear this marking. It is important to note that the negotiations surrounding this plan took place at the same time as official talks were under way to set up a Jewish fighting force within the British Army – the Jewish Brigade.

Reuven Zaslany met with American and British Intelligence officers in Cairo, and with Brigadier Clayton, the highest-ranking intelligence officer in the region, and intelligence adviser to the Resident Minister, Lord Moyne. All the military people Zaslany talked to at that time agreed on the necessity of the plan, which stipulated the insertion of agents from Palestine into Hungary in order to organize and activate the local Jewish communities as local resistance cells charged with carrying out acts of sabotage and subversion. The obstacles to the plan, as the people in Cairo stressed, were political, and it was up to Shertok to take action on this issue. Shertok and Zaslany heeded their advice and prepared a copy of the plan, which they presented to the High Commissioner to Palestine, Harold MacMichael, and to Lord Moyne.

At the beginning of March 1944 the Germans overran Hungary, and the fate of Hungarian Jewry was now in their hands. As the situation deteriorated, the pressures for approving the plan intensified. Reuven Zaslany travelled to Cairo once again, while in Palestine volunteers were already being recruited. Shaul Avigur coordinated operations in Palestine in place of Zvi Yehi'elli who was in Egypt at that time with the parachutists just prior to their departure. Ya'akov Salomon was appointed commander of the training course which was to take place under British supervision.

Despite initial opposition from various British authorities in the area, fears stemming from concerns such as: 'What will happen after the war is over?' or 'What would the Arabs say?', Shertok and Zaslany decided to stick with the original plan but to change their tactics. Both of them understood that the chances for the success of the plan were better now, provided it was put into effect outside the British political–military establishment in Palestine and Egypt. Shertok, who was in London at the time, told Zaslany to go to Bari in the south of Italy, since that was where the Allied forces in North Africa and the SOM had set up forward headquarters. Moreover, Resident Minister MacMillan, who was in Algiers, had set up an office there for his senior representative.

In order to understand Reuven Zaslany's actions in Bari, one must read the reports he sent to Jerusalem at the time, and the summaries that he prepared upon his return. It is also instructive to look through the reports submitted by the British officials with whom he met. Facing these men was a short, bespectacled man whose name was hard for them to pronounce or remember (and they devised several variations instead), who represented a small nation without a country that was asking to be allowed to take part in the British war effort in the Balkans, and requesting help for its persecuted brethren in Hungary. Zaslany's personal charm and powers of persuasion came together with British operational intelligence needs to produce the desired results. The high-ranking officials he met with in Bari were convinced of the urgency of the operation, and even told Zaslany, at some point in their talks, to return to Palestine and begin recruiting candidates for the operation.

When Zaslany later summed up the British support for the plan, and compared it with earlier opposition in Cairo and in London, he attributed it to three factors. First of all, despite all their efforts, British Intelligence and the British Army had not succeeded in setting up a viable resistance movement in Hungary. The 'Resistance Plan', as proposed, would help them realize this objective which, when it did finally succeed in the summer of 1944, turned out to be of vital importance to the British war effort.

Secondly, the British had suffered a number of bitter failures in their attempts to make contact with underground groups in Europe. The Jewish Agency proposal, by way of contrast, suggested that they work through the Jewish Agency which, naturally, neither had, nor ever would have, any larger strategic plans concerning the future of Hungary's regime or government.

Thirdly, Zaslany felt that the British were trying to redress at least some of the wrongs that they had dealt the Jewish people in the course of the war by repeatedly rejecting the idea of setting up a Jewish military unit within the British Army which could join the fight against the Germans and help the British set up underground Jewish resistance units inside Europe.

On 24 July 1944, the Political Committee of the Allied Headquarters in Bari discussed the plan submitted by Zaslany, approved it, and sent it on to London for final authorization by the British Chiefs-of-Staff in London. The Committee recommended that the number of volunteers be reduced from the hundreds suggested in Zaslany's original document to a total of ten, who would work in conjunction with the SOE in Hungary.

The Chiefs-of-Staff discussed the plan and sent it on to the Foreign Office for their reaction and comment before making a final decision. Zaslany remained optimistic throughout, and even reported to some of the High Commissioner's people in Jerusalem on his meetings in Bari. Things moved very slowly in London, and it was only on 10 August 1944 that the Chiefs-of-Staff met again for a final discussion on this issue. Ultimately, this would become the first instance of an agreement on a framework for cooperation between a British operational unit, the SOE, and representatives of the Jewish people.

Reuven Zaslany's tireless efforts and endless lobbying of the British authorities finally bore fruit. The British approval in principle was, in this case, far more important than the actual operation itself. The month of August 1944 was a very difficult month for the British in Palestine. Between January and July members of the LEHI underground movement[17] struck at a large number of British targets, including army bases, and local CID headquarters and facilities. Shortly before the final approval of Zaslany's plan, the LEHI made an unsuccessful attempt on the life of the British High Commissioner in Jerusalem. It was in this context that the approval of the 'Resistance Plan', even in its reduced format, was a beacon of hope for the people of the Jewish Agency, who strongly opposed all forms of terror committed by the Jewish underground movements, the IZL and the LEHI, for fear that they would severely hamper ongoing efforts to win official British approval for the creation of the Jewish Brigade and the implementation of the 'Resistance Plan'.

To Shertok and Zaslany's deep disappointment, the 'Resistance Plan' was shelved for two reasons: first of all, it turned out to be virtually impossible to find candidates who met the tough standards set by the British, and, secondly, prior to the approval of the plan, the situation in Hungary underwent dramatic changes. Mass deportations of Jews to concentration camps had begun, leaving intact only very few of the Jewish resistance cells – the mainstay of the original plan.

Faced with these developments, on 31 August 1944 Zaslany wrote to Major Morton, the SOE representative in Bari, who had supported the plan, and asked him to revise the criteria for recruiting candidates. He also proposed concentrating all efforts in this mission on Budapest and its environs. The British, led by Morton, decided instead to cancel the operation in order to avoid unnecessary casualties. Reuven Zaslany, who had worked so hard to realize the plan, received the official cancellation notice from Bari with a heavy heart.

Reuven Zaslany's activities as liaison between British Intelligence and the Jewish Agency now faced a time of change. He ended his service in this position in the autumn of 1944, and began preparing for a diplomatic mission to the United States. Both David Ben Gurion and Zaslany himself realized that the time had come to move on, and there was no one quite as well equipped as Zaslany to set about hitching the Zionist wagon to a new horse.

Reuven Zaslany summed up this period of activity in a detailed memorandum on 27 November 1944, and presented it to the members of the Political Department at the Jewish Agency before departing for the United States. In his memorandum Zaslany described in detail the chain of events leading from the initial contacts with British Intelligence at the outbreak of the war up to and including the summer of 1944.

At the end of his report, Zaslany wrote the following:

> I have submitted this general description of intelligence work for one reason: in the years to come, intelligence and the activity associated with it will continue to play an important role in Allied diplomatic and economic activities. Britain and the United States paid a high price for neglecting this field in the past. It is safe to assume that after the war they will leave operational intelligence units in Europe. We too will have to operate in Europe. That is where our immigrants will come from. We will have to continue this cooperation – or else find new ways of cooperating with these institutions.[18]

Reuven Zaslany, in his own way, with his sharp instincts and extraordinary powers of perception, understood all too well the biblical injunction 'And with cunning thou shalt make war'. His vitally important undercover activities with elements of British Intelligence at the time of the covert intelligence cooperation during the Second World War, remain to this day as a milestone and a challenge to all the men and women involved in covert activities on behalf of the State of Israel.

NOTES

1. 'Yishuv', literally 'settlement' in Hebrew, and, by extension, the term used to designate the entire Jewish community in Palestine before the establishment of the State of Israel.
2. An underground espionage organization established in 1915 in Palestine to help the British gather information against the Turks and complete their conquest of the country. The ring was uncovered by the Turks in 1917, and most of its members were executed.

The name is an acronym for the Hebrew – *Netzach Yisrael Lo Yeshakker* – 'the Glory of Israel will not lie' (I Samuel 15:29), one interpretation of which is that Israel's destiny shall prove itself, and redemption will be achieved.

3. Known as the MacDonald White Paper (after Commonwealth Minister Malcolm MacDonald), its principal aim was to pacify the more extreme factions among the Arabs of Palestine. It placed severe limitations on the sale of land to Jews in Palestine, and on Jewish immigration, limiting to 75,000 the number of Jews that would be allowed into the country over a period of five years, to ensure that the population of the Jewish Yishuv would not exceed a third of the total population of the country. This was the third such White Paper issued by the British Government concerning Palestine. The previous two (Churchill's in June 1922 and Passfield's in October 1930) also limited the number of Jews living in Palestine, ostensibly in order to uphold the rights of the local Arab population.

4. Yoav Gelber, *The Source of the Lilies* (Tel Aviv: Ministry of Defence Publications, 1992), pp.93–5; Haggai Eshed, *Reuven Shiloah – The Man Behind The Mossad*, trans. David and Leah Zinder (London: Frank Cass, 1997), pp.8–9.

5. Eshed, *Reuven Shiloah*, pp.23–5.

6. Criminal Investigation Department.

7. Eshed, *Reuven Shiloah*, p.53.

8. Eshed, *Reuven Shiloah*, p.54.

9. A spontaneously organized grass-roots self-defence movement, aimed at helping to protect Arab lives and property from the internal Arab terror that was rampant during the Arab Revolt and claimed up to 4,500 lives. For more see Eshed, *Reuven Shiloah*, p.31.

10. Eldad Harouvi, 'British Intelligence and the Covert Cooperation with the Yishuv during World War II', MA thesis (Haifa University, 1992). Chapter entitled 'First Steps', pp.73–9.

11. These secret code names were found among Reuven Zaslany's many papers that are kept in the Central Zionist Archives in Jerusalem, cat. no. S25/22352.

12. So called because of its use of Arab-looking men and women, fluent in Arabic, who could move easily in and out of Arab cities and villages to gather information.

13. It is interesting to note that this same concept of 'Fake Arabs' (using the same Hebrew word – *mista'aravim* – for the unit) is still being used by the IDF, this time for operations to quell disturbances in the West Bank.

14. A mission that became known as 'The 23 of the Boat' – after the 23 members of the group. They did not reach their objective and none of the men were ever heard from again, and to this day no evidence has ever been found to clarify exactly what happened to them.

15. The framework set up by the Jewish Agency to gather and bring to Israel Jewish refugees from Europe.

16. From the Hagannah Archives in Eliyahu Golomb House in Tel Aviv. Section 29, file no. 6, from 7/5/1949.

17. The LEHI (from its Hebrew acronym: Lohamei Herut Yisrael – the Israel Freedom Fighters) was an extreme right-wing underground organization led by Avraham Stern, that had split off from the slightly less militant IZL organization (the 'Irgun', from its Hebrew acronym: *Irgun Zeva'i Leumi* – National Military Organization), led by Menachem Begin.

18. Eshed, *Reuven Shiloah*, p.101. The original document is in the Central Zionist Archives, in file S25/7902.

4

Reuven Shiloah – Master of the Covert Contact: The First Attempt to Organize a Summit Meeting between Moshe Sharett and Gamal Abdul Nasser*

HESI CARMEL

Reuven Shiloah, the first head of the Mossad, has often been called 'a one-man Mossad'.[1] He was involved in every Israeli Intelligence operation in the 1940s and 1950s. At the same time, Shiloah was one of the few Middle East experts in Israel who regarded the Arabs not only as enemies and intelligence targets but also as neighbours and potential allies. He pursued his efforts to establish covert contacts with Arab leaders virtually simultaneously with his intelligence activities. He was one of a small group of people who handled the secret Israeli contacts with King Abdullah of Jordan, with the leaders of Syria and Lebanon, and with King Farouk of Egypt. The 'Young Officers' Revolt' in Egypt, which toppled Farouk in a bloodless coup, and raised the banner of social revolution, aroused great hopes in Israel. Ben Gurion's retirement to Kibbutz Sdeh Boker in 1953[2] together with Moshe Sharett's election as Prime Minister, created a slim window of opportunity for peace initiatives with Egypt.

The year 1954 was critical for the secret attempts to reach some kind of agreement with Egypt. Nasser's rise to power gave a small group of Israeli leaders the feeling that the young and ambitious army officer, who was trying to move his country in the direction of social progress, could be a suitable partner for peace talks with Israel.

Reuven Shiloah was one of the leaders of a group of Israeli officials who sought every opportunity to set up secret negotiations with Nasser. While serving as Minister in the Israeli Embassy in Washington, Shiloah spared no effort to make some form of contact with the Egyptian leader. The most

---

*Trans. David Zinder.

important conduit in this respect was the CIA, whose operatives were closely involved with the young officers who had led the coup in Cairo. What is more, there were persistent rumours that the CIA had been directly involved in the young officers' rebellion, as part of an overall strategic US plan to remove from the Middle East all the long-established rulers, as well as the British and French, and leave the United States as sole power-broker in the area.

The first feelers aimed at investigating the possibilities of secret negotiations with key Egyptian officials were sent out shortly after the conclusion of Israel's War of Independence in 1948. Two years later, in February 1950, Captain Yeruham Cohen, who had been ADC to Yigal Allon[3] during the War of Independence, took advantage of a special relationship that had sprung up during the war at the siege of the 'Faluja Pocket',[4] with one of the officers of the encircled Egyptian forces – Gamal Abdul Nasser.

Yeruham Cohen and Nasser met for the first time the day after the bitter battle over the former British police fortress at Iraq Suweidan.[5] On orders from Yigal Allon, who commanded the Southern Front, Yeruham took a Jeep with a loudspeaker and drove up to a forward Egyptian outpost waving a white flag, in order to make contact with the Egyptians following their defeat. Among the three Egyptians who came out to meet him was one whom Cohen described as young, impressive-looking but somewhat abashed – Major Gamal Abdul Nasser.

As the Israeli and the Egyptian officers waited for the commanders of the Egyptian brigade to show up, Cohen and Nasser exchanged views on the situation in Egypt and in Israel, on British colonialism, and on corruption among the Egyptian leadership. Two months later the two men met once again, on the final day of the Egyptian retreat from the Negev. At that meeting at 'Ouja (present-day Nitzana, on the Israeli–Egyptian border), Nasser appeared in the dress uniform of a full colonel in the Egyptian Army, and seemed much more self-confident than at their first encounter.

'Do you remember what I told you at our last meeting?' Nasser asked Yeruham Cohen. 'That you might not see your wife and daughters again?' Cohen replied. 'And I set your mind at ease, and told you that you would see your wife and daughters and that you would have a son too.'

'True,' Nasser said, 'and she did give birth – to a boy.'

'Well done!' Cohen replied joyfully. 'Congratulations, congratulations!'

Upon his return to Tel Aviv, Cohen immediately went out to buy a gift for the newborn son of *Bimbashi* (Colonel) Nasser. Through a complicated series of manœuvres he managed to get the gift to his 'friend', Nasser, in Cairo, and even received a thank-you note through a mutual acquaintance. Yeruham Cohen was in constant touch with his former Palmach commander, Yigal

Allon, who had left the army and gone to London to continue his studies. Allon encouraged Cohen to keep up the connection with the Egyptian officer, who seemed, even then, destined for greatness.

In July 1952 Colonel Nasser participated in the 'Free Officers'' coup against King Farouk, which toppled the king's rule, and, in a bloodless revolution, turned Egypt from a corrupt monarchy into a country ruled by a Revolutionary Council of young army officers bent on introducing major reforms and social justice to the country.

A short time after the coup, Yeruham Cohen sent another message to Nasser, this time congratulating the young officer on the successful revolution, and, a few months later, he even received confirmation that his message had reached its destination. In 1952 it still seemed as though peace between Egypt and Israel was just around the corner. Secret and indirect contacts between the two sides were conducted through many different channels simultaneously. Eliyahu Sasson, who was in charge of most of the contacts with the Arab countries, continued to exchange messages through intermediaries with leading figures in Egypt, and also arranged for the Israeli agent nicknamed 'Nicole' – Yolande Harmer – to return to Cairo and resume her previous contacts with leading members of Farouk's court. After the assassination of Jordan's King Abdullah in 1951, Egypt became the focal point of Israel's attempts to establish secret contacts with top figures in the Arab world. Many people in Israel believed that the talks between Egypt and Israel that had begun during the armistice negotiations at Rhodes, should be continued, and could lead to a permanent peace settlement.

The Free Officers' coup in Egypt generated a great deal of optimism in various circles in Israel. The feeling was that the young revolutionaries could be suitable partners for peace negotiations. Even Ben Gurion, who was generally pessimistic about the chances for peace with the Arabs, sent Muhammad Naguib, the figurehead leader of the Free Officers, a supportive cable, congratulating him on the success of their rebellion.

At the beginning of 1954 a small crack appeared in the otherwise solid wall of hostility in the region. The moderate Moshe Sharett replaced Ben Gurion as Prime Minister in Israel, and Nasser replaced Naguib as head of the Revolutionary Council in Egypt. Sharett, a native-born Israeli, and descendant of the early BILU pioneers,[6] fluent in Arabic, a socialist with moderate political views, seemed a perfect partner for the young Egyptian officers who declared their intention of introducing wide-ranging social reforms in their country, in order to move it out of the Middle Ages and into the twentieth century.

Opinion in Israel was divided concerning the chances and the risks presented by the young officers' regime in Egypt. Moshe Sharett and his people – Reuven Shiloah, Eliyahu Sasson and others – believed that the young officers were promising potential partners for negotiations on a peace settlement, while Ben Gurion and his 'youngsters' – Moshe Dayan, Shimon Peres, and the man who replaced him at the Ministry of Defence, Pinhas Lavon – regarded the Free Officers' coup as a potential threat to Israel's security.

The two camps also disagreed on security policy as a whole. While Ben Gurion and the majority of the top Israeli security echelons regarded the retaliatory raid policy as the appropriate response to terrorist infiltration from Jordan and Egypt, Sharett wanted to limit the policy of retaliation to only a few, small-scale actions, in order to retain the possibility of negotiating with the Arab countries, particularly with Egypt.

Consequently, two parallel, and at times totally disconnected, policies were at work in Israel *vis-à-vis* the Arab countries. Sharett, together with Shiloah and Sasson, searched everywhere for covert channels of communication with Egypt, while some of the top security people in the country, chiefly Lavon and Benyamin Gibli, sought means to undermine the new Egyptian regime – from the inside through subversive actions, and from the outside through numerous and large-scale retaliatory raids.

Following the major retaliatory raid in Kibya,[7] and before he relinquished the premiership, David Ben Gurion gave an apocalyptic forecast of future events in the region. He predicted that in 1956 a major war would break out between Israel and the Arab countries. Sharett, who did not contest the theoretical possibility of such a confrontation, tried to take every diplomatic and political step possible to prevent a 'second round' of warfare between the two sides. Sharett's policy plans focused on three different levels simultaneously: on the Palestinian level, he proposed a far-reaching plan of reparations for the Arab refugees of 1948; on the Arab level, he did everything he could to find ways of reaching some kind of high-level dialogue with leading Egyptian figures; and on the international level, he was a strong proponent of the American orientation, as opposed to the European orientation of some Israeli foreign policy-makers, among them Shimon Peres.

The American orientation dovetailed perfectly with the attempts being made at the time to establish a covert channel of communication with the Egyptians. The CIA had been involved in the Free Officers' rebellion in Egypt. The Americans were looking for every possible way to neutralize French and British influence in the region, as part of an overall policy of gaining an important strategic foothold for the United States in the region. The reasons for this were two-fold: first of all, the area's vast oil reserves, and secondly, the general anti-Soviet orientation of American foreign policy, which sought every way possible to head off Soviet penetration of the region.

In the course of 1954 two parallel tracks were set up for secret talks with the Egyptians, in an effort to bring about a summit meeting between Nasser and Sharett. These were the most important, and most timely efforts to find a basis for negotiation between Israel and Egypt. Many Middle East experts felt that 1954 was the last time it was possible – with good chances of success – to reach a settlement between the two countries, until Sadat's visit to Jerusalem in 1977.

The first channel of communication to Egypt was opened up in Washington between Shiloah and officials from the CIA, whose agent in Cairo, Kermit Roosevelt (the grandson of President Theodore Roosevelt), was one of the people closest to Abdul Nasser. Nasser received strong American backing, particularly from the CIA, in his attempts to remove the British presence from the Suez Canal Zone. The heads of the CIA regarded Nasser as an important partner in the anti-Soviet defence system they were busy setting up, the first two components of which were Iraq and Turkey. They gave the search for a solution of the Arab–Israeli problem top priority in their grand plan for 'a new Middle East'. When Shiloah arrived in Washington in September 1953 to take up his post as Minister at the Israeli Embassy, after leaving his position as head of the Mossad, he used his intelligence connections to nurture further contacts in the CIA, arousing profound envy in his successor at the Mossad, Isser Harel,[8] who regarded these contacts as his own private domain.

Shiloah had first made contact with officials from the CIA's wartime predecessor, the OSS, during the Second World War. The first American Intelligence officer to establish contact with representatives of the Jewish Agency and the 'Briha' organization,[9] had been Jim Angleton, the OSS representative in Italy. Later, as head of the Mossad, Shiloah developed a close relationship with the director of the CIA, Walter Bedell-Smith, General Eisenhower's Chief-of-Staff during the Second World War.

Reuven Shiloah renewed the good contacts he had nurtured in the past with Bedell-Smith, who in 1953 was serving as Assistant-Secretary of State, and with Jim Angleton, one of the senior directors of the CIA. Angleton, who was in charge of contacts between the CIA and the Israeli intelligence community, was a dyed-in-the-wool anti-Communist, who regarded Israel as the West's main bulwark against Soviet penetration of the Middle East. It was through Angleton and the CIA representative in Cairo, Kermit Roosevelt, that Shiloah managed to make contact with Egyptian officials. A short while after Moshe Sharett took over from Ben Gurion as Prime Minister, Sharett, on Shiloah's advice, used the good offices of the Americans to send a message to Nasser. He suggested to the Egyptian leader that they set up a kind of direct, secret 'hot line' between Cairo and Jerusalem in order to deal swiftly and effectively with border clashes and day-to-day security problems, and to prevent any unwanted escalation in the military confrontation between the two countries.

It was through this channel of communication, too, that Sharett's proposal for a secret summit meeting was first transmitted to Nasser. At the same time, a second channel of communication opened up, independently of the CIA connection. Two Israeli representatives, Ziyama Divon and Dan Avni, set up secret contacts with the Egyptian military attaché in Paris, Colonel Sarwat Okasha, who was close to Nasser, and had been given permission by the Egyptian leader to make contact with the Israeli officials.

The connection with Okasha was established a short time before the 'Lavon Affair' spy-ring was captured in Cairo, and one of the first problems discussed by Okasha and the Israeli representatives concerned Israel's efforts to prevent the execution of the captured agents.

Another connection to Egypt was set up through Haled Mouhi al-Din, one of Nasser's closest associates, who was often at odds with the Egyptian President on questions of ideology. Mouhi al-Din was in close contact with an Egyptian Jew by the name of Henri Kouriel, a leading figure in the Egyptian Communist party who was living in exile in Paris. Kouriel, who was very active in setting up secret contacts between Arabs and Israelis, maintained close ties with public figures right across the Israeli political spectrum. Years later, in the 1970s, Kouriel was even involved in an attempt to arrange a meeting between Arik Sharon, at that time a member of the IDF General Staff, and Yasser Arafat.

In October 1954 Shiloah and Sasson held a series of meetings in Paris with Colonel Okasha and an Egyptian official sent by Nasser as his personal representative. The secret discussions resulted in a four-point memorandum of understanding:

(1) Both sides would do everything in their power to prevent armed clashes along the borders.
(2) The two sides would set up a direct telephone link (a 'hot line') to allow adequate time to deal with conflicts promptly.
(3) The two sides would continue to maintain a conduit for direct talks through their respective representatives in Paris.
(4) Egypt would allow passage through the Suez Canal of ships carrying goods to Israel under foreign flags.

Following this agreement, Nasser agreed to receive an emissary from Israel to discuss the contacts that would have to made in order to arrange a summit meeting between Nasser and Sharett. Shiloah, who was the prime mover behind the meetings held in advance of the proposed summit, was notified by Colonel Okasha of Egypt's agreement to the meeting. However, it was agreed that the technical details would be handled through intelligence channels. The CIA representative in Cairo, Kermit Roosevelt, agreed to look after the Israeli representative during his stay in Cairo.

Sharett decided to entrust the Commission to Yigael Yadin, former Chief-of-Staff of the IDF, and later world-renowned archaeologist. Yadin was in London at the time, pursuing his studies in archaeology once again, after having suspended them for the duration of the War of Independence. He was regarded as the man best suited to this unique mission. As a former Chief-of-Staff, he had a solid security–military background; at the same time he was a university professor and a private citizen with no formal connection to the country's political establishment. The final coordinating touches for the Israeli emissary's visit to Cairo were taken care of by Jim Angleton of the CIA.

Memi De Shalit, a high-ranking official in the Prime Minister's office, was sent to Rome to meet Angleton and receive from him an envelope with all the arrangements for the Cairo summit. De Shalit later remembered very clearly his meeting with Angleton in Rome, and claimed that he knew nothing about the contents of the envelope he took back with him to Israel. On 26 January 1955, after all the arrangements for the meeting in Cairo had been finalized, Sharett used a Mossad courier to send Yadin his final instructions prior to his trip and the proposed meeting with Nasser.

Sharett asked Yadin to wait in London for the go-ahead, which would be sent to him in a coded cable. The Prime Minister postponed giving final approval to the meeting until the Egyptian court handed down its verdict in the trial of the Lavon Affair spy-ring, which was expected any day. In accordance with the original plans, Yadin made arrangements for the journey from London to Cairo, and then waited for Sharett's final approval.

Had the meeting between Yadin and Nasser taken place at the end of January 1955, as planned, it would certainly have changed Middle East history. However, on the morning of 27 January a Cairo court found the two leaders of the Lavon Affair fiasco, Azzar and Marzuk, guilty of espionage, and sentenced them to death. Sharett, who was taken by surprise by the move, sent a message to Nasser through the CIA, expressing his 'anger and amazement' over this development. International intervention on behalf of the Cairo defendants had led Sharett to believe, up to the very last minute, that Nasser would decide to pardon them. But the hoped-for miracle did not occur, and the two were hanged in prison on 30 January 1955.

That very day, Sharett, who was furious with Nasser, decided, in consultation with the head of the Mossad, Isser Harel, to postpone Yadin's trip to Cairo. Instructions to that effect were sent to Yadin in London via the Mossad. On that day Sharett wrote the following entry in his private diary: 'We will not conduct negotiations in the shadow of the gallows.' He was never given another opportunity to renew the contacts. Ben Gurion's return to the Ministry of Defence on 21 February 1955, in the aftermath of the Cairo hangings, put an end to the Israeli policy of secret negotiations and compromise.

On 25 February Arab infiltrators killed an Israeli cyclist in the town of Rehovot. One of the infiltrators, who was pursued by IDF soldiers and killed shortly afterwards, had a note in his pocket with reports of observations he had apparently carried out from Gaza, on orders from Egyptian Military Intelligence. The following day, Minister of Defence Ben Gurion, and Chief-of-Staff Moshe Dayan, demanded Sharett's approval for a retaliatory raid against an Egyptian Army base in Gaza. Sharett was willing to approve a raid, but only on condition that it be of a limited nature. In the discussions they held on the planned action, Dayan told Sharett that he believed about ten Egyptian soldiers would be killed in the operation. At the same time, however, Dayan had already laid much more ambitious plans. In a meeting of the General Staff, Dayan asked some of his generals to submit an operational plan for the conquest of the entire Gaza Strip. He presented this plan to Ben Gurion at the beginning of March.

On 28 February Arik Sharon, then commander of the Paratroop Brigade, was given the go-ahead for Operation 'Black Arrow' – a raid on an Egyptian army base in the Gaza Strip. That very night, 150 paratroopers, led by legendary Israeli paratroop commanders 'Soupapo', Aharon Davidi and Danny Matt, attacked an Egyptian Army base near the city of Gaza, taking it completely by surprise and killing 37 Egyptian soldiers.

The operation raised an outcry around the world. Moshe Sharett felt that he was losing control over matters of state. He sent a note to Ben Gurion, warning him of possible reactions from the United States and the United Nations. 'I assume', he wrote, 'that the deviation from the number ten, which I heard from the Chief-of-Staff, to 37, was an unavoidable result of the battle, but we must understand that in matters such as these, quantity turns into quality.' Ben Gurion responded with a strongly-worded letter. 'I understand that foreign governments play favourites among various countries', he wrote. 'However, I am not obliged to abide by such Hottentot morality.'

A few months after the Gaza operation, Ben Gurion issued a statement that was in time to become a motto for Israeli self-defence: 'Our future does not depend on what the Gentiles say, but rather on what the Jews do.'

The IDF action in Gaza caught Abdul Nasser off guard. In a meeting with an American official who had come to meet him in Cairo, he admitted that he had been caught 'with his pants down'. During this meeting, according to the American official, Nasser displayed an impressive understanding of the ins and outs of Israeli politics. He was aware of the fact that with Ben Gurion's return to the Ministry of Defence, many supporters of the hawkish 'Old Man' had also returned to positions of power. 'These days', Nasser said, 'I see that Ben Gurion is again taking steps to put his political ideas into practice.'

In Egypt, news of the Gaza attack sparked angry reactions. The top military commanders felt humiliated and threatened. In political circles, the feeling was that Israel was planning a much broader military action. Later, Nasser was to say that it was the Gaza operation that convinced him that he must supply his army with massive quantities of arms to offset Israeli aggression, and to set up units of *fedayeen* – or suicide squads – to carry the fight into Israel.

One last glimmer of hope for a continuation of the contacts between the two sides appeared briefly during a meeting held at Nitzana, on the Egyptian–Israeli border on 11 March 1955, between the Egyptian representative, Salah Gohar, and the Israeli representative, Yosef Tekoah, at a special meeting of the Joint Egyptian–Israeli Armistice Commission. The two representatives agreed to maintain regular meetings in order to try to lower tensions along the borders.

However, the situation along the borders deteriorated rapidly. On 24 March a band of infiltrators penetrated the *moshav* (village) of Patish, a settlement of Jews from Kurdistan, and opened fire on a wedding party. The party turned into tragedy, as one of the celebrants, Varda Friedman, was killed, and 22 others wounded. Ben Gurion visited the *moshav* the following day, and promised that they would not remain sitting-ducks for terrorist attacks.

That same day, Ben Gurion demanded that Sharett allow the IDF to occupy the entire Gaza Strip. When Sharett refused, Ben Gurion brought the issue to a vote in the Cabinet. There, too, he was turned down, when a majority of the ministers opposed the idea. But Sharett was aware that this would be his last such victory. His majority in the Cabinet rested on support from coalition ministers, rather than those from his own Mapai party. These, for the most part, voted with their venerated leader, Ben Gurion. Sharett knew that even though he had managed to ward off one military action, the atmosphere in the Government was no longer conducive to political negotiations.

And indeed, in April of that year the entire region underwent a dramatic change. Nasser returned from the Conference of Non-Aligned Nations in Bandung, Indonesia, crowned with glory as the undisputed leader of the awakening Third World. Sharett's extensive efforts to secure an invitation for Israel to the conference had been thwarted, and instead, Israel had become the object of unprecedented vituperation at the gathering. On his return from Bandung, Nasser placed a total ban on all further contacts with Israel.

Nasser's next move put Israel and Egypt on an unavoidable collision course. He ordered his Military Intelligence to set up a unit of 700 *fedayeen* suicide fighters, most of whom were Palestinians. These units embarked on a campaign of intelligence-gathering, sabotage and terrorist activities inside Israel, on direct orders from Colonel Hafez, head of Egyptian Intelligence in Gaza.

In July 1955, general elections were held in Israel, with Ben Gurion heading the Mapai party list.[10] Even though Mapai lost five seats in the elections, the Israeli public still gave strong, unequivocal backing to the activist policies propounded by Ben Gurion. The two parties whose platform advocated an active response to Arab aggression – the left-wing Ahdut Ha-Avoda (led by Yigal Allon), and the right-wing Herut (led by Menachem Begin) – made significant electoral gains. Sharett's conciliatory policies received little support among the Israeli voters.

On 27 September 1955, a 'commercial' agreement was signed between Czechoslovakia and Egypt. The same country that had saved Israel in 1948 by supplying the IDF with its only heavy weapons, now became Egypt's primary source of arms. According to the deal, Egypt was to receive 200 MIG fighters, 28 Ilyushin bombers, 100 Stalin heavy tanks, and six submarines.

At that time, Israel had no more than 30 jet fighter planes to field against this enormous air armada. Ben Gurion ordered Dayan to draw up plans for a pre-emptive strike at Egypt. The narrow window of opportunity, that had swung open only very briefly, offering a slim chance for Israeli–Egyptian negotiations – now slammed firmly shut.

NOTES

1. The word *mossad* in Hebrew means 'institute' or 'institution', therefore the phrase has a double meaning: the verbal relation to the Mossad, and a sense of Shiloah being a 'one-man institution'.
2. Ben Gurion's act was a demonstrative one, aimed at setting an example for the youth of Israel in the hope that they would follow him into the Negev desert to 'settle the wilderness and make the desert bloom'. The mostly barren Negev comprises nearly a third of Israel's territory, from Beersheba to Eilat. Kibbutz Sdeh Boker was one of a handful of successful settlements in the arid region, and is located some 30 kilometres south of Beersheba, near the ancient Nabatean city of Avdat.
3. Commander of the Palmach, the elite infantry unit of the Israeli Defence Forces during the War of Independence and a central figure in the development of IDF tactics. Later a major political figure, as Minister of Labour, Minister of Education, Foreign Minister and Deputy Prime Minister in Labour governments from 1961–74. Allon died in 1980.

4. So called because it was a pocket of Egyptian resistance around the Faluja junction some 50 kilometres southeast of Tel Aviv (near Kiryat Gat of today). The Egyptian forces, that had previously managed to cut off the Negev from the rest of Israel, were surrounded by the Israeli Army during Operation Horev, with no means of retreat back to Egyptian-held territory. The besieged Egyptians held off repeated attempts to dislodge them, but ultimately, after a series of successful assaults by the Israeli Defence Forces, the 'pocket' was reduced to one area near the Faluja junction itself, where 4,000 soldiers of the Egyptian 4th Brigade held on until the end of the war, when they were finally released as part of the Israeli–Egyptian Armistice Agreement of 1949.

5. One of the phases of the Faluja Pocket siege, fought in an effort to dislodge the Egyptian forces from the Faluja area. This bitterly fought battle took place over possession of a police fortress, near present-day Ashkelon, where the Egyptian troops withstood seven night attacks by IDF forces, and finally surrendered, on 9 October 1948, after an unusual daytime attack by combined IDF artillery, air force, armoured, and mechanized infantry units, led by legendary founder of the Palmach – Yitzhak Sadeh.

6. BILU – an acronym for *Beit Yisrael Lechou ve-Nelcha* – 'House of Israel, rise and let us go forth' – a Jewish youth group founded in Russia after the pogroms of 1881, dedicated to a return to the Land of Israel. They are regarded as 'The First *Aliya*' (wave of Jewish immigration), sending their first group to Palestine in 1882.

7. On 14 October 1953, the IDF carried out a raid on a village northwest of Jerusalem which resulted in the death of 75 of the local inhabitants. The extent of civilian casualties in this action resulted in very heavy international criticism of Israel's policy of retaliation.

8. Head of the Mossad after Shiloah, and instrumental in relieving Shiloah of his duties there. Harel became famous particularly for the kidnapping and bringing to trial in Israel of Adolph Eichmann in 1961.

9. An escape organization (*briha* means 'escape' in Hebrew) established in 1944 by Jewish partisan fighters and refugees from the ghettos to aid Jews to escape from Europe and Nazi persecution.

10. Until recently, Israel's electoral system was totally proportional, so that prior to elections, each party presented the voters with a list of 120 candidates for the 120-seat Knesset, Israel's Parliament. The figure topping each list was that party's candidate for Prime Minister.

Part Two

Intelligence in Israel in Times of Peace

5

Intelligence and the Peace Process in Israel*

SHLOMO GAZIT

'Intelligence' is an integral part of political decision-making in any government, and the reference here is to *all political decisions*, not just those pertaining to a peace process, and to the Government of *any* country that has foreign relations and security problems, not just Israel. Nevertheless, this article refers specifically and emphatically to the peace process embarked upon by the State of Israel.

The survey is divided into three parts. The first will present a theoretical analysis of the functions of Intelligence in the process of negotiations and peace-making; in the second I will relate a number of personal experiences connected with the contribution of intelligence to the peace process; while in the third I will attempt to draw some conclusions.

(1) METHODICAL ANALYSIS

The functions of intelligence as a supporting and contributory element in the process of making peace came into play in three stages. The first stage occurred before Israel had seriously embarked on the peace-making process or entered into any practical talks or negotiations. At this stage Israel had to constantly and systematically monitor events on the enemy side – our neighbours across the border. And let us not forget that, at that time, even when these borders appeared pastoral and serene, Israel was nonetheless constantly in a state of war – not only *de jure*, in view of the fact that Israel did not have formal peace agreements with any Arab country, but also, and perhaps most importantly, *de facto*, for we were aware that *at*

---

*Trans. David Zinder.

any moment, without prior escalation or warning of any kind, war might break out between Israel and one or more of its neighbours. Theoretically, war may break out again at any time, just like the surprise attack on Yom Kippur, 6 October 1973, or the Iraqi missile attacks during the Gulf War in January 1991.

Recently I took a group of foreign security specialists to the Golan Heights. One of them was Russian. As part of our visit we spent some time with an Israeli armoured unit located close to the border demarcation between Israel and Syria, and the tank unit's intelligence officer gave the group a review of the situation. The officer spread out a large map on which IDF forces were marked in blue and Syrian forces in red as 'Enemy Forces'. The Russian in the group chimed in at that point, asking, 'What do you mean "Enemy Forces"? Why "Enemy"? Are we talking about war here?' And the Israeli members of the group then had to explain to the Russian visitor the true nature of our situation: for Israel the present state is, for all intents and purposes, a state of war, and Israel must drill this fact into its army and its soldiers so as not to be deceived by any apparent quiet on the other side. As far as the tank unit was concerned, it had to be trained to think and believe that it might come under fire at any moment.

This then, as far as Israel was concerned, was the first step to the peace process, the stage where a 'ceasefire' was in place, but could revert to full-scale war in an instant. Nevertheless, to return to the main subject of this article – the duties of intelligence in the peace process – what is required of Israeli Intelligence may be summed up in a paraphrase of the following verse in Nehemiah (4:11) 'every one with one of his hands wrought the work, and with the other held the weapon' – the paraphrase reading: 'With one of his hands he uses Intelligence monitoring to foresee preparations for a surprise Arab attack, and with the other endlessly seeks signs of a shift in Arab policy toward the pursuit of peace.'

The second stage in the peace process was intelligence involvement in, and contribution to, the process of 'making peace' from the very beginning of the talks and throughout the negotiations, while the third stage was the work of intelligence during the actual implementation of the agreements, and, of course, during the 'peace' itself. Given the nature of Israeli–Arab relations over the years, it is fairly safe to assume that even after the peace agreements are signed – even assuming that they include every one of the Arab countries and that all their clauses are implemented to the letter – even so, an extended period of time must elapse before it will be possible for Israel to relinquish its precautionary measures or watchful monitoring of everything that happens across the borders.

The first stage: prior to the process of negotiation

Awareness: The most important aspect of this stage, which is still *de jure* a state of war, in which no talks of any kind are yet under way and no negotiations or active peace-making processes are taking place, is the *awareness* on the part of intelligence units that a change of heart in the direction of peace on the enemy's part is a real possibility. And yet this change of heart, if it does exist, cannot yet be made public by the opposing regime as an official government initiative directed toward Israel, for reasons relating to the nature of that particular regime or to public opinion. In such cases, a heightened awareness of the importance of careful intelligence monitoring, so as to detect the development of such a possibility, is an absolute necessity.

Let us go back for a moment to the experts' visit to the Golan Heights. Israel cannot, under any circumstances, regard Syria in any way that is substantially different from that presented by the Tank Corps intelligence officer. Quite rightly, he regards Syria as an enemy; quite rightly, he monitors the activities of the other side, looking for any signs of unusual military activity, to prevent potential surprise attacks. However, at the same time, the State of Israel and Israeli Intelligence must, with the same sensitivity applied to the search for signs of war, maintain close intelligence surveillance to ascertain the possibility of a change of official policy across the border, a political shift that could perhaps open up a channel for negotiations. And this is the reason for the emphasis on awareness: the fact that Israel has been in a state of war for over 47 years does not mean that we are doomed to remain in this state for all time.

It is the duty of the intelligence officer – and the reference here is only to Strategic Intelligence, the intelligence body responsible for the National Intelligence Assessment – to examine the policy shifts and any developing trends that might open a door to a new and different direction – in other words to seek what is referred to as a 'window of opportunity', an opening for diplomatic possibilities.

The opportunities offered by that window, should it indeed open up, must not be missed. The decision to take advantage of these opportunities and the ways of going about doing so are indeed an issue that must be dealt with by the highest political echelons. No intelligence body can assume that kind of responsibility. However, intelligence will be derelict in its duties if it fails to identify the 'window', fails to indicate its appearance at the right time, and fails to present to the political leaders of the country its understanding of the situation in a clear and unequivocal manner. Failure to do so would be entirely its responsibility, exactly as it would be its responsibility if, God forbid, it misread the signs and failed to give advance warning of a surprise attack.

Tell-tale signs: One of the most difficult questions in this context is how to discern such shifts. When the issue is a change in troop deployment that constitutes a clear warning sign of a possible military offensive, things are relatively cut and dried. Intelligence services have an inventory of 'tell-tale military signs', and if the intelligence apparatus has been given orders to gather information on them, and if it does so by intensively and systematically monitoring these signs as they appear in the enemy's land-based, air and naval forces, and among the members of their General Staff and War Office, chances are that developments indicating serious preparations for a premeditated military move of some kind, will be revealed.

The same does not apply when it comes to identifying a policy shift toward a political settlement. In matters such as these, it would be a mistake on the part of intelligence to rely solely on public statements or publications issued by the other side. Extreme anti-Israeli statements, attacking Israel and rejecting any negotiations or agreement out of hand, could conceivably stem only, or for the most part, from the unwillingness of Arab leaders and journalists to make their true intentions public, and their insistence on using their habitual rhetoric. It should be recalled in this context that Arab leaders are strongly influenced by pan-Arab consensus, by threats from their radical opposition at home, and even by fear of assassination for expressing views that may be regarded by some extremists as heretical. And the same applies to the other side of this coin: it is altogether possible that 'moderate' statements may appear, in support of negotiations and a political settlement, which are in fact PR stunts aimed at swaying world public opinion, or misleading Israel itself. How is it possible, under these circumstances, to reach a reliable conclusion?

In this instance, we still have not developed a pattern of tell-tale signs that can provide parameters for intelligence surveillance and gathering, which in turn can provide us a reasonable answer to this vexing problem. There is no alternative, then, but to devise a series of tell-tale signs which will become objectives for constant intelligence surveillance and analysis. This in turn – and this is its great importance – will provide us with material for comparative studies over an extended period of time, and the capacity to identify, from one year to the next, changes that may occur in a developing and shifting process. It is this comparative capability which makes it possible for intelligence to report on demand, at any point in time, whether the 'Dow Jones Index' of the peace issue is rising or falling, bearish or bullish. This is the primary importance of this kind of systematic surveillance.

Incidentally, one thing that could be attempted would be to carry out public opinion polls in enemy countries. Clearly, under the circumstances, we cannot ask an Israeli opinion-poll company to carry out such a survey in Syria, for example. However, if for example a prestigious newspaper such as the *New York Times* were to back the project, it would have no problem commissioning one of the American polling organizations, or a local Arab one, to do the job. A poll such as this, conducted on a yearly basis, could give indications of the tendencies and moods of the local populace, whether or not the 'index' of preparedness to recognize Israel's right to exist – the 'peace inclination' average – is on the rise or on the decline. Once again, the issues here are not clear-cut because we are dealing with countries which do not support free and democratic expressions of public opinion, and where public opinion, such as it is, has hardly any influence at all on decisions made by the Arab leadership. We do not have any information on public opinion in Egypt from 1977, just prior to Sadat's visit to Jerusalem. It is safe to assume that if such information were available, the polls would have shown a marked anti-Israeli tendency, no different from that which prevailed at the same time in other Arab countries. On the other hand, if a poll had been conducted in Egypt a few days *after* Sadat's visit to Jerusalem, we would have undoubtedly found a dramatic swing toward support of the President's move. Nevertheless, political decisions in the Arab world are not totally cut off from public opinion. What is more, if public opinion polls were conducted in the various Arab countries, they would give clear indications of the fundamental problems plaguing Arab society, such as the seemingly never-ending burden of enormous defence costs, a desire to improve living conditions and the quality of life, and a singling out of security considerations as the main obstacle to the attainment of these objectives.

Reporting on changes and tendencies: There is an additional point which is of prime informational importance both to intelligence personnel and to their political leaders, and, for that matter, to all recipients of the various intelligence summaries. It is of crucial importance that in the periodical intelligence projections, be they annual or semi-annual, a permanent section should be devoted to monitoring the possibility of policy shifts towards a political settlement. It is entirely possible that the information appearing under this heading might include no more than this brief statement: 'In preparing the Intelligence Assessment, we find that there has been no change compared to last year's findings.' And perhaps an equally brief summing-up: 'We find that since the last analysis, the situation in this matter has taken a turn for the worse.' Nevertheless, what is important is that everyone involved knows that someone is following these developments closely and noting any changes that may occur. Generalizations, though, are not enough, of course. Each enemy objective, every country, must be surveyed, analysed, and reported on separately, and specific developments, such as a drop in the 'peace index' in Jordan, or a rise in the 'peace index' in Syria must be noted.

A general, superficial overview is simply not enough. The nature of any new developments revealed that may have been on the other side must be analysed and reported on in detail. These tendencies must be noted very clearly – and given the same emphasis that might be accorded to a report on the inherent dangers of a war or military offensive.

The second stage: following the negotiating process

The second stage, the intelligence services' participation in and contribution to the process of talks and negotiations, is the most important.

We will not be saying anything radically new if we point out that intelligence services are not the decision-making forums for state policy. Intelligence is no more than a service, a highly important one, but a service nonetheless. And yet, the contribution of this service both to military decisions and actions, and to political decisions and actions, cannot be underestimated. This input can be the vital key to any decision, positive or negative, that may be taken.

Assessing the opponent's position: The first problem that has to be dealt with is projecting the other side's opening positions in the negotiation. Where is their potential for flexibility and what form will it take? What tactics will they employ? Intelligence must project the basic strategies and tactics that the other side may employ during the various stages of the negotiations.

Israel has been holding bilateral talks with Syria, Lebanon, Jordan and the Palestinians. It is of the utmost importance that Israeli Intelligence provides the members of the negotiating teams with a profile of the Arab representatives at the talks that is as reliable and as precise as possible concerning their character traits, backgrounds and any other information about them that might be of assistance to the Israeli representatives at the talks.

Then comes the main body of information – the Intelligence Assessment of the Arab delegations' positions and their room for manoeuvring; the measure of the representatives' freedom to negotiate; their relations with the leadership in their capitals, and their capacity to influence decisions made by the leaders at home. The more precise and succinct this assessment is, the easier it will be for the Israeli delegation to handle the negotiations. It is on the basis of these assessments that the Israeli Government will issue instructions to the heads of its own negotiating teams. Should the assessments be too optimistic, the Government of Jerusalem may be misled into entertaining false illusions, and will issue instructions that have no chance whatsoever of producing an agreement; and vice versa: should the assessments be overly pessimistic, they may weaken Israeli resolve and so sabotage attempts to achieve a potentially attainable agreement, or produce an agreement that is detrimental to Israel, or an agreement which, with tough and reasoned bargaining, could have been considerably more favourable to Israel.

Intelligence accompanying the negotiating process: Political negotiations between two former enemies immediately become the most important issue, or at the very least one of the most important issues on the intelligence agenda. That is why it is crucial for intelligence to deploy an information-gathering apparatus that will facilitate optimal coverage of the enemy's decision-making mechanisms and optimal coverage of their diplomatic activities. Furthermore, and no less important, intelligence must make the logistical arrangements to ensure that all information received is delivered, as far as possible, in real time. For the most part, this will probably be information of tactical value, information with a very short 'shelf-life', that must reach our negotiating teams no later than the beginning of their next negotiating session.

And this is by no means an easy matter. What we are talking about here is a operational standard that is very difficult to achieve in reality. It would be ideal, of course, if intelligence could show up every day before each negotiating session, update the heads of the delegation on developments and inform them of what they believe the Syrian, Jordanian or Palestinian delegations intend bringing up at the next session. In reality, that level of information-gathering capability is virtually impossible to achieve. What is more, even those elements of information that can be gathered by the intelligence services raise a number of problems:

(1) *Problems of dissemination*: making certain that the information reaches the right person at the right time so that it still has operational value.
(2) *Problems relating to the safety of intelligence sources*: in these situations, the risk of a slip of the tongue by one of the members of the delegation is substantially increased, bearing with it the danger of possibly compromising important intelligence resources.

Solutions to these problems are not easy to come by. Where does one draw the line between what the Israeli delegation requires in order to handle an effective negotiation, and what might be referred to as 'gossip' – information that the intelligence services would like to flaunt, but which, if revealed, might endanger both the personal safety of the source and any future information-gathering potential.

And then there is the question of how such intelligence should be handled. To whom should it be reported? Only to the Prime Minister? To the Foreign Minister? The need to protect intelligence interests is clear to all. The question is only whether or not the intelligence services will be strong enough to withstand pressures that may be brought to bear on them by politicians eager for them to reveal more and more.

Appropriate information-gathering sources: In this day and age, modern intelligence-gathering systems rely increasingly on sophisticated technologies such as spy satellites, aerial photography, laser systems, electronic listening devices, and so on. However, in a negotiating process such as the one we are talking about, these sophisticated, technical-electronic systems are virtually worthless. Information-gathering for such negotiations must find ways to deal with the most difficult problem of all: identifying and understanding enemy intentions. No satellite has yet been invented that can provide this kind of intelligence. There is no choice, therefore, but to return to the simplest, most elementary devices: Human Intelligence or HumInt. Under these special circumstances, of all the many gathering systems at the disposal of intelligence, the agent and the spy in the field are virtually the only ones who stand a chance of casting light on these areas.

Involving intelligence in the negotiating process: The problem that intelligence must deal with in this process is not just information-gathering. An area of equal importance is research.

Throughout the negotiating process, there must be a constant flow of intelligence assessments. Every day (and sometimes even twice a day), intelligence assessments are required in order to analyse responses or new proposals submitted by the Arab side. The negotiating team must scrutinize each proposal through Israeli eyes: what is new and/or different in the suggestion from our point of view? Is it beneficial to Israel's purpose and in what way? Or, looked at differently: what are the inherent dangers of the proposal? Scrutiny of the responses and proposals through 'Arab' eyes is no less important. What was the Arab concept behind this new proposal? Does it represent a step forward or a step backward in the Arab position? Does it give us any insight into the potential limits of their position? What do we know about the internal deliberations that took place in their delegation prior to making this proposal, and what was behind the decision to table it? Is this, to the best of our understanding, just a tactical manoeuvre, or a true shift in policy?

At the same time, our negotiating team also requires reliable information on possible Arab reactions to our proposals, for instance, what were the arguments, if any, that developed in their delegation in response to a given Israeli proposal, who was in favour and who against?

Receiving input of intelligence assessments like these on a regular basis and at the right time – before decisions need to be made – is often no less important than information coming in on broader shifts and developments that may have been observed in the Arab positions.

There is another problem of a different order, arising from the modern age of global communication that we live in. Leaders all over the world – and ours are no exception in this respect – are generally glued to their television screens, regularly watching news on CNN, BBC and Sky. These leaders tend (erroneously) to have blind faith in the truth of what they see on television. Thus they not only acquire incomplete, and often incorrect and distorted, information, but they also suffer from the sheer volume of news at their disposal, so much so that there are times when a leader simply does not have the time to deal in any depth with the authorized intelligence material that lands on his desk, or does not have enough time to read the reports in their entirety, or conduct joint sessions for updating and discussing various intelligence resources.

The main drawback of mass communications is its randomness. Media journalists do not file reports according to an Indicator of Vital Information (IVI: see p.75) imposed on them from above, nor they do deploy in the field in order to acquire optimal intelligence information. They set up wherever it is easiest to do so, or wherever they are allowed to; wherever it is most convenient for them to stay, or wherever the political–security leadership of the opposing country happens to be at that particular time – in other words wherever all the gossip can be found. Thus, for example, during the Gulf War, CNN provided us with daily reports from Baghdad and other places in Iraq, but these reports never gave us a true picture of what was actually happening on the battle front, or of the nature of the deliberations and activities of the political establishment in Baghdad. Instead what we saw was only whatever Peter Arnett's camera could pick up from the limited perspective of his hotel room window in Baghdad.

The CNN screen was indeed full of images from Iraq, but those were the wrong images and, for the most part, only those images that the Iraqi disinformation apparatus wanted Western viewers to see.

Intelligence needs in advance of a settlement: This is yet another area, on an altogether different level. Like any other player with vested interests seeking to make sure that its requirements will not be neglected at the negotiating table, intelligence is duty-bound, prior to the expected political settlement, to present its own logistic and organizational demands to our negotiating team. It is abundantly clear to everyone that history will not end once the agreement is signed, and intelligence will have the same, or possibly different and more difficult tasks to perform in the period following the signing of the agreement.

The top priority will of course be advance-warning intelligence – the need and the capability of intelligence systems to give advance warning of any intention or attempt on the part of the other side to breach the agreement in any way. As we face this intelligence responsibility, we are aware that it is entirely possible that the agreement between the two sides may include modifications of existing conditions on the ground, and that it is highly likely that this will bring about a significant deterioration in intelligence information-gathering capabilities.

And indeed, it is the duty of the intelligence services to advise the negotiating team from the outset as to which items in the agreement will be difficult – or impossible – for them to monitor satisfactorily on either side of the border. If the political echelons proceed through the negotiations in constant coordination with intelligence demands, they will be able to avoid including in the signed agreement any unverifiable conditions.

Furthermore, when we are about to sign peace agreements, diplomatic agreements and all that they entail, the basic working assumption must be that both sides have every intention of fulfilling the conditions of the agreement as signed. At the same time, however, another equally important working assumption must be borne in mind: that it is more than likely that one or both of the sides will try to pull the wool over the eyes of the other on one issue or another, and deviate in some way from the agreement. To be prepared for such an eventuality, intelligence must maintain optimal information-gathering capabilities.

Beyond all this, it will also be necessary to monitor and evaluate Arab policies relating to the re-indoctrination of their people, preparing them for true coexistence with Israel. On this issue too, we cannot rely merely on gut feelings.

It is, therefore, reasonable to assume that an alternative and orderly plan will be presented concerning the deployment of intelligence-gathering facilities and various other arrangements, to ensure future information-gathering capabilities after the implementation of the peace agreement. Some of these demands will no doubt be raised during the negotiations themselves – a series of stipulations, provisions and arrangements relating to what is to be allowed or prohibited in the area of mutual intelligence activities after the signing; others relate to budgets, manpower requirements and the setting up of alternative systems to replace capabilities that will be either seriously hampered or lost altogether following the signing of the agreement.

In 1975, while Israel was negotiating the interim agreement in Sinai with Egypt, the Israeli demand to retain its intelligence-gathering facilities in western Sinai, was one of the main stumbling blocks in the path of a final agreement. In the end, Egypt relented, and as a result, at various points along the demarcation line between Israeli and Egyptian forces, unusual bulges were created to accommodate the intelligence-gathering facilities inside Israeli-held territory.

One other point: a bilateral agreement such as this one will, in all likelihood, involve a third party (the United States, the UN, or an international surveillance mechanism of some kind) to ensure the implementation of the agreement and to monitor its progress. It is important to decide in advance which intelligence demands will be submitted to this third party for its consideration within the mandate of its duties both during and after the implementation of the agreement:

— systematic coverage of the area by satellite or aerial reconnaissance, and immediate, uncensored transmittal of these photos to the two sides;
— carrying out of regular patrols, monitoring of potential breaches of the agreement, with continuous reports to both sides on the findings of these patrols.

In August 1970 a ceasefire agreement was arranged between Israel and Egypt through the active intervention of the United States. One issue which was of paramount importance to Israel at that time was its categorical demand that Egypt should not take advantage of the ceasefire in the Suez Canal area to move its surface-to-air missile systems eastwards, closer to the Canal itself, where they would be able to function more efficiently and give better protection to any land-based Egyptian forces that might try to cross over from the western side of the Canal. The first thing the Egyptians did after the ceasefire went into effect was to move these missiles forward. Israeli Intelligence detected this movement, but American Intelligence – for political reasons – was not willing to verify the Israeli findings and support Israel's complaint and its demand for immediate withdrawal of those missile systems that had been moved eastwards.

Preventing intelligence coverage from the other side: Throughout the negotiating process, the intelligence objectives of the opposing side – in the field of information-gathering and assessment – are absolutely identical to yours. It is, therefore, absolutely clear that your counter-intelligence must closely monitor the intelligence activities of the other side, and close off every existing or potential breach from the probing eyes of their intelligence-gathering apparatus. Moreover, you must constantly bear in mind the intelligence ramifications of positions and demands presented by your opponent during the negotiations.

The chances that you will be able to get your hands on reliable and detailed information on the overall intelligence coverage available to the other side are very slim. Beyond taking every possible step necessary, in terms of precautions, compartmentalization and secrecy, in order to prevent leaks and unnecessary disclosure of information, you will also be required to make a careful analysis of everything made public by the other side, in the hope that this might give you some idea of the depth of information the other side has on you, and perhaps, too, on the possible sources for this kind of information on your side.

One of the possible counter-measures in these circumstances is to create a smokescreen to conceal your thoughts and intentions during the negotiations. For these purposes, it is of the utmost importance to embark on a campaign of disinformation, both through overt sources and through feeding the other side with false information via covert sources, designed to reach the other side and add an aura of enhanced reliability to the information.

Arab Intelligence will also be anxious to deploy in a way that is conducive to the achievement of its objectives during the implementation of the agreement, and will present its leaders and its delegations at the talks with various demands concerning border-lines, deployment of forces and facilities, and the nature of the activity that will be allowed in the field.

Under these circumstances, counter-intelligence will have to do the following:

(1) monitor these requests or reveal the intelligence objectives behind the demands raised at the negotiating table;
(2) analyse the meaning and potential dangers involved in agreeing to and accepting these demands;
(3) try to weigh the relative advantages and disadvantages of a mutual agreement on the implementation of both sides' intelligence demands, as opposed to the advantages and disadvantages of their mutual rejection.

Finally, another area altogether, this intelligence activity will have to take place concurrently with information-gathering and assessment efforts aimed at revealing possible enemy offensive intentions, under the cover of the ongoing political negotiations. Providing assistance to the peace process does not absolve intelligence from the need to prevent military surprises of any kind, and to give appropriate advance warnings of potentially dangerous developments.

The third stage – intelligence responsibilities after completion of the political agreement

Defining a new indication of vital information (IVI): The Indicator of Vital Information (IVI) is the basis for all intelligence work. This is the definition of objectives, of the questions that need to be answered. From this point of view, the 'Basic IVI' (as opposed to 'Current IVI', or 'One-shot', or 'Short-term IVI'), serves as the deciding factor in the preparation of work schedules for both the intelligence-gathering and the intelligence-analysis apparatus.

The first task of the intelligence services following the signing of a peace treaty between nations is to redefine the Basic IVI. Up until the signing of the agreement, all intelligence work has been based on an IVI derived from previous – and now outdated – assumptions; assumptions which related differently both politically and from a military–security standpoint to a hostile neighbouring country. Now a new relationship is required, and a new IVI that will provide answers for a new cluster of issues, questions and interests.

If we go 'by the book', it is the political leader who is supposed to define the new IVI by presenting intelligence with the issues and questions that concern him. In reality, it is more likely that the intelligence apparatus *per se* will have to define the new IVI for itself. And in actual practice, the body in charge of doing so inside intelligence is the research body responsible for the National Intelligence Assessment.

Without going into the details of the IVI – which in any particular case may be different and unique – we shall concentrate on a number of issues:

(1) The intentions of the other side to abide by the agreement, and a systematic monitoring of possible changes in its attitude to this question.
(2) The stability of the regime on the other side, threats of a possible over-throw and the stated positions of potential revolutionary elements toward the implementation of the agreement should they come into power.
(3) The manner in which the agreement is implemented by the other side. Note that it is important to remember that if we want to respond, complain, or demand immediate compliance with the agreement, then information must be available in good time.
(4) The nature of the relationship and coordination between the other side and the overall pan-Arab complex, on both the political and the military levels.

(5) The preparations – basic political and military activities not specifically dealt with in the agreement – which can give the clearest indication of the other side's true strategic intentions.

The intelligence system's basic assumption must be that the other side will try to cheat and deceive us in certain details of the implementation of the agreement. It follows therefore that a very careful intelligence monitoring will be necessary to uncover these attempts and enable immediate intervention to put them right.

Setting up a new information gathering system: Parallel to the process of implementing the new political agreement, the following items will have to be checked out:

(1) How will the existing intelligence-gathering system be affected by the agreement?
And within this question, special emphasis must be placed on:

   (a) carrying on existing information-gathering, or applying political limitations and new sensitivities to continued information-gathering inside the territory of the partner to the agreement (questions will arise, for example, concerning political licence to activate agents in the target country, or carrying out aerial reconnaissance over its territory, or recruiting agents who are citizens of the partner state in a neutral country);
   (b) new possibilities of information-gathering that will be opened up by the agreement, arising from the very fact of having an overt, official physical presence in that country;
   (c) the distancing of the optical and electronic 'sight-lines' as a result of the removal of physical presence in the field.

(2) Thus, for example, according to the terms of the Israeli–Egyptian peace agreement, Israel retreated east of the international border of what was defined in 1948 as 'Palestine' – a fact that forced Israel to move its intelligence installations some 250 km. away from the Suez Canal and from the centres of Egyptian activities. The intelligence services, which up to then had enjoyed immediate proximity only a few hundred metres from the Egyptian outposts, suddenly found themselves a great distance away and with no actual contact with the Egyptians.

(3) Can the present intelligence-gathering apparatus provide answers for the new IVI?

(4) What are the political, budgetary and technological problems involved in building a new intelligence-gathering infrastructure that will supply the following new needs?

(a) Constant and real-time flow of information from a third party to the agreement (for instance, American aerial reconnaissance flights serving both sides).
(b) Technological solutions necessary to replace lost intelligence resources and capabilities, and the ramifications of these solutions on:
 – a realistic time-frame for their construction;
 – research and development efforts for this purpose;
 – the necessary budgets;
 – the addition of new resources particularly specialist human resources.
(c) Receiving approval for these new plans for intelligence-gathering from the political leaders.

(2) INTELLIGENCE AND PEACE: A FEW PERSONAL EXPERIENCES

The decisions of the Arab Summit at Khartoum

A few years ago, while working on a research paper in the United States, I needed to find the exact wording of the decisions of the Arab Summit Conference that took place in Khartoum, Sudan, in 1967. I myself was not involved in intelligence work at the time of the summit, but I remembered very clearly – like most Israelis, I suppose – that this was the first Arab summit to convene following the Six-Day War, and its conclusions in the aftermath of the war were an outright rejection of any attempt to reach a political settlement or a peace agreement with Israel. After the publication of its conclusions, the Khartoum Conference became known in Israel as the 'Conference of the Three Noes': No peace with Israel! No recognition of Israel! And no negotiations with Israel!

My being in the United States gave me easy access to American press records of the time, and I read numerous articles that I had not seen or read in 1967. The headlines I found were surprising: 'Positive Notes at Khartoum', or 'Nasser and the King Plan Concessions' – the reference being to King Hussein of Jordan.

Below these headlines were articles by American journalists who analysed and interpreted the language used by the Arab heads of state in their joint statement at the end of the conference, and their conclusions were as follows:

(1) The discussions at the Khartoum Conference were the most realistic ever held by Arab leaders, and they should be seen as a step toward moderation and peace in the Middle East.

(2) Nasser was talking very clearly about a political settlement with Israel. The term [and I quote from those American newspapers] – 'removing the traces of Israeli aggression' was different and more positive than earlier statements that called for the 'removal of the State of Israel'.

(3) The fact that Houari Boumedienne, the President of Algeria, Hafez el-Assad, the President of Syria, and the head of the PLO at that time, Ahmad Shukeiry, were absent from the conference was an indication of the reasonably moderate inclination of the conference.

I couldn't believe my eyes, and decided to double-check to make sure that my memory was not playing tricks on me. I went to the Library of Congress and took out Israeli newspapers from that time. The facts concerning the decisions reached by the conference and their exact wording, as well as the reports about the discussions themselves and their proceedings, were identical in the English and in the Hebrew. Their interpretation, however, was very different. The Israeli press indeed presented its analysis – as I recalled it – in a very negative light, emphasizing the 'Three Noes'.

I am not qualified to judge which of the two interpretations of that conference is closer to the truth, and in any case such judgement today is irrelevant. Nevertheless, my surprise over the American view of the events brings a question to mind: did the Israeli Intelligence people in Israel in 1967 come to the leaders of the country at that time, and, after presenting the Arab Summit Conference decisions and their analysis of these decisions, add a rider: 'Ladies and Gentlemen, we must bring to your attention that there are other parties who have a *different* understanding of the summit decisions. Please look at these articles from the *New York Times* or the *Washington Post*.' Was there anyone there who said, 'Even though we stand by our interpretation of these decisions, the other interpretation is possible – although not highly likely. We believe that you should examine these matters for yourselves. You could possibly send out feelers to test these findings, and it is possible that, in spite of everything, there are issues that are open for discussion between the two sides, and people who might be willing to discuss them!' I did not pursue the matter any further and made no effort to find out if anyone did indeed say anything to that effect. I doubt very much if anyone did.

And this is the first lesson. There is nothing easier than to compare your assessments of events, speeches, decisions made by the other side, with assessments of a third party – journalists or foreign diplomats, for example. Since Israel still does not have diplomatic relations with the majority of Arab countries, and we have no way of conducting first-hand checks, there is always the possibility of asking a third party from a neutral country to do the job for you, and find out what exactly are your opponent's intentions, positions, and so on. You are under no obligation to accept these analyses, but you should hear them and pay attention. After all, the third party is supposed to look at these things from an unbiased viewpoint.

Tell-tale signs of peace

Somewhere around 1976, while I was still head of Army Intelligence, we began receiving information indicating an apparent conceptual shift in the Arab world in general, and in Egypt in particular – a shift in the direction of a willingness to seek a political settlement with Israel. This information came to us primarily from foreign diplomats and journalists.

These reports raised a few questions in our minds concerning the veracity of the information. I recall a meeting I held in my office before handing in a periodic Intelligence Assessment that we had prepared at the time. The conclusion we reached at that meeting – in accordance with our routine way of thinking, and possibly in accordance with concepts we were locked into – was that 'We do not see any fundamental changes in the Arab position'. We explained the information we received as Arab strategy (particularly Egyptian strategy) designed to better their relations with the United States and the other Western nations, and part of an overall strategy of attempting to drive a wedge between Israel and the United States, a move which required the proliferation of expressions of goodwill, declarations of moderation, and so forth.

Although I fully supported this assessment, I was not satisfied with it. I said so at the meeting and presented the researchers there with a question:

> Could you please explain to me the basis for all the things we are
> being told by these sources? We have just concluded our
> assessment and it is at variance with what we are being told by
> those foreign sources. Perhaps we are wrong and not they? Only
> three years ago the greatest minds of Israeli intelligence sat in this
> very room, and today we know that they made a colossal mistake,
> and did not foresee the Arab attack on Yom Kippur. Is it too far-
> fetched to think that we are wrong today, and that there are indeed
> shifts of attitude toward peace and a negotiated settlement on the
> Arab side that we are unable to detect?

What is more, when we are talking about the possible outbreak of warfare, within a very short space of time we will know, and with complete certainty, if we were wrong. It will happen when the guns begin to fire. Whether or not we gave advance warning, this will be a concrete fact that cannot be denied. When we are talking about a political shift of direction, things are not so clear-cut. There is no assurance of any kind that an inclination on the part of an Arab leader to examine the possibility of moving toward a political settlement will ever be realized in a measurable way. Such a shift requires a concomitant shift on our part, and if we do not respond correctly or in the right time-frame, not only is it possible that we might miss the chance for a political settlement, but we may not even know that we missed it.

The visit of Anwar Sadat, the President of Egypt, to Israel 18 months later was an extreme example of a decision he made to take the plunge when – so it would seem – he reached the conclusion that the diplomatic steps he had taken and the messages he had sent to Israel by various means concerning a change in his attitude towards the conflict, had elicited no response on the Israeli side. The meeting that took place in Morocco between Israel's Foreign Minister, Moshe Dayan, and Egypt's Deputy Prime Minister, Dr Touhami [see below], was final proof for Sadat that no breakthrough would ensue if he pursued this present course of action. Sadat was prepared to take what was, for him, a daring and highly dangerous step of approaching Israel without any preliminary assurances or promises of any kind that his initiative would be answered in kind or even welcomed. The chances that any Arab leader might be willing to take similar risks in the future are extremely slim.

Bearing in mind my remarks at the assessment meeting, a three-pronged directive was issued:

(1) First of all, we decided to embark on an ongoing and methodical exami-
    nation of possible political–diplomatic policy shifts on the other side. It
    was decided that from that point on, this issue would be a permanent
    fixture in discussions relating to periodical Intelligence Assessments.
(2) Secondly, we decided to accustomize our political leaders to the issue,
    and to do so by submitting ongoing reports – verbally and in writing –
    relating to changes and trends on the Arab side in this respect.
(3) Finally, and this was perhaps our most important decision, we decided
    that we must generate for our own purposes a graph of 'tell-tale signs of
    peace', in order to know what to look for in this area and where to
    find it.

As soon as we began working on this last issue we were surprised to discover that we were treading on virgin soil – we could not find any earlier research work on this topic anywhere in the world, nor did we find even a draft proposal that could serve as a basis for our work. And that was how our search for tell-tale signs began.

Our first move, naturally, was to apply to the academic community for advice. The reply we received, surprisingly, was absolutely unequivocal: they knew of no pattern of tell-tale signs for policy shifts of this nature, and even less about universal signs that could be applied at any time to any individual instance.

I took advantage of our good contacts with foreign intelligence services, and asked them for help. We went from one service to the next, and I even chided them on the issue, saying, 'You have repeatedly told us that we are misreading what is happening in the Arab world, and that there is a real change in their leaders' positions. Well, if that is the case, please give us a key to examining and assessing these changes. On what basis have you determined that these changes have occurred, and how do you suggest we deal with this challenge?' But almost everywhere we turned, as soon as they heard our request, their enthusiasm took a nose-dive. Again and again we were told: 'Sorry but even *we* don't know how to do that, all we can do is relay to you what we hear from those countries.'

Ultimately, we had no choice but to improvise as best we could. We applied to the Shiloah Institute for Middle East Research at Tel Aviv University and asked them to suggest a pattern of tell-tale signs for the intelligence we were looking for. After much deliberation, we finally isolated three levels of intelligence that should be monitored and assessed:

(1) *The schematic level*: What are the top echelons of leaders, politicians, and journalists from across the border saying? Is there any change in style, terminology, or attitude toward Israel and its right to exist in the Arab–Muslim Middle East? Are they signalling a need or a desire for, and indeed a possibility of, a political settlement to the conflict? Have certain derogatory terms and words frequently used in relation to Israel, its policies, its people, etc., disappeared from their vocabulary? And another very important question: are they expressing themselves on these issues similarly in Arabic as well as in English, French, or any other language, in publications designed for foreign consumption? We have a great deal of experience with varying versions of this nature, when certain words and expressions were used by the Arabs for local consumption, while different wording was used when dealing with identical issues in material produced in other languages for foreign consumption.

In this connection, it is also very important to monitor Arab thinking and statements in order to understand the Arab approach to and understanding of the concept of 'peace'. The Israeli approach is well-known – we desire a peace which will define the relationship between the two sides. The more signs there are of enhanced cooperation, a willingness to coexist, and the creation of mutual interests, the greater the chances for enhancing the viability of peace. The Arab position on these issues has always been, at the best of time, a demand for a 'cold' peace and no more than the establishment of formal relations, with no intention of expanding on them in any way. Is there, then, any change on this point?

And one further question: Are there in the Arab world, local equivalents to the Israeli 'Peace Now' movement, people who talk openly about the need for a political settlement and the need for reconciliation? And if such movements or people do exist, even if they do not attract a mass following, do they live in fear of violent responses or even assassination?

And of course, we established that the most important issue will be the need for comparative monitoring of these points over the years, since a given situation, on its own, contains neither innovation nor any intrinsic importance.

(2) *The level of public opinion*: To what extent does Arab public opinion totally reject Israel, recognition of Israel, or any possibility of negotiations with Israel? We have already noted the possibility of conducting public opinion polls in the Arab countries. It is not altogether too far-fetched to find a commercial company to do this for us. The most important aspect of these polls would be precisely the comparative capability it would give us, from year to year, to detect changes – and their direction.

(3) *The practical level*: What steps, if any, are Arab countries taking that we might be able to identify as an expression of a new position, or a change of attitude toward Israel and toward a resolution of the conflict? In this respect we can offer a number of examples. For instance:

(a) Can we detect any changes in national priorities? Is state funding being moved from defence needs to socioeconomic issues? Or, on the contrary, are defence investments on the rise?
(b) Are any steps being taken toward a quiet resolution to the problem of the Palestinian refugees of 1948, such as giving them full citizenship or launching local rehabilitation projects?
(c) And an example from a different area altogether: do maps of the region being printed now include the name and borders of the State of Israel?

Over the past two years we have discovered a new and interesting phenomenon in the official Syrian press. In a broad range of publications, particularly political cartoons, Damascus seems to be changing its attitude toward the Israeli–Arab conflict. In contrast to the past, Damascus is now being portrayed as the peace-seeker, as trying to find ways of obtaining a political settlement to the Arab–Israeli conflict. It is Syria that is trying to move forward rapidly, and make the most of the fruits of peace, while Israel is portrayed as hampering or even blocking any progress. This is a fascinating example of a measurable, positive change in Arab journalism. We have no way of knowing if this is an indication that the regime is responding to the feelings of the Syrian people, or an attempt on the part of President Assad to prepare public opinion in his country for the acceptance of Israel's existence.

Intelligence Assessments in 1976 and 1977

From that time on (near the end of 1976), we made it our objective to re-examine our basic assumptions and examine developments on an ongoing basis with reference to these signs, and to make sure that these issues will be raised at every meeting dealing with the periodical Intelligence Assessment.

In December 1976 we took our first reading of the situation using this new format, and tried to put together a clear picture of the possibility of progress on the Arab side toward a resolution of the conflict by political means. For the first time we asked ourselves if it might not be possible that we were mistaken in our assessments, and that what we defined as the 'Arab Strategic Objective' has ceased to be a 'holy objective' that must be obeyed to the letter. Perhaps, we said, this is merely an 'asking price', floated by the Arabs in advance of negotiations, and that it was possible that at the end of the process, they would settle for much less?

Since this was the first discussion in which these new parameters were examined, and since we did not yet have any historical basis for comparison, we were content just to ask the questions, and refrained from taking a stand on the findings.

The next round of discussions took place in March 1977. Once again we examined the 'tell-tale signs' that might indicate a shift in policy. At the conclusion of that meeting we wrote:

> Lately we see more and more signs of 'bells signalling the apparent coming of spring' and the message of peace. It is a veritable Egyptian 'peace offensive', a series of meetings between Israelis and leaders of the PLO, the initiatives of Austrian Chancellor Bruno Kreisky, etc. And we ask ourselves – are we not, once again, locked into a dangerous 'concept'?

> Our answer is, that what is happening is nothing more than PR lip-service … and that in fact, the ultimate Arab goal has not changed.

> Nevertheless, what I am concerned about is the possibility that we will fail to identify fundamental and positive changes or breaches in the traditional Arab stand.

Two questions come to mind here: One is intelligence-oriented, and the other touches on the required political decisions. As far as Israel's political decisions are concerned, Army Intelligence has neither control over them nor any responsibility for them. We are responsible only for the intelligence side, and as far as we are concerned, we will have fulfilled our duty if we focus attention on the changes in good time.

Let us take an example from real life. Recently we have heard the stories related by Lyova Eliav and Matti Peled, who, on a number of occasions, met with Sartawi, a high-ranking PLO official. If I could be certain that this is an indication of a true policy shift on the part of the PLO in the direction of a political settlement, this would definitely be an example that we would have to point out.

What is more, we know that what is right today may not be so tomorrow, and we must certainly refrain from embracing the slogan 'The Arabs are despicable people bent on the destruction of Israel – now and forever!'

And this is where the problem lies – How can we check up on Sartawi and assess his reliability? How can we check up on Sadat and the sweet-as-honey statements he has issued?

The Charlotte Jacobson affair

Close to that point in time we were given a fascinating example of the kinds of problems we were required to deal with. Mrs Charlotte Jacobson of the United States, the President of the World Hadassah Organization at that time, was invited by the Government of Egypt for a visit. Mrs Jacobson did not want to accept the invitation without consulting Israel, and she did in fact write to the Israeli authorities who advised her to turn down the offer and not go to Egypt. The feeling in Jerusalem was that the invitation was nothing more than a PR stunt, and that in accepting the invitation, Mrs Jacobson would be merely serving Egyptian anti-Israeli propaganda. However, Mrs Jacobson ignored the advice given to her by Israeli officials. She travelled to Egypt on a ten-day visit, and upon her return had only the highest praise for the red-carpet treatment that she had been given by the Egyptians at every stage of her visit. She was awed by the Egyptians' frankness, and by their warm and welcoming response to her visit. In short, everything about the trip was superlative.

We in Army Intelligence decided to use this opportunity to re-examine our criteria once again. We wanted to see how Mrs Jacobson's visit was presented to the Egyptian people, and which details were reported in the Arabic–Egyptian media. We were in for a surprise. If one were to judge by the Arabic-language media in Egypt – radio, television and newspapers – Charlotte Jacobson simply did not exist. It was as though she had never set foot on Egyptian soil.

Had the visit been given broad coverage in the Arabic-language Egyptian media, it would have been an indication that the Egyptian regime is preparing local public opinion for a change of attitude toward Israel, and, by the same token, such coverage would have been a direct signal to Israel of this new policy line. Under the circumstances, however, our astounding findings on this matter only strengthened what we had been thinking in any case, and actually had included in our Intelligence Assessment: 'There is no real, sincere change in Egypt in the direction of peace.'

The Intelligence Assessment in September 1977

In September 1977, a mere two months before Anwar Sadat's historic visit to Israel, we met once again to discuss the Intelligence Assessment. We had in hand an assessment that we received from Professor Nadav Safran, a world-renowned Middle East scholar from Harvard, who came to Israel after a visit to Cairo. His main point, which he reiterated again and again, was that the Arabs felt that time was working against them, and he suggested two weighty reasons for this feeling. In the first place, the Egyptians felt that they had failed in their efforts to drive a wedge between Israel and the United States that would bring about a political separation between the two countries. Secondly, the Arabs were absolutely convinced that Israel was in possession of nuclear weapons, and that therefore they had no real chance of ever achieving a military resolution to the conflict.

In our own Army Intelligence Assessment, we did not accept Safran's positions, and put forward three points which we felt were counter-indicative to his claims:

(1) The United States was now putting the full weight of blame on Israel for the ongoing political deadlock.
(2) President Carter was about go public and condemn Israeli policies.
(3) There were signs of a rapprochement between the Americans and the PLO.

In our Assessment we repeated things we had already said before: 'We do not believe that Egypt is prepared to cut itself off from the pan-Arab collective.

Even though we have detected some semantic modifications, we believe that at this point in time there is nothing more to it beyond semantics and propaganda tactics. Therefore, there is no discernible change in the Arabs' basic stand *vis-à-vis* Israel.' Nonetheless, we did add a rider to this: 'If these tendencies continue, it is possible that in the future they will carry some practical weight.'

There was another unusual thing that happened during the discussions on the Intelligence Assessment we held at that time. We tried to respond to the question of how Egypt would behave in a year's time, i.e. in October 1978 – at the conclusion of the third and last year of the Israeli–Egyptian Interim Agreement on Sinai.

We felt that this was a dilemma for which we could provide no solution. We were convinced that it would be impossible to find suitable topographical features in Sinai to support a viable new Interim Agreement. Israel was not in a position to offer a new unilateral withdrawal without Egyptian commitment to real political concessions, while the Egyptians, for their part, as far as we could judge, were not capable of making any significant political concessions.

Looked at from another point of view, the Egyptians did not really have a military option. Egypt was simply not ready for war; nor did we envision it having any such capability in a year's time. Following the Yom Kippur War the Egyptians put diplomatic activity at the top of their list of priorities, with the result that the Egyptian Army had not yet begun to regroup after the losses it had suffered during the war. What is more, the deterioration of Egypt's relations with the Soviet Union made it impossible for the country to receive spare parts or ammunition to replace what was lost in battle. So we asked ourselves: if a political settlement was out of the question, and war was out of the question, what options were left? And then one of the officers seated at the conference table threw out an idea: 'Egypt does have a third option. Egypt can make peace with Israel!' – and burst out laughing, with all of us soon following suit.

If you will, this was the most difficult problem that we as an intelligence service had to deal with – how to think the unthinkable. How could we determine that we were facing a dramatic turnabout on the part of the Egyptian President when his own Foreign Minister was not aware of it, and handed in his resignation two months after the announcement of Sadat's Jerusalem initiative because he was not consulted or informed? How were we to deal with the need to examine and re-examine our Intelligence Assessment, over and over again, and change it if necessary in relation to things that at that point in time seemed totally improbable?

Dayan's position and the Army Intelligence Assessment

On 6 October 1977, Israel's Foreign Minister, Moshe Dayan, met with Egypt's Deputy Prime Minister, Dr Touhami. The meeting was an Israeli initiative: the head of the Mossad, acting on instructions from the Prime Minister, asked the Moroccans to act as intermediaries, and help organize a top-level Israeli–Egyptian meeting.

Army Intelligence, the military body in charge of the National Intelligence Assessment, was not brought in on this secret initiative, nor did it have a hand in its development. This decision – to exclude Army Intelligence – was a serious error. An intelligence research body, in charge of no less than the state's National Intelligence Assessment, cannot possibly arrive at a correct evaluation of Egyptian policies if it is not informed about these kinds of diplomatic moves. The head of Army Intelligence was personally notified of the fact that such a meeting took place (and even then in the strictest secrecy), but without any details as to its contents except for a very general statement that the meeting did not yield any agreements.

And indeed, today, now that the details of that meeting have been revealed, we know that it was very preliminary and exploratory: a meeting in which the two men did not arrive at any agreement save the need to meet again.

In retrospect it would appear that this meeting was one of the events that influenced Sadat's decision to come to Jerusalem. When Sadat received Touhami's report of his talks with Dayan, it became clear to the President that meetings of this kind would not be an effective conduit for a potential political agreement, and that a diplomatic move of a different kind was necessary if a true breakthrough was to be achieved.

Incidentally, six weeks later (one month before Sadat's visit), Foreign Minister Dayan appeared before the forum of the IDF General Staff, and presented his evaluations of the situation. These evaluations were no doubt based upon his own personal conclusions from the meeting with Touhami. Dayan's main points at the meeting were as follows:

(1) There is not a single Arab country that is prepared to sign a separate peace treaty with Israel at this time.
(2) Egypt, and possibly Jordan, are prepared to come to a partial agreement, along the lines of a 'cessation of the state of war', but even that will require American intervention.
(3) And the question must be asked if Israel will be willing to go along with such an arrangement. I, Moshe Dayan, am prepared to go ahead with it. In my opinion it would be foolish on our part to stick to a concept of 'all or nothing'.

Given all these, it was not surprising that Army Intelligence did not foresee the possibility of Sadat's visit to Jerusalem and its political ramifications.

The way in which these events developed, by the way, is not a uniquely Israeli phenomenon. It is characteristic of top political echelons everywhere to demand that the intelligence services serve them and give them every scrap of information and evaluation that might possibly contribute to their decisions. What they are not aware of is *their* duty to reciprocate and keep the intelligence services abreast of everything that is happening, provide them with every bit of information – even the most intimate – that might help them in their research analyses and the development of their Intelligence Assessments. Some similar cases have become well-known around the world, such as the contacts between the US President Richard Nixon and the Chinese (in the years 1967–71): contacts that were kept secret from the CIA, and of course prevented the Agency from producing a realistic assessment of Chinese policies at that time.

Sadat's visit to Jerusalem

The announcement of Sadat's planned visit to Jerusalem came to us, therefore, as a complete surprise. The first question we asked ourselves was whether this was not just a grandiose PR stunt designed to cause Israel grave political embarrassment by showing the world, and particularly the United States, that Sadat was willing to go to the extreme limits of his mandate, while Israel remained the hard-line, intransigent party in the conflict. And if indeed this was the plan, Sadat would, at the same time, achieve yet another success on the way to Egypt's strategic objective at that time – driving a wedge between Washington and Jerusalem.

A few days later, when it became clear to us beyond a doubt that Sadat was resolved to make good his announcement and was determined to come to Israel, we had to provide an Intelligence Assessment in advance of the visit. I say we 'had to' even though no one actually asked us to do so.

We treated the event as an extraordinary one which justified a totally different attitude on our part. Therefore, the forum that was invited to the Assessment discussion was truly unorthodox. Apart from Army Intelligence researchers, we also invited members of the research departments of both the Mossad and the Foreign Ministry, as well as senior representatives from the universities – Middle East experts from the Hebrew University in Jerusalem and from Tel Aviv University. In an effort to provide a suitably dramatic opening to the discussion, I began the meeting by pressing a button on a cassette recorder and playing the Egyptian national anthem: 'This anthem', I said, opening the session, 'will be heard here in a week's time as

President Sadat descends the steps of his presidential plane at Ben Gurion Airport.'

In fact, we held two sessions at that time. The first was an Assessment session, an attempt to analyse Sadat's motives and expectations regarding his planned visit to Jerusalem. The second, in a more limited forum, was aimed at proposing a number of practical recommendations for the Israeli Government – the steps it could take and the options it had at its disposal in response to the Egyptian President's initiative, based on our assessment of his motives, decisions and expectations.

I do not want to deal here with an analysis of the motives that brought Sadat to Jerusalem. For the purposes of this analysis it will suffice to note that we immediately transmitted two papers to Jerusalem – one, a position paper analysing Sadat's motives, deliberations and expectations, and a second paper which proposed a number of suggestions for possible Israeli responses – all this in the belief that our Assessment papers would serve as a basis for a discussion in the Government prior to the visit.

Two interesting things happened in this context. First of all – and I believe this was the first such case in our brief history – I received instructions from the Prime Minister to recall and *destroy* all copies of the second paper we submitted, i.e. the recommendations for government responses. The Prime Minister's complaint was, 'How dare intelligence suggest to the Government of Israel what it should do?' We, of course, did as we were told, and I recalled all the copies of the document that we had distributed, even though I was less than pleased about it. I had hoped that at such a rare moment in our history, our suggestions would be discussed at face value and not viewed from a strictly formalistic point of view – who was or was not authorized to make suggestions. What is more to the point, I know of no regulatory procedure whereby any official body is denied the right to submit policy suggestions, as long as the actual decision-making remains strictly in government hands.

A no less fascinating problem arose in connection with the first paper, the one evaluating Sadat's positions. From the moment I sent the paper out, I expected a government meeting to be convened in order to discuss the forthcoming visit. I spoke again and again with Brigadier-General Ephraim Poran, the Prime Minister's Military ADC, asking him to persuade the Prime Minister to call a meeting as soon as possible. Finally, on Friday, 18 November 1977 – one day before the scheduled landing of the presidential plane – I was at last called in to meet the Prime Minister. I took my files and drove to the Sdeh Dov airfield in Tel Aviv to take a helicopter to the capital. At the airport I was joined by the Chief-of-Staff, Lieutenant General Motta Gur, and the head of the Mossad, Yitzhak Hofi.

We found the Prime Minster's office in Jerusalem in a state of panic –

everything and everyone was at fever pitch in preparation for the visit. We waited for a few minutes and then were ushered in to meet Prime Minister Menachem Begin. To my utter surprise – we were not shown into the conference room, but to the Prime Minister's personal office. What is more, there was no one there except the Prime Minister himself and the Deputy Prime Minster, Professor Yigael Yadin. There wasn't a single Cabinet minister present.

The Prime Minister opened the meeting by turning to me and saying:

> Tomorrow evening we expect to receive the President of Egypt. And I hear from the Deputy Prime Minister, who is also acting Minister of Defence (Ezer Weizman, who was then Minister of Defence, had been hospitalized shortly before that following a serious car accident), and he tells me that he is afraid that the story of this entire visit is nothing more than an Egyptian trap that might serve the Egyptians as a cover for a surprise attack on Israel. And this is my question to the head of Army Intelligence: How do you view the possibility of a surprise attack?

The fact that the Prime Minister raised this issue, instead of holding a full-scale assessment meeting prior to Sadat's visit, as I had hoped, to discuss the Egyptian President's intentions and expectations from the visit, stunned me. I took a deep breath, regained control, waited a few seconds to recover, and said:

> Mr Prime Minister, I think there is no basis in reality for this concern. It is true that over the past few days there has been some tension along our borders with Egypt in Sinai. We carried out a large-scale military manoeuvre in Sinai that the Egyptians were not aware of, and they raised the alert level of their forces. However, I do not think that there is any reason to believe that the Egyptians are preparing any kind of military deception. I recommend that you ignore this possibility, and you should certainly not take any steps that might be interpreted by both the Egyptians and by the world at large as an Israeli move to sabotage the visit tomorrow evening.

The Prime Minister then turned to the Chief-of-Staff and to the head of the Mossad: 'What is your opinion on this issue?' Both of them supported the position I had presented. Then the Prime Minister turned to his Deputy. 'Mr Deputy Prime Minister, what is your opinion?' and Professor Yadin answered briefly, 'Even if the head of Army Intelligence is right, I don't think we should take any risks. I suggest we call up two reserve divisions immediately, and deploy them in Sinai.' The three of us – the Chief-of-Staff, the head of the Mossad and myself – tried to argue with him and convince the Prime Minister and the Deputy Prime Minister to drop the idea of calling up reserve units, but they were adamant.

The Prime Minister's summing up was brief: 'Since Ezer is in the hospital, and the Deputy Prime Minister is Acting Minister of Defence, I leave the question of mobilizing reserves for you to decide among yourselves. If you decide to mobilize the reserves – as far as I am concerned you have my approval.'

We did not see any point in continuing the argument any further. We boarded the helicopter and asked the pilot to put us down first of all at Tel Hashomer hospital, outside Tel Aviv. We went directly to see Ezer Weizman. He was lying in bed in great pain, his arms and legs completely bandaged and in traction. We told him about the meeting with the Prime Minister, and begged him, 'Ezer, you're the only one who can save the situation!' And indeed Weizman immediately understood the gravity of the situation. Groaning with pain, he called the Prime Minister and said to him, 'Mister Prime Minister, even though I am hospitalized, I am still in full possession of my senses. I ask you not to take any decisions concerning mobilizing reserves without consulting with me first and getting my approval.' The Prime Minister agreed, and the proposal was dropped then and there.

At that time, I was very angry with Prime Minister Begin. How was it possible that he did not convene even one political evaluation meeting on the eve of an event of such momentous significance as this visit of President Sadat to Jerusalem? I could not understand how Mr Begin or his government could formulate a policy without analysing, understanding and evaluating Egypt's potential flexibility.

Later, after thinking these things through and learning more about the decision-making processes of governments in Israel, I changed my mind. I found myself understanding and justifying the Prime Minister's position in this case. What is more, I witnessed a repeat performance of this attitude prior to Mr Begin's departure for Camp David ten months later, when he avoided convening any policy meeting to flesh out the Government's position on the eve of the summit conference. It is only because of my understanding of the Prime Minister's considerations at that time that I decided to raise this issue in this article.

I never heard an explanation from the Prime Minister himself, but I believe that I do understand his reasons. Had he brought up these issues in a government meeting, of necessity 'decisions' would have been made that would have tied the Government's and the Prime Minister's hands prior to Anwar Sadat's visit. And I have no doubt that any decisions that might have been discussed before Sadat's visit, before seeing the guest in person and hearing what he had to say, would have been extremely hard-line, in the spirit of Moshe Dayan's famous saying ten years earlier: 'It is better to have Sharm e-Sheikh without peace than peace without Sharm e-Sheikh.'[1]

At the same time, the Prime Minister could have found a middle way – a way of holding discussions on the issues without binding him in any way. One possibility would have been to have held an intelligence meeting with the Cabinet, at which time the intelligence services would have presented their assessments prior to the visit, analysed the positions that the Egyptian President might present, and answered any questions put to them by the ministers. At the same time, the Prime Minister could have seen to it that no further discussion took place in the Government before the visit on Israeli policies. The second option would have been to have held a meeting on the issues in a limited forum – the Prime Minister and one or two of his senior ministers, together with intelligence units, without involving other ministers.

This historic event – Sadat's visit to Jerusalem – is worthy of note for another reason. Israel is surrounded by Arab countries none of which is governed by democratic rule, and none of which is committed to a parliamentary and democratic decision-making process. Any decision or change in official policy is always the outcome of the initiative and decision-making of one man. He does not have to consult with anyone or reach decisions based on the majority opinion of the people around him. It was not only Israeli Intelligence that was caught off guard, surprised by Sadat's initiative: the Egyptian Foreign Minister, Ibrahim Fahmi, was no less surprised by the decision, having first learned of the visit from a radio broadcast.

This phenomenon makes life very difficult for intelligence services that are required to assess the decisions of an all-powerful leader of an enemy country.

(3) CONCLUSION

In summarizing the contribution of Israeli Intelligence to the peace process, I would like to emphasize the following points. The first of these (discussed earlier) concerns the awareness on the part of intelligence officers and the intelligence system in general that they must monitor any possible shifts toward a political settlement, or a shift toward peace, no less intensely than they monitor signs of an imminent attack or outbreak of war. It is important to stress that the intelligence services do not only focus on military problems. On the contrary, the higher one goes up in the ranks toward the top of the political pyramid, the greater is the relative weight of the political Intelligence Assessment as opposed to that of the military assessment.

The second point concerns the need to formulate a system of tell-tale signs that can detect a potential policy shift. Such signs must be monitored both by intelligence-gathering and by research and analysis in a systematic, consistent and orderly fashion.

The third point is the need to present an accurate National Intelligence Assessment, free of any political preconceptions held at the time by the people or their leaders. This Intelligence Assessment must examine every development in the region in a completely objective manner. And analysis is not enough: the intelligence services must report and present their Assessments in a clear, unadulterated fashion. In this context it is of the utmost importance that intelligence, more so than any other government body, must be allowed to present its findings in total freedom, even if the presentation is not to the liking of one political element or another in the country at large or in the Government. Evaluating enemy policy positions must be a permanent fixture in any Intelligence Assessment, both for the purposes of examination and evaluation, and for the purposes of orderly reporting and presentation to the country's political leaders.

One more point that we have already mentioned directly concerns the relationship between government and intelligence: the Government must not initiate secret contacts with the other side without consulting intelligence, particularly the section that is responsible for the National Assessment. There are (at least) five good reasons for this:

(1) In all likelihood, reports of these meetings will show up in material arriving at the intelligence services through their information-gathering systems. Without prior knowledge of these meetings, intelligence might cause damage and sabotage the meetings themselves by reports made in good faith, and wide dissemination of received information, possibly even responding to them derisively as 'rumours about negotiations and peace talks that are making the rounds on the other side'.

(2) Naturally, intelligence must present its Assessments without reference to the significance of such contacts. This, in turn, may cause the Assessments to sound absurd to the leaders, and lead to a sweeping denigration of the Intelligence Assessment as a whole – and all this when it is the leaders themselves who are responsible for the erroneous Assessments.

(3) Keeping the gathering and research arms of the intelligence services out of the picture prevents the leader from receiving important intelligence

input which could be very helpful to him in the ongoing talks and negotiations. We have already mentioned and analysed this important attendant
intelligence input.

(4) The sensitivity and concern over leaks about the ongoing secret contacts
    are quite understandable. Leaks of this nature can destroy the entire
    process. However, our wealth of experience in this matter has taught us
    that these leaks never originate from inside the intelligence system.

(5) Finally, the Government must consider the potentially serious damage
    that can be caused to the morale of the people in the intelligence
    community. To ignore their work is an expression of contempt, of a lack
    of confidence in and appreciation of all those people who do the work.
    This attitude could have repercussions in the future, when a new and
    revised assessment is required.

It is very important that the greatest latitude should be given in this
research/assessment area relating to policy shifts on the other side. There is
always the danger that one assessing body may have a pronounced preference
for a particular way of thinking, and therefore it is extremely important and
beneficial that at least one other body, if not more, examine these same trends.

An understanding between the political leader and the intelligence
research unit is necessary in relation to the contents and details of the
National Intelligence Assessment as it is submitted. Under no circumstances
should the leader adopt only those chapters of the Intelligence Assessment
that suit his policies or serve his political interests, while ignoring those
chapters that are less comfortable for him politically.

Finally, the other side of that same coin: the Intelligence Assessment must
be totally free of any concerns such as 'I, the intelligence officer, run the risk
of upsetting my political superiors'. Any intelligence officer who is afraid of
speaking out, for fear that what he has to say will displease someone who is
likely in turn to exact revenge on him or stall his promotion, will not be able
to carry out his duties as an intelligence officer. In the course of Israel's brief
history we have come across a number of such incidents. They were isolated
and rare, but the fact that they occurred at all indicate a danger of the first
order.

NOTE

1. Sharm e-Sheikh is a point on the southern tip of the Sinai peninsula. A small village under
   Egyptian rule, it later became the Israeli city of Ophira, and was evacuated when Israel
   withdrew from Sinai. In many ways it became a symbol of Israeli control over the Sinai
   peninsula which is why Dayan used it in his catchphrase.

6

Intelligence in a Time of Peace-making[*]

ALUF HAREVEN

'Knowledge is always a correction of previous knowledge.'

(Karl Popper)

THE NEED TO UNCOVER HIDDEN KNOWLEDGE

The subject matter of intelligence as well as the motivating force behind it is the need to know. If we knew in advance everything we needed to know, there would be no need to know anything, and no need for intelligence.

The main subject matter of intelligence, therefore, is what we do not yet know – that which is still hidden knowledge.

The constant challenge of dealing with hidden knowledge is the fascinating aspect of intelligence work, since hidden knowledge has many faces, faces that are not a permanent and unchanging depiction of reality, or even a permanent paradigm for the interpretation of reality. They are, rather, constantly, and occasionally surprisingly, in flux.

Hidden knowledge may be found, first of all, in ourselves and in our ability or refusal to see things of which we were previously unaware. Thus for example, when President Sadat informed the Egyptian Parliament in November 1977 that he was prepared to visit Israel, some people in the Israeli political and defence establishment refused to see in his declaration the beginning of a new direction in regional diplomacy, preferring rather to interpret it as a trick, a deliberate deception. They even insisted on placing the Israel Defence Forces (IDF) on alert in response. In other words, their implicit assumption was: once an enemy of Israel, always an enemy of Israel. Therefore even a seemingly peace-oriented proposal on Sadat's part could only be interpreted as a hostile action. However, there were others in Israeli political circles who immediately understood that Sadat's initiative could herald the beginning of an historic turnabout in Egyptian–Israeli relations,

---

[*] Trans. David Zinder.

and believed that Israel must dare to take up the challenge, and invite the Egyptian President to Jerusalem.

In view of the above, before setting out to fulfil their obligation – seeking hidden knowledge, intelligence personnel must first deal with a basic self-referential question: are they influenced, either individually or as a group, by implicit assumptions concerning the person or persons they intend to investigate, or are they, rather, willing to put any hypothesis at all to the test, provided it can be backed up by hard facts?

This perspective breeds an unusual paradox: only a situation of all-out conflict provides both sides to a dispute with the highest degree of certainty about each other – the sure knowledge that the other side is indeed the enemy. For in a state of total conflict, the two sides entertain a completely polarized world view which, for each of them, is a certainty. From there it is but a small step to a paradoxical syllogism: the world of conflict engenders more certainty than the world of peace-making. For in peace-making, the two sides are engaged in an encounter with neighbours who have been their enemies for decades and still have the potential to inflict considerable damage. This is an element in their relationship, dangerous both in theory and in practice, of which they are both well aware, and contains the potential for floating another basic assumption: namely, that perhaps despite the fact that they (the Arabs, the Israelis) are in the process of making peace, they have no intention of really making peace at all. Perhaps all this peace-making is part of an overall strategy whose hidden agenda is a continuation of the conflict by different means? Thus, for example, on the Israeli side, certain fundamental conceptions may persist concerning what they have labelled as the Palestinians' 'step-by-step doctrine', according to which, making peace is nothing more than a step on the road to the ultimate destruction of the State of Israel. By the same token, on the Arab side, certain fundamental conceptions may persist concerning Israel's ('secret') aspirations to gain hegemony over the entire Middle East, and instead of doing so by military force Israel now prefers to exploit its economic power for the same purpose. The major difficulty in dealing with basic conceptions such as these is that proof of their ongoing applicability to the present situation can be found not only in evidence from the past (*The Palestinian National Covenant*, or 'Two Banks to the Jordan'),[1] but also in statements made by both sides during the peace-making process (e.g. the Arab call for '*jihad* [holy war] on Jerusalem', or Israeli statements such as 'Israel will be the focal point of all advanced industry in the Middle East').

In contrast to the weight of our knowledge of the enmity-laden past, what we know of the peace process, at least in its first few years, is for the most part laden with uncertainty. Therefore the most difficult question facing either Israeli or Arab intelligence personnel in this time of peace-making is how to weigh the one against the other: basic concepts steeped in a conflict-ridden past with which both sides are all too familiar, as opposed to basic concepts emerging from a present marked by peace-making, and a future we cannot predict.

This is the greatest difficulty in intelligence work at a time of peace-making: the need to proceed on the basis of a dual and seemingly paradoxical assumption: that, on the one hand, the leading political figures in the Arab–Israeli conflict have indeed reached an understanding that their overriding historic interest now lies in making peace, and that the peace process is indeed gathering momentum; while on the other hand, that despite the historical imperative at work here, many dangers still lurk on the way to the achievement of peace, and the process itself may collapse in one area or another, or in a number of areas simultaneously.

Up to now we have dealt with one personal element, relating to the individual intelligence officer's need to examine his own concepts and assumptions for hidden agendas of which he may not be aware. However, intelligence work is, of course, all about the Other – someone else whose hidden intentions and actions we wish to reveal. Two questions come to mind in this context:

(1) What are the objectives of intelligence work in a time of peace-making, and what information are we seeking about these objectives? (In professional terms: what is the IVI – Indicator of Vital Information – for the decision-makers?)
(2) How do we set about acquiring the desired intelligence?

These two questions are of course not new to intelligence work. However, the conceivable answers are undergoing many changes, and the rest of this article will be devoted to an attempt to illuminate them.

TWO SUPER-OBJECTIVES OF INTELLIGENCE IN AN ERA OF PEACE-MAKING

A super-objective for intelligence in a time of peace-making may be defined as follows:

(1) Identifying peace-enhancing elements and the ways in which they may be encouraged to advance peace initiatives.
(2) Identifying peace-endangering elements, and the ways in which their threats may be deflected or deterred.

These super-objectives are based on the assumption that in a time of peace-making (and in all likelihood even after peace is established between Israel and all of its neighbours), the decision-makers will have to adopt a double-edged strategy: strengthening peace-enhancers on the one hand, and deterring the enemies of peace and pre-empting their hostile initiatives, on the other.

Peace-enhancing elements

Who are the peace-enhancing parties?

Peace-making, as we see it, is a highly intricate task of fitting together many disparate parts: a task that must be performed simultaneously on a number of different levels. The broader and more profound the peace-making work is, the greater are the chances for a long-lasting peace. We can differentiate between two types of peace-enhancing parties:

The first comprises *people whose decisions and actions may help launch initiatives and foster contacts that will strengthen the structure of peace.* Clearly, we are referring, first of all, to the political leaders with the authority to make decisions, and to their close advisers, and secondly, to other influential figures on the political scene, among them leaders of the opposition. A third group comprises people who can help strengthen economic ties, such as business entrepreneurs, and the fourth – people who can assist in developing contacts in the fields of science, technology and culture. Finally, there are people of the media – journalists who play an important role in shaping public opinion in any country.

But the term 'peace-enhancing elements' refers not only to people but also to issues that the people mentioned above can help promote – issues touching, for example, on international relations and agreements, or on joint economic enterprises, or any of the other areas mentioned above.

At the same time, intelligence services must also monitor certain basic elements in each country, whose encouragement, while not necessarily directly connected to the establishment of peaceful relations with Israel, may further the cause of peace. To begin with, we will deal with three such interrelated factors:

First of all, there is the stability of the regime involved in the peace-making. This is important if we assume that a different regime in the country in question may repudiate the peace agreements.

Secondly, there is *the rate of economic growth in each country.* This is important if we recognize that economic prosperity is a fundamental stabilizing factor, and thus a peace-enhancer, while a shaky economy is a destabilizing factor and therefore poses a danger to peace.

Thirdly, there is *the extent to which the country in question is integrated into major international systems* headed by the United States, Europe, Japan and China. The assumption here is that the more deeply the country in question is involved in these systems, and the more dependent it is on them, the greater its incentive to keep the peace, and the more effective the ability of the international systems to tone down and/or pre-empt trends that could lead to a resumption of hostilities (we say all this with a clear understanding of the limitations of international diplomatic systems – with the recent events in Ruanda and Serbia serving as a harsh reminder).

This process of identifying peace-enhancing elements is therefore not limited to the Middle East region, but rather encompasses the entire world, with special emphasis on its major centres, while at the same time not neglecting other, less central possibilities as well, such as, for example, specific people in some of the major countries who might be able to assist in furthering the peace in any one of the key areas we noted above. (Thus, for example, Norway's Foreign Minister played a crucial role in furthering the talks between the PLO and Israel, that eventually led to the Oslo Accords of 1993. Is it totally unthinkable, for example, that certain people might be found in non-Arab Muslim nations who could help set up peace-enhancing/ danger-preventing contacts with Iran?)

Peace-endangering elements

Who are the peace-endangering parties? Here we must differentiate between two groups: those who endanger the peace in actual fact, and those who have the potential to do so.

The people who might be considered under the heading of peace-endangering elements are those both in the Middle East and beyond it, who have both the political need and the ability to hamper the progress of the peace process, to halt it altogether, or even to turn it in the direction of war.

The greatest threat to peace in the Middle East comes from the direction of Iran, and from extremist Islamic elements throughout the world. These constitute a danger on two levels.

The first of these is the strategic level. In the coming decade, the greatest danger of all on this level is that Iran and parties connected with it will either develop independently, or somehow acquire, *nuclear or other weapons of mass destruction.* Such weapons in Iranian hands would pose a threat to many countries in the Middle East region, including Israel. From the point of view of intelligence, the danger resides not only in Iran or extreme Islamic elements, but in forces throughout the world, particularly in Europe and the Far East, who have had a hand in assisting Iran in developing these capabilities. Furthermore, the acquisition of nuclear weaponry by one country provides powerful motivation for other countries in the region to seek similar capabilities.

The second level is the day-to-day operational and/or tactical level, where *the danger of terrorist attacks* will undoubtedly go on unabated, attacks aimed either at targets inside Israel or Jewish targets elsewhere in the world, or at supporters of the peace process, chiefly the political leaders, anywhere in the world. Terrorist attacks also have political/strategic significance of the first order, since as far as the Israeli public is concerned, preventing such attacks, or at least limiting their numbers and scope, is the primary and most important test of peace. Above all, the super-objective of the perpetrators of these terrorist attacks is to sabotage the peace process and even initiate a chain of events that will eventually lead – so they hope – to its complete collapse.

To this list of peace-endangering elements, we must also add *extremist religious–nationalistic elements inside Israel*, who might resort to their own brand of terrorism, with the aim of undermining the peace process or destroying it altogether. The massacre at the Tomb of the Patriarchs in Hebron is one such example,[2] and one can think of other, even more extreme examples. The Islamic holy places such as the Temple Mount in Jerusalem and the Tomb of the Patriarchs, are obvious targets for such attacks, but these people could very well operate against other random targets as well.

At the same time as intelligence pursues its objective of acquiring as much information as possible on peace-endangering forces, it must also continue its traditional task of gathering information on *armies that might at some point launch a war against Israel*, their weapons systems, and their ability to deploy offensively against Israel, including the use of missiles and non-conventional weapons against civilian targets. In this context, *Iraq, too, poses a threat stemming from the potential use of non-conventional weapons against Israel*. It does seem, however, that the international community is more capable of curbing this tendency in Iraq than in Iran, though there is no guarantee that this will be the case over an extended period of time.

There are two main reasons for the need to acquire information on the military forces in the countries of the Middle East. First of all, as long as peace is not a totally stable and reliable factor in the region – a development that will require at least a generation – Israel has no choice but to treat the armies of all the countries in the region, even those formally at peace with Israel, as armed forces that may launch a military offensive should the peace efforts collapse, Secondly, as long as the danger exists – however infinitesimal – that one or more of the regimes in those countries that have made peace with Israel, may fall, their military forces must be regarded as a potential threat, since a new regime may renounce the peace agreements altogether.

THE PALESTINIANS AS A CRITICAL ISSUE FOR INTELLIGENCE

Peace-making in the Middle East is at present proceeding simultaneously on a number of parallel tracks:

— between Israel and Egypt;
— between Israel and the Palestinians;
— between Israel and Jordan;
— between Israel, Syria and Lebanon;
— between Israel and other Arab countries (Morocco, Tunisia, the Gulf States), and between Israel and non-Arab Muslim countries;
— between the countries of the region and the United States;
— between the countries of the region and other countries of the world.

Clearly, progress along any one of these tracks generally strengthens the inclination to make progress along other tracks (although there are exceptions to this rule). Nevertheless, the most crucial relationship in this context is almost certainly the relationship between Israel and the Palestinians.

As far as the Arabs are concerned, Israeli–Palestinian relations have been the main reason for the Arab–Israeli conflict, and for their refusal, for well over a generation, to even consider establishing ties with Israel. The Israel–PLO agreement of 1993 provided the Arab countries of the region, and beyond, with the legitimacy necessary to establish channels of communication and take the first steps toward establishing diplomatic relations with Israel. It follows, then, that the continued strengthening of the peace between Israel and the Palestinians in the West Bank and Gaza, will provide continued legitimacy to the development of ties on the other tracks. Any breakdown of relations with the Palestinians will no doubt have a destructive effect on these relations.

The ties between Israel and the Palestinians are also the closest to have been established between Israel and other Arab nations. It is a relationship with complex connections to virtually every aspect of their mutual existence: diplomacy, the nature of the regimes, security, public administration, employment and the economy, tourism and scores of other areas. These contacts are, by their very nature highly ambivalent – particularly for the Palestinians. On the one hand the Palestinians need the contacts with Israel (for example in the area of employment), yet on the other hand, they want to realize their independence and become self-sufficient. The proximity of the two populations, and their complex interdependence, are also high-risk factors in terms of potential terrorist attacks. Consequently, intelligence is faced with a crucial question on two interrelated issues.

The first issue concerns the degree of stability and effectiveness of the new regime established by the Palestinian Authority in the Territories,[3] particularly with regard to the prevention of terrorist activity, which bears directly on Israel's security, but also in other areas as well, especially economic development. Since the stability of the Palestinian regime is a peace-enhancing factor of the first order, a key issue for investigation by intelligence is the identification of factors conducive to the stability of the Palestinian administration.

The second issue concerns the peace-enhancing parties in the Palestinian population both inside the Territories and beyond; how can they be strengthened, and can this be achieved through direct intervention or only indirectly?

The Palestinian issue also bears on an internal Israeli issue: the question of the Arab citizens of Israel.[4] To date, the overwhelming majority of Israeli Arabs have never been involved in any form of aggression against the State of Israel, or ever threatened its security. This pattern of behaviour has differed markedly from that of the Arabs living in the Territories. The question for the future is whether or not this peaceful, civil coexistence will continue in Israel during an era of peace-making, and what effect the establishment of Palestinian self-rule in the Territories will have on Israeli Arabs and their national aspirations. Will more strident demands for autonomy or, indeed, for separation from the State of Israel, be heard, or will the demand – now voiced only by a few Arab scholars – to abolish the definition of Israel as the homeland of the Jewish people, gain wider support? Could this possibly become a rallying cry for the Israeli Arabs, leading to a polarization between the Arab minority and the Jewish majority in the country? Looked at from a completely different angle, it is worth examining those parties with the potential for enhancing cooperation between Jewish and Arab citizens in Israel and seeking ways to strengthen them.

MODUS OPERANDI FOR INTELLIGENCE IN AN ERA OF PEACE-MAKING

We may safely assume that all the information-gathering agencies employed by Israeli Intelligence services in times of war and conflict will continue to function in a time of peace-making, though a major portion of their work will now be devoted to dealing not only with peace-endangering factors, but also with peace-enhancing factors. The intelligence services will most certainly continue to exploit overt sources (radio and television broadcasts, newspapers and other printed publications), as well as covert sources such as electronic eavesdropping, satellite and aerial reconnaissance, agents and local supporters, and other special means.

A time of peace-making will, however, lead to fundamental changes in these operational methods. Some of the activities – particularly those dealing with peace-enhancing factors – will be a great deal easier to carry out than in the past.

The main reason for this is that in times of conflict, the activities of both sides are, to some extent, hidden from each other, without open lines of communication, or the possibility of direct contact between the two sides. In other words, in times of conflict, both sides conceal information about their military forces, their weapons systems, and their intentions (unless it is information employed for deception or deterrence). In a time of peace-making, on the other hand, both sides have a vested interest in strengthening peace-enhancing factors on both sides.

Some people will no doubt claim that the duties of intelligence do not include locating and/or identifying peace-enhancing factors, arguing that this is a matter that should remain entirely in the hands of the diplomatic service, or whoever else is involved in cultivating ties in the area of economic affairs, tourism, technology and culture. We believe that regardless of the nature of the information-gathering body dealing with this kind of information, proper procedure must be observed so that decision-makers at the various levels of government are given, on a regular basis, both comprehensive and specific intelligence on all the peace-enhancing factors in all of the relevant countries, as well as suggestions concerning possible ways of strengthening them.

SETTING UP COALITIONS OF INTELLIGENCE SERVICES

Peace-making is made possible by a coalition of regimes that support peace (in the Middle East and beyond), or at the very least, by a broad consensus among them. In the same way, it is possible to conceive of collaboration between a coalition of intelligence organizations from various countries. The objective of such a coalition would be to locate peace-strengthening and peace-endangering factors in the region. This kind of coalition might operate on a bilateral basis, as for example between Israeli Intelligence services and those of a given Arab country, or else a multi-lateral arrangement between a number of countries. The latter possibility means, in effect, the creation of a joint intelligence network in these areas, with an ongoing exchange of intelligence information among its members, with representatives meeting from time to time for direct clarification of outstanding issues.

The establishment of such a network, made up of intelligence elements from different countries, is in itself a peace-enhancing factor. We can conceive of a situation in which, within the framework of such a coalition, each side would table for investigation not only peace-enhancing factors within and beyond its borders, but also issues relating to neighbouring countries that give cause for concern, such as organizations bent on harming the peace process, or military issues such as the size and nature of a neighbouring country's armed forces or a weapons system that it is either being purchased or developed independently.

From the point of view of intelligence work, this latter area – the mutual exchange of information relating to the armed forces of the countries involved in a peace process, or weapons systems they have at their disposal – is the most sensitive. What, then, are the means of information-gathering that countries at peace with each other are allowed to employ against each other in their quest for information on potential dangers posed by their neighbours' military forces? Should they be satisfied with culling information only by technological means – including satellites and electronic devices – and through direct contacts between the military of the two countries, and direct channels of communication for mutual clarification of the issues so as to avoid misunderstandings? In this area, there may be some overlap between intelligence work and any direct contacts that may take place between military leaders of both of the countries involved in the peace process.

WOULD IT BE PROPER TO EMPLOY AGENTS AS WELL?

Beyond all the above, can a country also permit itself to employ secret agents inside a country with which it has peaceful relations? This is a tough question, which most decidedly does not have a clear-cut answer one way or the other, either on the Israeli or the Arab side. Is it conceivable, for example, that the Arab countries, or many other countries for that matter, would be willing to forego attempts to find out whatever they can about Israel's military capabilities in both conventional and non-conventional modes of warfare? By the same token, is it conceivable that Israel would be willing to forego attempts to find out whatever it can about developing military capabilities of its neighbours in these modes of warfare?

All this poses a serious dilemma: how to go about acquiring intelligence on potentially dangerous issues from a country with which Israel has peaceful relations, and this without endangering the peace-making process in any way. There are no easy solutions to this dilemma, and it most certainly requires serious consultations between the heads of the intelligence community and the political leaders of the country.

THREE PARTICULARLY DIFFICULT OBJECTIVES

Among the primary targets of intelligence-gathering in a time of peace, there are several which pose particular difficulties:

(1) *Iran* is a difficult target for intelligence since it is one of the most cloistered nations in the world, even though it does seem to want to emerge from its isolation and develop contacts, at least in the economic sphere. Iran is a difficult objective not only because of the essentially secretive nature of its regime, but also because of the complexity of the relationships among its leaders, and the difficulty of evaluating, or knowing, to what extent certain publicly-stated positions and decisions represent a broad and binding commitment, or are just the personal opinions of certain individuals in power. Consequently, where Iran is concerned, the question remains open as to whether official government decisions are in fact binding, or if there are forces (terrorist organizations for instance) that will ignore any decisions that have a direct bearing on their activities.

(2) *Terrorist organizations* are a difficult objective, since most of them are very small, and operate mainly underground. Therefore locating their agents and monitoring them on an ongoing basis requires local efforts in the field by conventional or unconventional means of information-gathering.

(3) *Organizations trading in non-conventional weapons* (and in material or information that may be instrumental for their development). These, too, are small, mostly clandestine groups that operate out of a number of different countries. Locating them and preventing them from carrying out their transactions requires intensive international cooperation.

THE HUMAN FACTOR: INTELLIGENCE AS AN INITIATOR OF INVESTIGATORY DIALOGUE

The most absorbing issue in an era of peace-making is the human factor (Israeli or Arab), which both Israeli and Arab Intelligence services are asked to assess. What, for instance, are the peace-enhancing or the peace-endangering factors in Rabin's mind?* What are they in Arafat's mind? In Assad's? In the minds of the leaders of Hamas and the other Islamic movements? In Sadam Hussein's mind? In Rafsanjani's mind or in the minds of other Iranian leaders?

---

*This article was written in 1995, prior to Yitzhak Rabin's assassination, and while Rafsanjani was still in power in Iran.

Our assumption is that for all these leaders, peace-enhancing and peace-endangering factors shared a kind of simultaneous, ambivalent and highly charged coexistence, although their relative magnitude for each of these leaders is different and variable. Just as Rabin, whose central objective [was] to make peace, was not prepared to do so at any cost, so we may assume that Rafsanjani, despite the extremism of his ideology, [was] not prepared to make war at all costs.

Therefore, intelligence must give high priority to revealing the full complexity of the leaders' views, and the extent of their willingness to endorse changes. For example, Israeli Intelligence must ask itself which peace-enhancing factors might strengthen Arafat's commitment to the peace process? Or which of the peace-endangering factors that affect Arafat can be mitigated, and how can that be achieved? These kinds of questions are relevant with regard to the leader of Iran as well: are there factors that could modify those of his positions which pose a danger to peace? This will become a crucial question if and when Iran acquires non-conventional weapons, since their acquisition might engender a powerful ideological temptation to use them for propaganda purposes against Israel or against other targets both in the Middle East and elsewhere. Under these circumstances, is there an effective deterrent that can be employed against the Iranian leaders? And how is it possible to ensure that hard facts about Israeli and American (and other countries') deterrent systems – and the terrible price they will exact from Iran itself – will come to the attention of the Iranians and be fully comprehended by their leaders?

All this leads to the conclusion that one of the crucial objectives of intelligence work in relation to leading figures in the region is to initiate an ongoing investigative dialogue. The basic assumption of the investigative dialogue is that there is no cast-iron imperative that irrevocably binds the leading political figures in the region to concepts they held in the past. One may note, in this context, President Sadat of Egypt, Moshe Dayan, Yitzhak Rabin, Yasser Arafat, Hafez el-Assad, and perhaps even Muammar Gaddafi and Sadam Hussein. Therefore, the investigative dialogue must explore the depths of their readiness to enhance peace or to head off peace-endangering initiatives. It is not at all clear whether or not the Israeli intelligence community has a unit today which is responsible for this area of intelligence work.

At the same time, profound changes are taking place in the very nature of the dialogue between intelligence and decision-makers in various countries. In situations of total conflict, when there has been no direct communication between leaders of enemy countries, intelligence has been the policy-makers' main source of information about their enemies and their leaders (although there have been cases when heads of state of countries in conflict met and exchanged information that was not made available to the intelligence services).

Today, when policy-makers on both sides meet on a more or less regular basis with their former enemies, it is intelligence that asks the leaders for information about these people. This is not, however, a one-way exchange in which one side has vital information and the other has none. It is rather an exchange in which intelligence must note and bring into sharp focus the questions policy-makers should be asking about their opposite numbers on the other side. In the past it was the decision-maker who indicated to intelligence the nature of the vital information he required. In the course of a peace-making process, it is the intelligence officer, rather, who establishes the IVI for the political leader to concentrate on, in his meeting with a leader of a country with which a peace process is in progress.

In this dialogue the intelligence officer must also give psychological guidance to the decision-makers. It is up to him to present the entire spectrum of potential requests and real difficulties of the other side, and the principal ways of responding to each of them (it is, of course, the decision-maker's prerogative to choose among the various suggestions). Furthermore, between leaders and between nations, the choice of words and of formulations are of great significance, as is the ungrudging recognition of the other side's dignity and fundamental problems, even when the intention is to accede to only part of their demands. Intelligence, whose duty it is to locate peace-enhancing factors, must deal with these psychological issues as well. Naturally, the *sine qua non* of all this is the decision-makers' receptiveness to the various intelligence bodies, and their willingness to maintain a continuous dialogue with them.

INTELLIGENCE FACING SUDDEN (AND POSSIBLY UNEXPECTED?) CHANGES

A substantial part of intelligence work involves monitoring ongoing processes that will, in all likelihood, continue to develop along the same lines in the years to come. For example:

- monitoring the peace process between Israel and the Arab countries, and between Israel and the Palestinians;
- monitoring military build-ups, conventional and non-conventional, in various countries;
- monitoring extremist Islamic movements, and the degree of danger they pose to various regimes.

This area of intelligence activity – which probably constitutes the greater part of its work – is for the most part fairly easy to monitor, since it deals with ongoing parameters with which we are already familiar, and minor, piecemeal changes in one area or another of the overall picture. These might include, for example, the willingness of each side to add economic ties to existing diplomatic relations; or the willingness to broaden diplomatic contacts through frequent top-level meetings; or the acquisition of new and hitherto unknown weapons systems.

Sudden changes, involving unexpected and radical shifts into totally new situations – known as 'second degree' changes – are the difficult part of intelligence work. The difficulty for intelligence in these cases is that while in most instances the theoretical possibility of a sudden change of one kind or another can be foreseen, the same does not hold true for either the certainty or the timing of their occurrence. The reason for this is that historical processes do not develop as an ordered and more or less predictable continuum of pre-existing relationships. Rather there is, at times, a sudden conflux of events and decisions that develop very rapidly, with no advance warning whatsoever. It is not at all clear if there is a unit in intelligence whose principal task it is to deal with changes such as these.

There are abundant examples from the past of such dramatic occurrences. In the first few decades of Israel's existence, the outbreak of war between a coalition of Arab countries and Israel was always a possibility, regardless of the fact that during the greater part of the period in question no such war ever erupted. Thus, for 45 years, from 1949 on, anyone who said, 'It is possible that the Arabs will launch a war against Israel, but it is not likely to break out next year,' was right 43 times and mistaken twice: in 1967 (even Nasser, at the beginning of that same year, rejected the possibility of war) and in 1973. In October 1977 a conference was held at the Van Leer Institute in Jerusalem to try to foresee the nature of a possible peace between Israel and her neighbours. One of the participants, a well-known professor of political science, dismissed out of hand the very subject of the conference, referring to it as 'science fiction'. Only one month later, President Sadat publicly announced his willingness to come to Jerusalem. Similarly there were people in Israel who predicted, some time before 1987, that a popular uprising could erupt in the Territories. No one, however, could have foreseen the exact chain of events which began by accident (literally: a car accident in which six residents of the Gaza Strip were killed in a crash with an Israeli semi-trailer) and led eventually to the outbreak of the *intifada*.

A parallel could be drawn between predicting political events and weather forecasting. Experts are able to tell us that a storm is brewing, or is about to reach a certain area, only after the first signs of the storm become visible. At that point, they can foresee that within hours or days, as the case may be, it will gather force in one direction or another. One week earlier, the only thing we could have said for certain was that a storm in this area was likely though by no means certain. The actual onset of the storm system in our area can be announced only very close to its appearance in the area.

We can, then, point to some possible – though not absolutely certain – events, that could bring about a sudden political–military change of direction. The very fact that we define them as 'possible', means that they may also *not* occur, or that they could come as a complete surprise.

THE DANGER OF A SURPRISE ATTACK BY NON-CONVENTIONAL WEAPONS

The worst eventuality of all is the use of non-conventional weapons, nuclear or other, against a civilian target in order to deal a crushing blow to the country in question, either in retaliation for an earlier action, or as a blow designed to bring about submission or total annihilation, or possibly even as an ideological showpiece. The difficulty of foreseeing such an event stems from the nature of the enemy or enemies that intelligence is facing, and the uncertainty surrounding the decision-making process in their regime. One will probably never know whether the decision to use weapons of mass destruction is in fact rational and sane. After all, a totally rational process of deliberation would lead to the inescapable decision *not* to use such weaponry, if only because of the grave dangers facing the perpetrators as a result.

Can we be certain that the leaders of Iran today (if indeed they remain in power) and the terrorist organizations associated with them, will be prepared to subordinate their political enmity and zealous ideology unconditionally and for all time to a pragmatic consideration of the price Iran itself might pay for such an action? And if some of them are indeed pragmatic and sane, is there any certainty that they will be able to maintain complete control over their country – and that Iran will never allow other forces, with access to such weapons, and the determination to go ahead and do this terrible deed, to function within its borders?

So far as the use of non-conventional weapons is concerned, it is also worth noting that a sovereign country might make use of a terrorist organization as a cover for any initiative on its part to use such weapons, thus reducing the retaliatory risk to itself.

These scenarios may sound somewhat far-fetched and paranoid, but they stem from a new admixture that may develop (at least in our region) of the existence, on the one hand, of weapons of mass destruction and, on the other, of leaders in power whose distorted understanding of world systems may cause them to make grave mistakes (such as the mistake Sadam Hussein made when he decided to invade Kuwait).

In this respect, there are profound differences between signs of the imminent outbreak of war and signs of an intention to use non-conventional weapons of mass destruction. The order of magnitude of today's armies is such that any redeployment in advance of offensive action – particularly in a time of peace – is bound to feature prominently in reports submitted by information-gathering agencies. Deployment for the purposes of launching weapons of mass destruction, on the other hand, is for the most part limited to specific and very limited locales, and can be revealed only through first-hand contact with the decision-maker (or makers), and with the unit that is actually going to fire the weapons – a unit which, by its very nature, is a very small one.

Given the tremendous obstacles intelligence must overcome in order to be able to provide sufficient advance warning of such attacks, the danger of the outbreak of non-conventional warfare must be placed at the top of the region's national security priorities. This poses the practical question: is it possible to set up a monitoring system that can provide information that will be precise enough to prevent such initiatives occurring?

A key question in this context is the reliability of regimes and their leaders. While in the realm of diplomacy and ideology the United States and the former Soviet Union were in constant conflict for over 40 years, as far as nuclear weapons were concerned the two countries remained highly reliable enemies, their leaders over this period of time being firmly committed to avoiding the use of the nuclear weapons at their disposal. Thus, at the same time as they squared off against each other on many issues in many places all around the world, they also maintained direct channels of communication and contact at the highest levels to prevent the occurrence of a nuclear disaster on either side. Is it possible to develop a similar relationship in the Middle East between Israel and Iran? This is one of the more difficult questions that intelligence – and the decision-makers in Israel – will have to deal with in the very near future.

THE DANGER OF SPECTACULAR SURPRISE ATTACKS BY TERRORISTS

Terrorist organizations are not military powers. Their aim, therefore, is to carry out attacks that have as spectacular an effect as possible, either for their own sake, or in the hope of causing the peace process to collapse. Experience gained in this regard in the world and in our own region has shown that no country threatened by such actions has ever managed fully to eradicate terrorist activities, unless (as in Northern Ireland) agreements are reached with the organization behind these attacks. Therefore we must expect acts of terror in the future that will be more terrible and unexpected than anything we have experienced in the past. The difficulty in attempting to provide protection from such attacks is that their human objectives are chosen totally at random.

THE DANGER OF THE COLLAPSE OF REGIMES

Another potential area for surprise developments in the area of intelligence, is the collapse of political regimes. With the exception of Turkey and Israel, there is hardly a single country in the Middle East that is immune to such reversals. The reason for this is that Turkey (despite its cruel suppression of the Kurdish minority) and Israel are democracies, in which governments rise and fall solely through democratic processes,[5] while in the other countries of the region no such mechanisms exist. In these countries the only way a leader can be deposed is either by military coup (involving relatively small forces) or by mass, popular uprising (like the one that took place in Iran).

In the Middle East (although it is far from certain) the regimes of the following countries are relatively unstable and may topple:

- *Egypt*: as a result of domestic socioeconomic problems that are gathering momentum. To date these are marked by the increased influence of fundamentalist Islamic movements with which the Government is finding it difficult to deal effectively.
- *Jordan*: because of pressures from Palestinian and Islamic groups.
- *The Palestinian Authority*: as a result of its failure to develop an effective and successful administration that is accepted by the majority of the residents.
- *Syria*: because of instability that may follow the eventual death of Hafez el-Assad. The 'domino effect' following such an eventuality will no doubt bring down the Government in *Lebanon* as well.
- *Iraq*: due to the instability that will occur when, sooner or later, Sadam Hussein's rule comes to an end. Iraq's very future as a nation, its geographical integrity and borders will be open for discussion.
- *Saudia Arabia*: as a result of pressures brought to bear by elements within the country opposed to the current regime's style of government.
- *Iran*: because of growing popular dissatisfaction with the results of the Islamic revolution.

The collapse of a regime can follow two possible patterns. In the first, the old regime is replaced by a new one that effectively gains control over most of the country. In the second, no new regime effectively controls the country, and a protracted armed conflict ensues between rival forces for control of the country. In the latter case, it is likely that other countries will intervene on behalf of one side or another in the conflict.

This is what happened in Lebanon during the civil war that lasted from 1975 to 1990. This is what is happening now in Iraq where the Kurds, with the help of foreign nations, have created a *de facto* autonomy that has cut itself off from the central government in Baghdad.

Thus, for example, the collapse of the regime in Jordan might precipitate intervention by its neighbours – the Israelis or the Palestinians, as well as Syria, Iraq or Saudi Arabia. The collapse of Palestinian self-rule, on the other hand, might force Israel to try to set up a new governing body in the West Bank and Gaza. Intervention from the outside in the case of the collapse of a regime, can also deteriorate into clashes among the armed forces of the intervening nations within the borders of the country on whose behalf they intervened in the first place.

The worst-case scenario is the collapse, one after the other, in 'domino' fashion, of all the peace-supporting regimes in the region, and the rise of new regimes in their stead led by Islamic extremists. This is an apocalyptic scenario that some Western scholars (not necessarily Middle East experts) propose as the next world-wide conflagration: a conflict between the countries of revolutionary Islam – which abhor Western-inspired, secular democratic culture – and the rest of the world, with Israel located right in the geographical epicentre of the conflict. On the other hand, there are other scholars (mostly Middle East experts) who caution against sweeping generalizations in relation to the Islamic movement, and against apocalyptic scenarios of this kind, and point out that even among the Islamic fundamentalists there are those who categorically reject murder as a legitimate weapon in their struggle. We do not know, of course, who is right – the 'apocalyptics', or those propounding a more complex view of the issue, and it is more than likely that a good many years will pass until we do know. Therefore this question – or this concern – must remain high on the agenda of the decision-makers and of intelligence, as one of the most crucial questions in an era of peace-making.

Beyond all the above, we must also consider the real possibility that a new regime, taking over from a regime that has collapsed, may totally endorse the previously-signed peace treaty with Israel, giving added strength and authority to the peace itself.

We can close this part of the discussion with the observation that for the

Arab nations and the Palestinian administration, the possibility of a political reversal in Israel following general elections, and the creation of a government opposed, either in part or *in toto*, to the peace treaties, is a major – and threatening – change, although they will all, no doubt, at first try to understand the overall significance of such a change before taking any action.

PEACE TREATIES WILL REDUCE THE DANGER OF A SURPRISE ATTACK

Contrary to these scenarios, which may occur suddenly with no advance warning, it is more likely that the danger of a surprise attack on Israel by a coalition of Arab countries will diminish over the next few years, provided of course, that the regimes committed to the peace process remain in power. We can point to two main reasons for this assumption. The first is the very difficulty of putting together such a coalition for the purposes of waging war against Israel, when the Arab regimes that may be included in it have a long-term interest in maintaining the peace (as Egyptian President Mubarak said in the mid 1980s, 'Peace is a strategic interest for Egypt'). The second reason is that the peace treaties themselves provide Israel with strategic depth for early warning:

– In Sinai, which is mostly demilitarized, any incursion of Egyptian military units into the area will in itself constitute a warning, particularly when the demilitarized zones of the Sinai Desert are monitored by an international force headed by the United States.
– The peace treaty with Jordan contains a clause obliging both sides to prevent the entry of hostile external forces into their territories. Practically speaking, this means the continuation of Jordan's ban on the entry of armed forces from other Arab countries into its territory (first implemented by Jordan in 1970). Accordingly, the entrance of any foreign Arab military force into Jordanian territory will constitute a clear warning of the possible outbreak of war against Israel.
– The demilitarization of southwest Syria, just beyond present ceasefire lines on the Golan Heights, will in all likelihood play an important part in any peace agreement between Israel and Syria, and will be monitored – as in Sinai – by an international force, with the United States playing a central role in its implementation. Any incursion of Syrian forces into this demilitarized zone will be tantamount to an early warning of hostile intentions.

On this issue of early warning of a surprise attack, it is more than likely that overall the work of Intelligence will be easier in an era of peace-making than in an era of prolonged conflict.

INTELLIGENCE AND THE INFORMATION AGE

We began this article by stating that intelligence's primary motivation is the need to know, and we will conclude by stating that intelligence has never been omniscient, and that the fundamental tension in intelligence work is between the attempt to uncover as much as possible and the certain knowledge that we will never acquire all the information that we need – particularly as regards advance warnings on critical developments in the region. Even in an era of peace-making, the uncertainty that attends decisions made by inherently fallible human judgement will continue to generate surprises, some bad and some good.

Nonetheless, the era of peace-making has coincided with the beginning of the era of information systems. The world is organizing itself as a world-wide system of knowledge and information. Every telephone directory instructs us on how to dial directly to almost any destination in the world, with no borders or boundaries to stop us. The Internet enables subscribers all around the globe to exchange information by way of their computers on almost any subject under the sun, and there are many other such net-works.

Despite the clandestine aspect of its work, intelligence too must not remain secluded behind its own closed doors. Conceivably, if indeed peace does take root in the region, intelligence will also emerge from the dark in many of its areas of operation, and will function in a totally open manner to satisfy its curiosity about the identity of peace-enhancers in our region, the means that may be employed to strengthen them and the identity of peace-endangerers and the ways of stopping them. Any intelligence service in this new age adhering to outmoded attitudes toward its sources of information will find itself lagging far behind events, whereas the flow of vital information can be at one's fingertips in a multitude of easily accessible data bases.

Bearing this in mind, it is entirely possible that in an era of peace-making part of the output of intelligence will be made totally available to the public at large. It is the public's right to know who the peace-enhancing forces are in the various countries, and the periodic publication of material on them can conceivably assist in initiating contacts among like-minded people. Bearing this in mind, the duty of intelligence in an era of peace will be to function as a facilitator that exploits the widespread availability of information to enable contacts on many levels, despite the fact that intelligence itself is usually not involved in such initiatives.

At the same time, in the struggle to uncover peace-endangering factors in the Middle East, intelligence may also shed some of its clandestine attributes. In the same way as the stability and resilience of the peace are the result of a coalition of peace-supporting nations, so too the struggle against peace-endangering factors can be presented to the public in all these countries as the attempt to strengthen the peace and head off any possible continuation of armed conflict with the heavy price it exacts from all sides. The conditions for such integrated and overt action by a coalition of intelligence agencies do not yet exist in the current peace process. But the longer the peace holds, the more its very durability becomes the measure of its reliability. And the greater its reliability, the easier it will be for a coalition of intelligence agencies to make their information public, and request information on those forces that endanger the process.

DOMESTIC INTELLIGENCE VERSUS FOREIGN INTELLIGENCE

In an era in which the threat of war is likely to be radically reduced, public attention will turn to terrorist attacks which are regarded as a daily danger. Consequently, for Israeli decision-makers and its intelligence services, the prevention of terrorist attacks inside Israel must become a top priority in the operational and tactical spheres (though not necessarily in the area of strategy, where the dangers are of a totally different order of magnitude).

What all this signifies is the increased importance of internal security forces in Israel and its neighbouring countries, those manning the front lines of the battle that is still being fought. The security services are responsible for uncovering terrorist elements, and preventing them from carrying out their operational plans. This is highly localized and painstakingly detailed work, which requires continuous effort in order to locate potential terrorists, either among the residents of the country, residents of the Territories, or among the millions of foreigners who visit Israel and its neighbours every year, as tourists or for other purposes.

One of the most important components of this battle is the creation of regional and international information networks that will assist in the daily monitoring of terrorists wherever they are, their movements, their plans and the means of concealment they employ in their operations.

HOW CAN INTELLIGENCE ACHIEVEMENTS BE MEASURED IN
AN ERA OF PEACE-MAKING?

In conclusion, we might ask what are salient features in assessing intelligence achievements in an era of peace-making.

The following criteria seem relevant in this context:

(1) As regards peace-endangering elements, the crucial factor in assessing intelligence achievements is the extent to which intelligence acquires and places at the disposal of the decision-makers information that will facilitate the prevention of initiatives for the development and use of non-conventional weapons (nuclear and other) and, as a corollary, the extent to which intelligence succeeds in helping set up channels of communication that will prevent the use of such weapons. The dangers involved in this area are so horrifying (to all sides) that it must be given the highest priority in intelligence work and in the evaluation of its achievements.

(2) At the same time, intelligence success will be measured by the extent of its prevention of terrorist activities, and the degree of its success in reducing these to a minimum. To put it bluntly, we might say that intelligence success in this area will be measured by the number of victims of terrorist attacks – the fewer the victims, the greater its achievement.

(3) Also important is the extent to which intelligence can present an accurate picture of the size of the ever-growing conventional forces of nations in the region, together with any changes in their deployment.

(4) As regards peace-enhancing factors, the criterion for evaluation will be the quality of information and assessments intelligence provides for the decision-makers, on the political level and on other – not only state-related – levels as well, as a result of which further actions can be taken to enhance the peace.

(5) The success of intelligence work will also be influenced by the setting up and operation of a regional network of intelligence services, the primary common objective of which is to locate local peace-enhancing or peace-endangering factors.

(6) One of the fundamental bases of peace is the growing and unimpeded flow of information between nations and countries. Intelligence, whose primary function is to know, must be integrated into this exchange, both as one of the enabling factors in the flow of information between peace-enhancing factors and as one of the parties reaping its fruits.

NOTES

1. *Translator's note*: The Palestinian National Covenant is an official PLO document which includes, among other things, the demand that all Jews who came to Palestine after 1917 (when the British Balfour Declaration set the stage for the creation of 'a national home for the Jews') should return to their countries of origin; 'Two Banks to the Jordan' was the rallying cry of the right-wing Revisionist Movement founded by Ze'ev Jabotinsky, calling for Jewish sovereignty over biblical Israel – from the Nile in the south to the Euphrates in the north, and from the Mediterranean in the west to the Moab (present-day Jordan) in the east – including both banks of the Jordan River.

2. *Translator's note*: On 25 February 1994, Baruch Goldstein, a resident of Kiryat Arba near Hebron, walked into the building on a day of Muslim prayer, and opened fire indiscriminately, killing 29 worshippers and wounding many others, before he himself was killed. Twenty-four Arabs later died in clashes with Israeli security forces that erupted following the massacre.

3. *Translator's note*: A term used in Israel to designate all of the West Bank and Gaza – the 'Territories' taken over by Israel following the Six-Day War. Generally, the Golan Heights are not included in this definition.

4. *Translator's note*: Those Arab residents of Palestine who remained inside Israeli territory after the establishment of the state in 1948. They are bona fide Israeli citizens, with all civil rights and obligations save the requirement to serve in the Army.

5. It is true, however, that in Turkey the army has on occasion intervened in order to restore the Government's authority.

7

Intelligence Research in the Middle East Peace Process (From the Madrid Conference to the Peace Treaty with Jordan)*

'COLONEL SHMUEL'

INTRODUCTION

The past few years have seen rapid changes in the world: new countries are rising out of the ruins of the former Soviet Union; Europe is moving slowly ahead in the process of unification – the original objectives of which are by now largely unattainable; and the United States, the only remaining superpower, defines the limits of its own involvement. The old world order has made way for a unipolar world, with a few areas of instability (parts of the former Soviet Union, eastern Europe, the Persian Gulf and North Korea), and a few dictatorships – Iran, Iraq, Libya and North Korea – attempting to rebel against the new rules of the game. At the same time, tensions have increased between the economic blocs, the United States, western Europe, and East Asia, with Japan and Germany – both of which were defeated in the Second World War – leading this economic front.

The demise of the old world order and Sadam Hussein's defeat in the Gulf War – after trying to take on the new world in the waning years of the old – have once again opened up a window of opportunity for peace between Israel and the Arab countries. Up until now this has produced two agreements with the Palestinians: the 'Agreement on Principles', relating to the Interim Agreement, which was signed on 13 September 1993, and the 'Jericho and Gaza First Agreement', which facilitated the implementation of the first stage of the Interim Agreement. Following on these, a peace agreement was reached by Jordan and Israel, and signed on 25 October 1994 at Ein Evrona in the Arava desert.

---

*Trans. David Zinder.

These new realities have initiated highly significant repercussions in the world of intelligence. Under the old world order – both in the Middle East and in broader world systems – life was easier: ideologies were clear-cut, political processes were for the most part predetermined, and dialogue was a rare commodity. Now, with the collapse of some of these ideologies, the pace of events has accelerated and political dialogues are proliferating, creating a new reality. Under these circumstances, the challenge facing intelligence is much greater than before.

This article (written in the spring of 1995) is devoted to political intelligence analysis in the peace process between Israel and the Arabs from the Madrid Conference in October 1991 to the beginning of 1995. The reference here is to intelligence analysis carried out by the Army Intelligence Branch of the Israel Defence Forces (IDF). However, it should be pointed out that most of the assessments we shall present below were shared by other state intelligence bodies. The analysis presented in this article is offered from a personal point of view and does not necessarily represent the opinions of other bodies or persons in the Israeli intelligence system. It is the aim of this article to discuss intelligence assessments from the perspective of methodology. Broadly speaking, the article contains three main messages:

(1) It is impossible to guarantee accurate predictions of policy shifts. Intelligence can greatly enhance the level of prediction and narrow down the areas of uncertainty, but it is ultimately incapable of preventing surprises. In any case, intelligence is not meant to foresee the future but rather to evaluate opponents' capabilities and intentions. The future depends to a great extent on the decision-making echelons in Israel, which are beyond the purview of intelligence investigation.

(2) Since the beginning of the 1990s, intelligence notched up a number of impressive successes in predicting the positions taken by the two sides in the peace process: after the Gulf War, intelligence foresaw the tendency toward a renewal of the political momentum, and the consent of Syria, Jordan, Lebanon and the Palestinians to join the Madrid Conference. Since then, Palestinian positions (including those that led to the Oslo Accords) have been predicted with a high degree of accuracy, as have the positions held by Syria and Lebanon (it is still too early to evaluate all the assessments in these two areas). The demands made by the Jordanians, their desire for peace and their willingness to make progress in the negotiations – all these were accurately forecast. Intelligence erred, however, when it predicted that King Hussein would not sign a separate peace treaty with Israel as early in the process as 1994.

(3) Intelligence analysts often find it very difficult to carry out their duties in the political arena because of their deliberate exclusion from information by the political leaders during secret negotiations. There are reasons for employing such compartmentalization of information, but there is also a price to be paid: possible distortion of the National Intelligence Assessment ('friendly forces' are off-limits for intelligence investigation, consequently intelligence officers are often misled by an incomplete and ultimately false reality that emerges from the open negotiations they do have access to); not exploiting the advantages inherent in state intelligence services, in which hundreds of millions of dollars are invested every year, and where the best minds are concentrated, all this precisely at a time when such qualities are needed most – a time when fateful decisions must be made. For example, there are people who believe Intelligence involvement in the secret negotiations at Oslo might have produced an improved version of the 'Agreement of Principles' with the Palestinians; might have prevented the obfuscation found in certain clauses of the Agreement that later led to disagreements; and might have given the policy-makers insights into the Palestinians' reading of the Agreement and their ability to implement it. Therefore, a methodological solution should be found that would provide sufficient leeway both for intelligence needs and for the political echelons' desire to safeguard the secrecy of their diplomatic contacts.

INTELLIGENCE FORECASTING CAPABILITY – THREE METHODOLOGICAL REMARKS

'God does not gamble with dice.' This statement was made in the 1930s by Albert Einstein as part of the battle he waged against the conclusions of two of his renowned colleagues, Niels Bohr and Werner Heisenberg. These two physicists claimed, on the basis of their findings in the new field of Quantum Theory, that a basic uncertainty prevails in the realm of elementary particles since we can never truly predict the exact location of a particle in space. The best we can do, they said, is to indicate the probabilities of its presence at a given point. To Einstein's chagrin, the scientific world embraced their findings, and recognized, for the first time, that basic processes in our universe are determined at random. This concept of randomness in physical processes is all the more applicable when it comes to processes determined by human beings. What this means is that the desire to be able to predict the behaviour of political leaders or population groups on the basis of past events cannot be guaranteed any measure of success, even if we are in possession of all the relevant information and have a complete understanding of the processes involved. In other words, even if one draws the correct conclusions from historical events, and knows everything there is to know (and one cannot!), one will still be left with a great many factors of uncertainty that are impossible to foresee.

To illustrate this issue, here are three examples of random events that took place in 1992–93. Each one of them had a direct influence on political processes in the Middle East, even though no causal relationship existed between these events and the process itself:

(1) King Hussein's contracting cancer – he himself has said that his illness was a motivating force behind his signing of the peace treaty with Israel.[1]
(2) The death in a car accident of Bassal Assad, son and heir-apparent of Syrian President Assad.
(3) Arafat's plane crash in the Libyan desert. It is hard to tell what would have happened in the Palestinian camp had the PLO leader been killed in that crash.

Events such as these were totally unforeseeable, and it was extremely difficult to assess just how they would affect the three leaders involved. Nonetheless, it is clear that they gave them an added awareness of the uncertainty of their survival, and perhaps of the legacy they would leave behind – both from the personal perspective (who would take over?), and from the collective perspective (what prospects for the future would the leader leave behind after his demise?). All this may have had a crucial effect on their decisions in the peace process. It is possible that in the final analysis these events will appear to have had a positive influence on the process, but it is too early to predict the real extent of their influence. What all this means is that no one should expect any behavioural model to predict the future with any measure of precision. Nonetheless, the era of such behavioural models is not over by any means. The trivial conclusion – that a good model has better chances of predicting the future than no model at all – holds water in a world riddled with randomness, on condition that it contains a hint of regularity; and if we can discover it, we are duty-bound to take advantage of it.

A second point relates to the way in which intelligence influences reality. The great physicists mentioned above reached another interesting conclusion: that the instruments chosen to measure any phenomenon affect the reality they reveal. To my way of thinking, the same is true of intelligence work: when Intelligence is involved in diplomatic negotiations it is not merely an onlooker, but actually influences the development of the reality being negotiated. Suffice it to note that the way in which data is presented to the policy-makers – Prime Minister, Defence Minister, Foreign Minister and Chief-of-Staff – serves not only to present them with a particular view of the facts, but can also influence their ultimate choice of a solution.

A third point touches on intelligence forecasting and the political leader's influence on reality. The leader may take decisions, based among other things on intelligence, and in so doing create a reality that could conceivably turn the intelligence forecast itself on its head. Here are three examples:

(1) Let us assume that intelligence accurately assesses that the enemy has no intention of attacking Israel in the next few years. The political leader, for his part, uses this forecast to further non-military national objectives, and in so doing drastically reduces defence spending – which in turn detracts from the army's readiness and military capability. When the enemy learns that the balance of power has tilted in his favour, he changes his mind and launches an attack.

(2) Let us assume that intelligence identifies preparations for an enemy attack, and gives an accurate warning of the imminent outbreak of war. The political leader then takes steps to defend his country and deter the enemy from taking the offensive, as a result of which the enemy desists from its offensive intentions. In this instance, it could be said that both intelligence and the political leader did their duty by heading off the realization of their forecast.

(3) The attempt by the Israeli Ministry of Finance to enact a law taxing stock market gains (in September 1994), is an interesting example of belying a forecast through government intervention. Before this law was enacted, conventional wisdom had it – apparently correctly – that share prices would rise in the following year. Therefore – based on the average volume of trade on the stock market – the country's leaders expected the new tax to yield in 1995 a revenue of NIS 500 million. However, as soon as the tax was imposed, the public reacted with a massive sale of stocks, sending prices tumbling. In these new circumstances, the government managed to collect only a fraction of the projected revenues, and ultimately had to withdraw the new tax.[2]

Finally, in this context, it should also be pointed out that a political leader may embark on a policy that is not in keeping with the intelligence forecast, because his decisions are influenced by considerations which are of no interest to intelligence, such as political factors (the stability of his coalition and public opinion) and personal considerations (a desire to leave a mark on history, etc.).

INTELLIGENCE OBJECTIVES IN ISRAEL DURING THE
PEACE PROCESS

A few years ago, when intelligence people were asked to characterize their main objectives and areas of responsibility, they talked about their sense of identification with the lookout mentioned in the Book of Ezekiel (33:6–7): 'But if the watchman see the sword come, and blow not the horn, and the people be not warned, and the sword do come, and take any person from among them, he is taken away in his iniquity, but his blood will I require at the watchman's hand. So thou, son of man, I have set thee a watchman unto the house of Israel ...'. And indeed, the main objective of intelligence in Israel – since its very beginnings – has been to maintain a careful watch over enemy armies and give advance warning of a surprise attack. The technique for achieving this objective is clear: in all probability, the actual decision to launch the attack will not be discovered in advance, however from the moment the order has been given until the attack actually gets underway, the enemy forces must complete a series of feverish preparations which can hardly be kept secret. Observation and interpretation of these signs will give intelligence the information it requires to issue a warning to the country's leaders.

Knowledge of the enemy's intentions is a prime objective during diplomatic negotiations as well, although they are much more difficult than obvious military preparations to uncover. Such intentions may play in a leader's mind – often without crystallizing into a decision – and be revealed only at a much later stage to a select group of top aides (as was the case in 1977 with Sadat's visit to Jerusalem). Therefore, attempting to uncover these intentions is a very difficult task indeed, and the best one can do is make an educated guess. Given this state of affairs, there is one all-important fact that must be made available to the political leader: the answer to the question – is there a real opportunity to achieve peace? Does the opponent have a genuine desire for peace? Which of his positions are truly important to him, and which of them are merely tactical? To what extent is he likely to be flexible? And is there a connection between these positions and his willingness to sign a peace treaty, and external factors (such as the prospect of American aid, progress in the peace talks between Israel and other Arab countries, the extent of their opposition at home, their leader's state of health and public opinion)?

At the same time there are also certain tactical issues that are of paramount importance: the sequence of presentations of the two sides' positions, the other side's overall approach to negotiations, the level of official representation at the talks, their location, and more. Tactical surprises during the process itself, however, are relatively insignificant. For instance, if the Palestinians surprise the Israeli delegation at the negotiating table with a new negotiating position, no immediate damage will ensue if the Israeli delegation asks for time to study and weigh the details. Furthermore, rejection by one side of diplomatic efforts undertaken by the other to break a deadlock in the negotiations is in no way comparable to a defeat on the battlefield. Nevertheless, missing out on the chance for peace, or following through on an essentially erroneous diplomatic move, can exact a very heavy price, the severity of which will only be revealed in time and history.

TESTING POLITICAL RESEARCH FORECASTS IN REAL LIFE

Most intelligence forecasts, even those not based on sensitive intelligence material – are not released to the public at large. Those that do become public knowledge are generally revealed following intelligence assessment failures, or political controversies arising from their fallout. In most cases, too, such assessments generally reach the public in a distorted, unmediated fashion (e.g., without either taking into consideration or understanding intelligence's tasks and capabilities). One prominent example of this phenomenon is the well-worn claim that 'Intelligence failed to foresee the Oslo Accords.' A few brief questions can reveal the gap between claims such as these and a true professional understanding of the events:

– Was intelligence expected to foresee the concrete results of negotiations it knew nothing about (following a Prime Minister's decision not to involve intelligence)?
– Was intelligence supposed to flout the Prime Minister's express wishes and use its resources to uncover the existence of secret negotiations and assess their status?
– Is intelligence indeed expected to assess the outcome of negotiations that depend for their success on a fundamental change in Israeli positions?

The answer to all these is a clear and simple 'of course not'! Intelligence is responsible solely for the assessment of the opponents' positions. And even granting that this is the primary responsibility of intelligence work, we should reconsider its objective ability to assess positions held by the other side when these are determined in a secret negotiating process that develops over a period of many months without intelligence being apprised in any way of its existence, or having access to any of the intelligence material submitted by the opposite side in those secret negotiations. Be that as it may, as far as the Oslo Accords are concerned, when comparisons were drawn between the research reports drawn up by intelligence analysts on the Palestinian issue before the Oslo talks, and the results of the secret negotiations, the intelligence assessments proved to be very precise. At the end of a long and exhausting negotiating process, the Palestinians still clung to principles which intelligence had identified a year earlier as the 'red lines' which the Palestinians would not cross under any circumstances.

FORECASTING PALESTINIAN PRINCIPLES FOR AN AGREEMENT WITH ISRAEL IN THE INTERIM PERIOD

Two children were watching a fisherman on the shores of a lake: the elder of the two saw a man catching fish, while the younger saw a man drowning worms (and the outcome of his efforts proved the elder child's case). In other words, identical data is interpreted differently by different people because of the different way they view reality, because everyone of us has his or her own set of data and contexts. Both Israel and the Palestinians signed a complicated diplomatic agreement (the Oslo Accords), and each side has its own interpretation of the Accords and their objectives: Israel sees them as a first stage in the implementation of autonomy for the residents of the 'Territories', while the Palestinians regard them as the basis for a Palestinian state whose capital is Jerusalem.

Analysing the Palestinian problem is regarded as the most complex and intricate issue in the negotiations, and this is true from the point of view of intelligence as well. While in other areas of the Middle East conflict, issues are argued between states, the negotiations with the Palestinians are part of the creation of a new political entity whose fundamental nature, character and chances for survival are still open to question..

The model for researching the Palestinian question was put together in the latter half of 1992, before the preliminary feelers that eventually brought about the Oslo Accords of September 1993.[3] At that time it was becoming clear that the talks being held in Washington, headed by a delegation of Arabs from the West Bank, were close to a dead end. On the one hand, it became clear that the Palestinians had no intention of accepting the Israeli model of autonomy, which called for self-rule for the residents of the West Bank without giving them control over any part of the land, while on the other, it was clear that Israel had no intention of accepting – at the Interim Agreement stage – the Palestinian model, which was very close to a *de facto* Palestinian state.

The Palestinians' negotiating posture clearly illuminated their guiding principle: striving over the long run for the creation of an independent Palestinian state with its capital in Jerusalem. Consequently, it was thought that the Palestinians would never agree to anything that might pre-empt this possibility. However, it was believed that in order to facilitate the continuation of the process – which is the only way to further their interests – they would agree to postpone the more difficult issues until later discussions on the permanent settlement.

In light of this understanding, intelligence research pointed out five areas on which it believed the Palestinians – faced with the basic Israeli positions – would be willing to compromise in the interim stage:

(1) *Sovereignty over Jerusalem (the Eastern section)*: The feeling was that the Palestinians would accept a decision not to include the city in the area of Palestinian 'self-rule' – on condition that its Arab residents be allowed to vote for, and be elected to, its institutions, and that Israel withdraw its objection to including the fate of the city in the agenda of the Permanent Status talks.

(2) *The continued existence of Israeli settlements in Judea, Samaria and the Gaza Strip*: The feeling was that the Palestinians would understand that their demand to dismantle these settlements was unrealistic and would retract it, but would, at the same time, insist on imposing a freeze on settlement in general, i.e. no new settlements, and no significant expansion of any existing settlements, and demand that negotiations on the future of the settlements be made a part of the Permanent Status talks.

(3) *'The Right of Return' (for Palestinian refugees)*: It was felt that the Palestinians would agree to postpone discussions on this issue until the Permanent Status talks, but would insist on the rights of smaller, clearly identifiable groups to return to their original homes (e.g. the refugees of 1967).

(4) *Control over borders and external security*: It was quite clear that the Palestinians understood the need for – and were willing to accept – Israeli control over the international borders, and Israel's total responsibility for external security in the Interim Stage (even though during the negotiations on the 'Jericho First Agreement' they tried to chip away at the details of this agreement).

(5) *Geographical boundaries*: It was felt that the Palestinians would seek to demarcate the boundaries of the Interim Agreement along the borders of 4 June 1967 – the day before the outbreak of the Six-Day War, but that they would be flexible on this point on condition that most of the 'Territories' be included under 'Palestinian self-rule'.

It was also believed that the Palestinians would want to proceed toward a settlement with Israel regardless of the status of negotiations between Israel and other Arab nations, mainly because, as far as they were concerned, unlike the sovereign Arab countries, for them this was a case of 'to be or not to be'.

The Intelligence Assessment also noted that PLO leader Yasser Arafat had tied his fate to an overall political strategy that would eventually lead to an agreement with Israel.

These assessments also emphasized that the Palestinians would show no flexibility in those parts of the negotiations which, from their point of view, were the building blocks of a future entity on the way to an independent Palestinian state. These included:

– Control over large and contiguous geographical areas (as opposed to control only over Arab population centres).
– The right to formulate their own laws and statutes within their self-rule.
– The right to concrete signs of independence (air- or sea-ports), and symbols of independence (flag, coins and stamps).

As we have noted, the intelligence model and the results of the Agreement of Principles were, in the end, very similar, leading me to conclude that this was a very good example of successful intelligence work on a highly complicated issue, and this despite the fact that the intelligence analysts were totally unaware of the ongoing secret negotiations in Oslo.

Regardless of their ignorance of the developments in Oslo, intelligence people definitely felt that the model of Palestinian behaviour in the peace process outlined above was entirely plausible, and consequently were not surprised by the actual contents of the agreement when they were finally made public. Even earlier, when the idea of withdrawing from the Gaza Strip as a first step was aired in the media, it was thought that the Palestinians would accept this as one stage in an overall solution within the framework of an interim agreement. Before the details of the Oslo Accords were made available to the media – and to intelligence – a number of senior members of the PLO Executive Council (the decision-making forum of the organization) handed in their resignations. While academic analysts read this as a sign of Arafat's impending demise, intelligence analysts felt that some very tough decisions were being made in the Palestinian camp in connection with an interim agreement and the question of 'Gaza First', and that there were those among them who were strongly opposed to these decisions, preferring to resign than having to live with them.

Nevertheless, despite all the above, it is no wonder that intelligence was surprised by the timing of the agreement. Not only were the analysts unaware of the negotiations in Oslo, they were also misled by their intimate acquaintance with all the details of the Washington talks. The fact is that at the same time that rapid progress was being made in the Oslo talks, the Israeli delegation to Washington was travelling back and forth between Israel and the United States in an effort to keep the negotiations with the Palestinians going. Hence the very existence of the talks – not to mention the Accords that were eventually signed in Oslo – came as a complete surprise to the research people, particularly to those closely involved in the Washington talks (where the stated Israeli positions made it patently clear to everyone that an agreement based on the above model was out of the question). And indeed, in Oslo, Israel agreed to many things that it had not been willing to concede in Washington.

Moreover, it transpired later that the very fact of the Oslo channel's existence had a decidedly negative effect on the Washington talks, and only those who were in on the secret of the simultaneous existence of both channels, could truly understand the Palestinians' behaviour in Washington. Among the issues that had an important effect on the Washington talks was, for example, that in Oslo the Palestinians had been promised recognition of the PLO and of Arafat's leadership. Less clear-cut in its impact, but nonetheless there, was the behind-the-scenes struggle between the leaders of the PLO (referred to as 'PLO Tunis') and local leaders from the 'Territories'.[4]

To my way of thinking, there are two positive lessons intelligence can learn from these events. The first of these is that a good research model has its own intrinsic worth, even if the analyst proposing it is not in full possession of all the facts about the negotiations themselves. What is more, proximity to the talks, to the official participants, or even to the leaders, can at times lead to misconceptions. Decision-makers have their own agenda concerning the time and the place for revealing diplomatic initiatives, and analysts may find themselves being misled by what is, in effect, an erroneous picture of the reality they are dealing with. The second lesson is that even under complex and highly uncertain circumstances, a research model has its own merits. Nonetheless, in my opinion, given the wide scope of uncertainty surrounding this particular issue, a totally different outcome would not have been too surprising. The research people continued then, and are continuing now, to monitor the implementation of the Oslo Accords. It should be noted that even to this day their predictions concerning the model of Palestinian self-rule and Palestinian interpretation of the Accords, and, on a different level, the continuation of terrorist activities by Palestinian opposition groups,[5] all proved to be accurate.

THE RESEARCH FORECAST IN RELATION TO THE
PEACE WITH JORDAN

Unlike the Palestinian problem or the dispute with Syria, the issue of Israel's relations with Jordan seemed easy to resolve to everyone's satisfaction, and indeed was regarded as less important – relatively speaking – than the solution of the Israeli-Arab problem as a whole.

The research model in this instance included the following elements:

(1) It was felt that since the Madrid Conference Jordan regarded peace with Israel as a strategic choice, particularly in view of the Hashemite monarchy's fundamental weaknesses (both demographic and economic).[6]
(2) The Jordanians would take a strong stand on most of their demands relating to water resources (because of the kingdom's severe water shortages), and on border demarcations (King Hussein would not be willing to appear as having voluntarily ceded Arab lands to Israel).
(3) The Intelligence Assessment of 1993 suggested that in 1994:
   – Jordan would be prepared to make progress in talks with Israel and conclude the negotiations on the major points, sign a public Agreement of Principles, and put into effect a number of joint projects.
   – Jordan would not be given any significant aid package as an incentive, save a restructuring of outstanding national loans.
   – Jordan would not sign a separate agreement with Israel, as long as the Syrian track of the peace talks remained deadlocked and no interim agreement with the Palestinians had been signed. This was because the advantages Jordan might gain from a separate peace agreement paled in comparison with the potential political damages to the King from such a move on his part, both on his own domestic front and *vis-à-vis* the Arab world. Consequently, the idea was that once the negotiations with Jordan were successfully concluded, the peace agreement would be 'put on the shelf' – as a draft – until significant progress was made on the other tracks.

As late as November 1993 this model still held true: Israel's attempts to bring the King round to signing a separate agreement – virtually identical to the agreement that was eventually signed – failed, after Hussein recalled, and in fact retracted, the so-called '3rd of November Document'.[7] However, after further negotiations – some secret and some public – a separate peace agreement was signed between the two countries on 25 October 1994, without either a significant breakthrough in the negotiations between Israel and Syria, or the completion of negotiations with the Palestinians on the Interim Agreement. The American administration promised the King that they would waive repayment of up to $700 million in Jordanian debts to the United States.

In short, in the Jordanian model, two major items did not materialize as predicted. It should be noted at this point, though, that immediately following the 'Washington Declaration' of July 1994 it was felt that Jordan could be persuaded to sign a separate peace treaty.

I believe there are three possible explanations for these inaccurate forecasts relating to the signing of this separate peace agreement in 1994.

(1) One of the hidden assumptions in the analysts' report was that although King Hussein is a very brave man, as a political leader he would avoid taking any real risks. In other words, given a choice between the maximum gain and minimum loss, Hussein would always opt for the latter. One example of this way of thinking on his part was evident in his stand during the Gulf War: responding mostly to public opinion in Jordan at the time, Hussein came out in support of Sadam Hussein, despite the heavy price he eventually had to pay in his relations with the West and with other Arab countries. Accordingly, the analysts felt that this time too the King would avoid unnecessary friction both in his domestic and foreign relations.

(2) All the constraints affecting his rule were in fact still in place, but their effect was weaker than originally estimated. This was true of constraints relating to the Syrians, the Palestinians and his own home turf (the latter being closely tied to his relations with the Palestinians). In fact, the Syrians did not go out of their way to condemn the Jordanian move (they even broadcast the signing ceremony in the Arava live on Syrian television), and the Palestinians expressed only guarded opposition to the agreement. On the domestic front there were sharp reservations about the agreement, but no actual disturbances that might have posed any kind of threat to the King.

(3) The American administration gave Jordan by way of incentives more than was originally estimated, and from the outset the model did not attempt to assess potential Jordanian reactions to possible Israeli offers. Another hidden assumption, at least on the part of some of the analysts, was that in the final analysis the border between the two countries, which had never been properly demarcated, would be drawn in accordance with compromises agreed to by both sides. In fact, Israel accepted Jordan's version of the exact location of the international boundary – a move that made it much easier for the King to sign the agreement. In return, the Jordanians were helpful in finding solutions for continued Israeli cultivation of some of the land returned to Jordan, and even agreed to an exchange of territories, albeit on a small scale.

Ultimately, it seems as though the offers made by Israel and the Americans tipped the scales against the internal and external constraints facing the King. The whole affair may be likened to the case of a junior government official being given a surprise offer to buy a luxurious, new Mercedes Benz. The official quickly rejects the offer and gives two reasons, 'I don't have $100,000 to buy this beautiful car, and I don't want the neighbours to be jealous', he says. But the people offering the car say to him, 'You've got it wrong, you'll get the car for a sweet deal, only $10,000, but we can't solve your problems with your neighbours.' To which the official replies, 'The hell with my neighbours, bring on the car!' adding, 'Once in a lifetime I deserve to live like a king.' The moral of the story is clear – the returns received by the King from Israel and from the United States, altered the balance of the issue, tipping the scales clearly in favour of signing the treaty – despite all the constraints, such as the need to take the Syrian position into account. What is more, Hussein made it quite clear that the *quid pro quo* he received pulled the rug out from under his critics' complaints.[8] There is a lesson to be learned from all this: political constraints and diplomatic returns should not be discussed separately, since some of the constraints can be overcome with the help of appropriate returns, which might seem totally out of reach to both the decision-makers and the analysts at the beginning of the negotiating process.

And yet, beyond all the above, a number of factors made it extremely difficult to predict with any accuracy the possible signing of a separate treaty:

(1) The Jordanian leadership had, on more than one occasion, rejected the possibility of a separate treaty. Top Jordanian officials did say that Jordan should move forward on solving its problems through negotiation, without waiting for progress in the other negotiating tracks, but they also made it clear that Jordan rejected the idea of a separate settlement with Israel.[9]

(2) King Hussein's hesitations about a separate peace treaty and the way in which it would be received – at home and in the Arab world – remained unresolved up to the very last minute, and only when he was convinced that he had been given everything he could hope to achieve – thus heading off potential domestic and foreign opposition – he signed the agreement[10] (see Note 8). It seems as though Jordan managed to keep these intentions secret and eventually surprised even the Syrians by the move.[11]

(3) In retrospect one does get the impression that the Jordanians were overly optimistic about future developments – both in relation to the status of the negotiations along the other tracks[12] and to the economic gains it expected as a result of the agreement (this is borne out by the expressions of disappointment in Jordan after the signing when many of these expectations did not materialize). Jordanian projections in 1995 concerning potential American loan waivers also proved to be overly

optimistic, as the House of Representatives agreed to waive only some of the loans and not all of them as expected.

(4) The negotiations with Jordan were also handled covertly, and once again intelligence analysts were not brought in on the secret. It later transpired that the breakthrough was achieved during secret contacts between Prime Minister Rabin and King Hussein during May–July of 1994, and made public in the 'Washington Declaration'. Even afterwards, when talks were underway between working committees from both countries, it transpired that the agreement was in fact hammered out in direct negotiations between the Prime Minister and the King (see Note 10).

Intelligence's failure to foresee King Hussein's willingness to sign a separate peace agreement with Israel in 1994, caused some people to claim – once again – that intelligence had proven itself incapable of truly assisting a political leader to make progress on diplomatic initiatives. In my opinion, the assessment of the constraints King Hussein was under – even if erroneously exaggerated – caused Israel's leaders to seek, with American help, creative solutions to the outstanding problems in order to facilitate the signing of the agreement as early as 1994. Intelligence should have indeed proposed solutions it felt would be acceptable to the opposite side, but only a country's political leader can actually decide what he is willing to concede. All in all, Jordan's strategic move to seek peace with Israel was accurately assessed (unlike the case of Sadat, when even his intentions were incorrectly understood by the Head of Army Intelligence at that time), and even the inaccurate assessment – 'Jordan will make progress on the negotiations in 1995, only up to, but not including, the signing of a treaty' – did not deter Israel from initiating diplomatic moves, even though intelligence predicted there would be fewer returns for the effort.

THE NEGOTIATIONS WITH SYRIA

In his book *Philosophical Investigations* (written between 1929 and 1945), Ludwig Wittgenstein states that words do not have a single unique meaning, but rather depend for their actual meaning on situational context and specific usage – a concept which endows words with an endless number of meanings and, at the same time, teaches us that human language is far from being precise and predetermined. Here are two examples:

(1) A young student of languages sitting in a cafe near the university, raised his hand to catch the waitress's eye, and said, 'Black, please'. A few minutes later, the waitress brought him a steaming cup of Turkish coffee.

He added a spoon of sugar from the bowl on the table, slowly stirred the coffee, and mused, 'One code word was enough – "black" – for there to be an understanding between myself and a girl I have never met before. If I were to say "black" during a lecture at the university, or just in passing in the street, I would be considered – at best – unintelligible.'

(2) As he was stirring his coffee, a classmate walked in, a civil service pensioner. They knew each other only very superficially. But when asked by the old man, 'How are you?' the young man answered politely, 'Well, thank you'. The older man was at pains to give a full reply, and gave a long and detailed report on his troubles and joys, and in so doing took up the bored young man's entire coffee break. By analogy, ever since the Madrid Conference (1991), the leaders of Israel and Syria have been calling upon each other to 'make peace', but while both leaders have been using the same term – peace – their individual perception and understanding of the term are widely at variance.

On this issue, intelligence was asked to provide the Prime Minister with an interpretation of the Syrians' positions and a clarification of their understanding of Israel's stance. Intelligence was called upon to forecast the positions on which the Syrians might be willing to make concessions, and those on which would they dig in and refuse to compromise. At the time this article is being written, spring 1995, it is too early to make public the intelligence assessments on the negotiations with Syria, since the gap between the two sides is still very great, and there is no way of knowing when the negotiations will be concluded. Nevertheless, part of the picture, which has been made available to the media, may already be revealed. Intelligence believes that today the Syrians have a much better understanding of Israel's demands, and that they may prove flexible on some of their positions if their own demands are met. Damascus is certainly no 'Lover of Zion',[13] but in order to regain its control over the Golan Heights and improve its relations with the United States it might be willing to make concessions on security arrangements, and might even agree – in the end – to provide at least some of the elements of normalization that Israel is demanding (unrestricted passage across the borders in both directions remains a major stumbling block for Assad's totalitarian regime). Irrespective of all this, no matter how the process develops, Assad will not back down from his demand for a complete Israeli withdrawal from the Golan Heights.[14]

In the final analysis, intelligence has refrained from offering its assessment of whether or not – or when – Syria would sign a peace treaty with Israel, since the answers to these questions depend greatly on the positions adopted by the Israeli government, and intelligence, as we have mentioned, is barred from investigating government actions. Intelligence also does not know if Israel will be willing to make compromises, and likewise is prohibited from expressing its opinion as to whether the equation of 'the Golan Heights in return for a peace treaty' is good or bad for Israel, since that is a political call, and as such outside the army's purview.

FORECASTS CONNECTED TO THE REGIONAL AND THE INTERNATIONAL CONTEXT

In the wake of the peace process, Israel and the Arab countries found themselves caught up in processes and events of immense significance, all of which had been correctly predicted by intelligence over the past few years. Among these were Russia's basic weakness and the instability of most of the independent states that rose out of the Soviet Union's demise; the continuation of Islamic terror carried out by opponents of the peace process; the continued survival of Arab regimes despite severe domestic problems, as well as developments and trends – both conventional and non-conventional – in the military arena in the Arab countries and Iran. Various crises that plagued the peace process itself: Israel's Operation 'Grapes of Wrath' in Lebanon, the deportation of over 400 Hamas leaders to Lebanon and the Hebron massacre (when an Israeli settler from nearby Kiryat Arba killed 29 Arabs and wounded scores in the Tomb of the Patriarchs in Hebron) – were also accurately assessed as being temporary and having only a short-term effect on the peace process.

INTELLIGENCE AND THE POLITICAL LEADER IN THE PEACE NEGOTIATIONS

Elyakim Rubinstein, who participated in the negotiations that led to the peace treaty with Egypt in 1978–79, served as head of the Israeli delegation to the talks with the Palestinians and the Jordanians in Washington from 1991, and led the negotiations with Jordan in the Arava, is regarded as one of Israel's best negotiators. In his book *Pathways to Peace* (written before the Madrid Conference), he praises intelligence and its capacity for contributing to the political process, and comes out strongly in favour of involving intelligence in the negotiations and revealing to it the maximum amount of information available to the negotiators.

Nevertheless, decision-makers in Israel preferred to keep intelligence out of the picture both in the secret negotiations in Oslo and the secret talks with

King Hussein. This situation was not altogether new to intelligence, since it had been similarly kept out of the picture in the secret negotiations with Egyptian President Sadat in 1977. In fact, to date, intelligence analysts have not been included in any of the secret negotiations that eventually led to peace agreements. True, the Prime Minister is not obliged to involve intelligence in negotiations, or to accept its assessments, and refraining from involving intelligence in the negotiations can be explained (see below), but there is a price to be paid for keeping intelligence analysts out of the larger picture. Secret negotiations are an intelligence source of the first order, and keeping the intelligence people in the dark about them may result in serious distortions in the overall intelligence picture and, consequently, in their forecasts. In any case, the net result of such compartmentalization of information is that intelligence capabilities are not exploited for the benefit of the negotiations themselves, where fateful decisions relating to the future of the country are made.

These conflicts between the political echelons and intelligence are not uncommon and, all in all, they are fundamentally beneficial, since agreement across the board on all counts is not really conducive to creative thinking, and an ongoing dialogue between intelligence and the political leaders is vital for fine-tuning national policies. Nonetheless, on occasion, Intelligence Assessments do leak out from the conference rooms to the media, and the leaders immediately react.[15] It is reasonable to assume that the political echelons' need to react publicly to these events stems not only from considerations relating to their professional stance on a given issue, but also, and perhaps mostly, from their awareness of the possibility that intelligence might have an influence on public opinion (contrary to its intention), thus creating a situation that might be uncomfortable for the Government. This is particularly true given the uses political opposition parties make of Intelligence Assessments.

In this context, intelligence may very well find itself influencing public opinion on a sensitive political issue, despite its efforts to distance itself from any such involvement, and consequently may slide into an open conflict with the Prime Minister instead of serving as his right hand on policy matters. This raises a sensitive question concerning the necessary connection between the country's leaders and intelligence. According to Israeli law, national intelligence bodies are subordinate to the Government (including Army Intelligence, which is subordinate to the government through the army). The question is, then, what happens when an Intelligence Assessment is at odds with government policy, and may be potentially harmful if revealed to the opposition. This has been solved in Israel by requiring intelligence to present the National Intelligence Assessment to the Knesset Foreign Affairs and

Defence Committee which is a legislative body, and includes opposition MKs among its members. This creates the danger of having intelligence information leaked to the public at large, and then used as a legitimate political weapon by the opposition[16] – and this notwithstanding efforts on the part of intelligence to avoid being pushed into that kind of corner.[17] This, in my opinion, is one possible explanation for the fact that political leaders are wary of involving intelligence in covert diplomatic initiatives, and often voice their annoyance with Intelligence Assessments.

As a footnote, and contrary to the above, it should be noted that among Israel's negotiating partners there are those who believe that Israeli Intelligence services have the ability to influence Israeli policy in directions which are detrimental to Palestinian aims. One example is Yasser Arafat, who blamed 'a senior official in Israeli Intelligence' for attempting to 'sabotage' Palestinian efforts in the peace process.[18]

It is difficult to find an appropriate solution that will satisfy everyone. Elyakim Rubinstein wrote in his book that 'the solution to this is probably, unfortunately, an informal one: creating a relationship between intelligence people, the political echelons, and the negotiators, based on reciprocity, and enabling the flow of informal information through personal trust, feedback to the intelligence community, and requests for vital material. This kind of reciprocal system has been established satisfactorily only very rarely.'[19] Intelligence people who worked closely with Rubinstein recalled that he kept strictly to his side of the deal, but it is hard to believe that as he was writing those lines in his book he ever imagined that he himself – as head of the negotiating team with the Palestinians in Washington – would be kept in the dark about the existence of secret negotiations, and would be as surprised as he was by the signing of the Oslo Accords. What he said afterwards could have been said by anyone in intelligence: 'This is not surprising. You carefully and religiously monitor, investigate, and become involved only with what is going on in the Arab world. You do not look into what is happening on your side of the fence.'[20]

POSTSCRIPT

Over the past few years, intelligence research analysts in Israel have had the privilege of taking on very difficult research challenges in a changing world, and amid political processes the complexity of which is unparalleled in the history of the State of Israel. The strategic trends and the changing face of the Middle East were, I believe, accurately predicted. Parts of this assessment were signal successes, while others were clear failures (particularly in relation to the negotiations with Jordan).

At this point in time, the peace process has come a long way, but the finishing line is still a long way off and there are many obstacles to be overcome. If and when the process is completed, there will remain the difficulties of monitoring the implementation of the peace agreements, assessing the stability of the signatory regimes, and the process of inculcating the concept of peace among the peoples of the region. For it seems that the weakness of the peace at this point stems from the fact that for the time being it is dependent on the conscience of leaders who are still unwilling to relinquish the use of arms, and that it has not yet developed out of the status of formal, written treaties between regimes to a 'warm' peace between nations.

In the Analysis Division of Army Intelligence there is a notice board listing the unit's basic precepts, and there is a quote from Deuteronomy: 'Then shalt thou inquire, and make search, and ask diligently …' (Deuteronomy 13:15), and this is a succinct summation of the analysts' tasks.[21] It is up to them to point out the capabilities of enemies and opponents and at times even to reveal their intentions. They have the ability to discern trends and point out threats and opportunities – all this in order to enable the political leaders to prepare for impending dangers and help them reach more advantageous diplomatic agreements. They do not, necessarily, hold the future in their hands. Intelligence should not assess the political leaders' policies or make qualitative judgements about them. Once it has completed its task to the best of its ability the entire responsibility for the outcome rests on the leaders alone.

NOTES

1. King Hussein revealed that his cancer – from which he initially recovered before relapsing and dying in February 1999 – caused great concern and uncertainty in Jordan regarding the future of the country. It appears from his story that his illness spurred him on to 'fulfil his duty' to his people and to the future of his country and of the nations of the region (interview with Hussein, in the Israeli daily *Yedioth Aharonoth*, 25 October 1994).
2. Israeli journalist Sever Plotzker wrote a detailed analysis of the stock market tax, which was rescinded between September 1994 and February 1995. I have included this example in this article merely to illuminate the present issue, on the basis of newspaper articles, through the use of a well-known event in recent Israeli history. Its inclusion in the article should not be construed as a statement of opinion on the matter itself. In any case, the affair is a case in point concerning the enormous difficulty inherent in predicting behaviour or events, even when they are within our jurisdiction and under our control, and when there is no difficulty whatsoever in gathering information on factors that may influence them. Incidentally, the reaction of a 'very senior official' to the affair should be noted: 'The public reacted in a totally unbalanced way. It took us by surprise. The public deserves a zero grade in economic behaviour, while we deserve 100' (*Yedioth Aharonoth*, 3 February 1995). It is simply a good example of the great difficulty human

beings have in recognizing the collapse of their assessments.
3. Ron Pundak (one of the architects of the Oslo Accords who handled many of the early top-secret negotiations) claims that the first meeting in Oslo between Palestinians and Israeli representatives (Pundak and Ya'ir Hirschfeld) took place on 20 January 1993. According to Pundak, by May a first draft had been proposed, and it was decided to make the Oslo channel official – albeit still secret (Israel Television, Channel 2, 5 December 1994).
4. Mamdoukh Naufal, a senior PLO official, reported that Arafat was interested in undermining the ninth round of talks in Washington held between 27 April and 13 May. He did so by dictating extremely tough guidelines for the Palestinian delegation, including instructions to bring up the question of Jerusalem in the negotiations, and to oppose any tripartite meeting – Israel, PLO, United States – even though the PLO had in the past been interested in holding just such a meeting. Naufal relates that among Arafat's reasons for this move was his determination to prevent Feisal Husseini from gaining any successes in the talks. Husseini is one of the most prominent of the Palestinian leaders from the 'Territories' and was brought in to lead the Palestinian side in Washington in order to get the talks moving. According to Naufal, the failure of this round of talks was what caused Prime Minister Rabin to 'gamble on the Oslo channel' (see, in this context, Note 3); (*Ma'ariv*, 1 February 1995).
5. The Head of Army Intelligence reported to the Foreign Affairs and Defence Committee of the Knesset that terrorism would wane inside the autonomy, but would continue and perhaps even intensify in other areas of Judah and Samaria, and inside Israel proper. He added that the PLO would not prevent the Hamas from attacking Israeli targets (*HaModi'ah*, 4 May 1994). I would like to point out that including the briefing by the head of Army Intelligence in this article is aimed at giving a firm basis to the presentation of Intelligence Assessments, which are not usually presented by research officers. While the Head of Army Intelligence does not always agree with the researchers they were in agreement on the issues dealt with in this article.
6. *Translator's note*: The royal family is of Bedouin lineage, while Palestinians comprise nearly 60 per cent of the country's population.
7. Foreign Minister Shimon Peres pointed out that, 'The November 3rd document includes virtually all the elements of the present agreement. The only thing that is missing is a final, formulated and orderly agreement with maps and clauses. The contents are identical' (interview with Sima Kadmon, *Ma'ariv* Supplement, December 1994).
8. King Hussein stated that he expected President Assad of Syria to read the agreement and only then criticize his actions, 'if he has any criticism at all' (interview with Hussein, *Yedioth Aharonoth*, 25 October 1995).
9. Some of the more prominent Jordanian statements against a separate agreement with Israel were:
   – In answer to a question as to whether or not Jordan would go for a separate treaty with Israel, King Hussein said, 'A separate solution has been out of the question since 1974' (Radio Amman, 9 November 1993). This statement was made six days after he held talks with Israel in an effort to bring about a breakthrough in the talks.
   – On 18 October, Abd-el Salam Al-Majali, Jordanian Prime Minister and the leader of the Jordanian delegation, was asked if there was a possibility that Jordan might sign a separate peace treaty before Syria concluded its negotiations on all the clauses in its negotiating track. Al-Majali replied, 'I don't see the possibility of such a thing happening, and if we want a true and lasting peace, all sides must be partners to the

agreement' (interview given by Al-Majali to the BBC on 18 August 1994). Eventually it transpired that Al-Majali was the main opponent in Jordan of a separate peace treaty (*Yedioth Aharonoth*, 28 October 1994). After the signing of the treaty he expressed his disappointment over the partial implementation of the economic aspects of the agreement, and later left the government.

10. After all the agreements were concluded in Aqaba between Prime Minister Rabin and King Hussein, a major, albeit secret, controversy broke out in the negotiations with Jordan. The King sent a message to Israel saying: 'Everything we agreed to is null and void. Jordan cannot forfeit even one centimetre of Arab land.' Earlier, so it had been reported, palace circles had reached the conclusion that the agreement was unacceptable to the kingdom, since it could be interpreted as forfeiture of Arab lands, an act which would arouse fierce opposition in the Arab world and in Jordan itself. As a result, Rabin decided to 'give up a few kilometres of barren land' in the Arava desert and reach an agreement within the framework of an exchange of lands between the two countries (*Yedioth Aharonoth*, 28 October 1994).

11. The Syrian Foreign Minister Farouk al-Shar'a, said that before the 'Washington Agreement' (the agreement on principles between Israel and Jordan, signed in Washington in July), the Jordanians did not brief the Syrians on the expected breakthrough in the Israeli–Jordanian talks. This despite Hussein's visit to Damascus close to the date of the signing (interview with al-Shar'a on MBC – Middle East Broadcasting Company – on 13 September 1994).

12. Here are two Jordanian statements – one prior to the breakthrough in the negotiations, and the other, on the eve of the arrival of Jordan's ambassador to Israel – both of which underscore Jordan's excessive optimism prior to the signing of the treaty with Israel and the later disappointment concerning the lack of progress being made along the other negotiating tracks:
   – King Hussein stated, at the end of January 1994, that Jordan and Syria maintained constant contact, and that he was glad to hear of the results of President Clinton's meeting with President Assad. He estimated 'personally' that there would soon be real progress between Israel and the Arabs on the other tracks. He said once again, that Jordan was in favour of an overall peace settlement, but made it clear that Jordan was not bound to hold back on dealing with its problems until everyone else had dealt with theirs (King Hussein, at a meeting with representatives of the Jewish communities of America, from a Jordanian news service, 26 January 1994).
   – Marwan Al-Ma'ashar, the first Jordanian ambassador to Israel said, 'The waning of enthusiasm over the peace process is not a call to end the process, but a call to re-evaluate it, which is a normal development, in relation to the state of affairs along the Palestinian track' (*Jordan Times*, 6 April 1995).

13. *Translator's note*: The reference is to the early Zionist movement *Hovevei Ziyyon* (literally, 'Lovers of Zion') that sent pioneers to Palestine in the 1870s and established some of the first Jewish settlements in the country.

14. In the Intelligence Assessment for 1994, the head of Army Intelligence at the time, Major-General Uri Sagi stated that Syria had softened its positions on the definition of peace, but insisted on its demand for a full Israeli withdrawal (*Ma'ariv*, 17 February 1994). General Sagi estimated that in Syria it was understood that in return for the complete restoration of the Golan Heights to Syria, it might be willing to reach a peace agreement which would include diplomatic relations. Nevertheless, Assad refrained from disclosing the elements of the peace. The head of Army Intelligence made it clear that there were

no signs of any Syrian willingness to compromise on the Golan Heights (*Yedioth Aharonoth*, 25 March 1994). As for the Intelligence Assessment of 1995, it was reported that Assad had not budged from his willingness to reach a peace treaty with Israel, but progress might be slowed down (*Ha-aretz*, 8 January 1995), and Assad would continue to take a hard line on this issue as long as Israel did not make its position on the Golan Heights clear (*Ha-aretz*, 26 February 1995).

Information coming in from Syria on the issue of the complete withdrawal is unequivocal, but the information about normalization is not as clear-cut:

– A member of the US House of Representatives, Tom Maltus, related that at the beginning of January 1995 Assad said to him, 'We say full peace in return for full withdrawal. When I say full peace I mean the normal peace that exists among 187 countries in the world. Israel is seeking more things ... they want cooperation. They want much more than we have with Jordan or with other Arab countries ... What they are asking for is too burdensome for us ... If that is the condition for peace, then there will be no peace. *Yedioth Aharonoth*, 16 January 1995).

– The Foreign Minister of Malta related that at the end of January 1995, Assad told him, 'There is no need whatsoever to hold talks on the principle of the return of the Golan Heights ... I will not be willing to think of any form of compromise on this issue. Within the framework of peace, Syria will maintain good relations with Israel, just like Egypt and Jordan' (*Ha-aretz*, 1 February 1995).

15. Furthermore, an example of this is the conflict that erupted between the head of Intelligence Analysis Division in Army Intelligence, Brigadier-General Amidror, and Prime Minister Rabin. In November 1994 it was reported that the head of the Intelligence Analysis Division estimated, in a presentation before the Knesset Foreign Affairs and Defence Committee, that President Assad of Syria did not always honour agreements, and he would only abide by them in the future if it was worth his while or if he felt threatened (*Davar*, 9 November 1994). These remarks were made following complaints by Turkish officials that the Syrians were not keeping to agreements they had reached with them. The Prime Minister hurriedly countered this assessment in public, stating that the Syrians had kept to their side of the Separation of Forces agreement on the Golan Heights to the letter (*Ma'ariv*, 10 November 1994).

16. The head of the Tsomet Party in the Knesset, former Chief-of-Staff, Rafael Eytan, when he was in the opposition, entered a no-confidence motion in the government for ignoring the warnings issued by the head of the Intelligence Analysis Division (*Davar*, 15 November 1995). The head of the opposition Likud Party, MK Benyamin Netanyahu, told the Knesset that Army Intelligence had prepared a paper listing the threats to the country following the implementation of the Oslo Accords (*Davar*, 22 December 1993).

17. Following the responses to the report made by Brigadier-General Amidror, head of Intelligence Analysis, the head of Army Intelligence made it quite clear that, 'It is our duty and the duty of the political echelon to avoid exploiting Intelligence personnel for political infighting' (*Yedioth Aharonoth*, 10 November 1994).

18. Following remarks attributed to the head of Army Intelligence, Arafat said that a senior Israeli Intelligence officer tried to sabotage the Palestinian efforts to make peace by spreading a rumour that once Palestinian Autonomy was established it would suffer the same fate as Lebanon (interview by Arafat to the Saudi Arabian newspaper, *Alsharak Alouest*, 8 January 1995).

19. *Pathways to Peace*, Elyakim Rubinstein (Israel: Ministry of Defence Press, 1992) (in Hebrew), p. 245.

20. Interview with Elyakim Rubinstein by Semadar Peri (*Yedioth Aharonoth*, 21 October 1994).

21. 'Then thou shalt inquire, and make search, and ask diligently; and, behold, if it be truth, and the thing certain, that such abomination is wrought in the midst of thee' (Deuteronomy, 13:15). This verse highlights the biblical roots of intelligence 'analysis' (and it is interesting to note the order of the activities mentioned: 'inquire', 'make search', and 'ask'). On the purely verbal level this is applicable to any intelligence research analyst. In fact, this was a stern injunction to the people of Israel to determine, before carrying out judgement, who among them had strayed to idol-worship. In this sense it is probably more appropriate to those involved in internal security.

8

Secret Diplomacy and the Arab–Israeli Peace Process*

DAVID KIMCHE

Few events so characterize the change from the old world order to the new as the demise of the Arab–Israeli conflict. As the twentieth century draws to a close, and the new, post-Cold War era takes hold, the wars of Arab and the Jew – so prominent a feature in the latter half of the outgoing century and of the Cold War – have finally come to an end as well. Admittedly, a full, comprehensive peace in the Middle East has not, at the time of writing, been ushered in. But the Arab–Israeli peace process has passed the point of no return. Whatever happens, there will be no going back to the *status quo ante*, to the old days of tension and war.

Contrary to the fears of many, the establishment of a Likud Government in Israel in 1996 did not derail the peace process. The new reality that the process had created proved stronger than the desire of so many in the rightist camp in Israel to reject the Accords that Israelis and Palestinians had hammered out in Oslo, in what must be seen as one of the most classic examples of secret diplomacy of the century. Those in the anti-Oslo camp discovered that there was no turning the clock back: Likud could not move back into Gaza or into the West Bank towns that had been taken over by the Palestinians, nor could they freeze the talks with the PLO leadership. The new realities could not be reversed, nor could the Arab–Israeli conflict continue in its old traditional patterns. The Arab–Israeli conflict had been governed by three concentric circles of interrelationships: international – and in particular the Cold War; regional – Arab–Arab, Arab–Israeli; and internal – the unfolding relations and events within the countries themselves, and in particular in Israel and among the Palestinians.

Throughout the existence of the Cold War, the US–Soviet rivalry

---

*Part of this article is based on David Kimche's 'The Arab–Israeli Peace Process', in *Security Dialogue* (Sage Publications), 27: 2 (June 1996).

impinged on events in the Middle East, and made any meaningful Arab–Israeli peace process virtually impossible. The Soviets, at least from 1967 onwards, consistently encouraged the Arab regimes to take a tough, uncompromising attitude towards Israel, and they backed up their advice with massive supplies of arms. After the Six-Day War in 1967, when the UN debated the possibility of an Israeli withdrawal to its pre-war positions in return for an end to the state of war, the Soviet Central Committee addressed a warning to President Nasser in which it stressed that 'such a move on the part of the UN should not involve a request for any concessions from the Arab countries to Israel ... it should not be linked to an obligation on the part of the Arab countries to recognize or negotiate with Israel'. The Soviet *démarche* was later embodied in the Khartoum declaration of September 1967: no recognition, no negotiations, no peace. The Soviet Union, moreover, gave its support particularly to the most radical of the Arab states – Iraq, Syria, Libya, plus the PLO – which were also the most adamant in their opposition to any move toward peace with Israel. The departure of Egypt from the Soviet camp was, in effect, an essential prerequisite to the subsequent moves of President Sadat, which eventually led to peace between Egypt and Israel. Similarly, the efforts of the US administration, which culminated in the historic gathering in Madrid in 1991, would have never succeeded if the old Soviet hard-line policies of the Brezhnev era had still been in place.

The disappearance of that old Brezhnevian policy toward the Middle East was thus the first element which made the peace process possible. The United States, as sole world power, made good use of its new position. The visits of Secretary Baker in the Middle East on the eve of the Madrid Conference were a *tour de force* which hardliners such as Yitzhak Shamir in Israel, and Hafez el-Assad in Syria, were unable to withstand.

The second element came from within the region – the decisive role played by Anwar Sadat and by Egypt. The Madrid Peace Conference would never have taken place it had not been preceded by the Camp David Accords. The Arab consensus of no fraternization with the enemy, laid down in Khartoum, could only have been broken by a country with the stature and political weight of Egypt. Once the consensus was breached, and particularly after Egypt was invited back into the Arab fold, it was simply a question of time for the others to follow suit. For Egypt could not be ignored in the Arab world. Its primordial position is uncontested. The inter-Arab relations existing at the time made it possible for a man like Sadat to ignore the consensus and to brush aside Arab objections and protests. I heard him say, during one of his visits to Israel, that Egypt is more important to the Arab world than the Arab world is to Egypt. Sadat took the lead and was convinced that the others would eventually follow in the direction that Egypt was taking. In every sense of the word, Egypt has been the king-pin of the peace process, and it says much for the present leadership of Egypt that it has steadfastly followed along the road that Sadat took. The Foreign Minister of Egypt, Amru Mussa, told me late in 1996 that if the peace process collapsed it would be a calamity for Egypt, for it would mean that the decision of President Sadat to visit Jerusalem had been mistaken, and the policy followed by Egypt ever since that visit had been wrong.

There was need, however, of an outstanding event in order to jolt the other Arab countries into following the path Egypt had taken. That event was the Gulf War, which had the effect of a powerful electric shock on the body politic of the Arab world. Iraq's invasion of Kuwait, and the war that followed, shattered old, conformist stereotypes regarding Arab unity. It made a mockery of the Arab League. It pitted Arab against Arab, and divided the Arab world between the Coalition partners and those who stood aside or supported Saddam Hussein – none more so than the PLO, whose stand in favour of Saddam isolated it internationally, and cut it off from the financial and political backing it had enjoyed from the Gulf countries, and particularly from Saudi Arabia.

It was, perhaps, the greatest mistake Arafat had made in his long career as the leader of the PLO, but it was a mistake that was consistent with PLO thinking at the time. Saddam Hussein's vitriolic attacks on the United States, on capitalist decadence, and on the Arab regimes supporting the West, well-suited the PLO. Saddam was viewed by many in the Arab world – and none more so than by the PLO and by many in Jordan – as the champion of the underdog pitted against the might of the Western industrialist states, and against the wealthy Arab rulers of the Arabian Peninsula. His threats against Israel were greeted joyfully in the ranks of the PLO. But the effect of Arafat's support for Iraq was to prove devastating for him and his followers.

The PLO's change of fortune was the third element which made the peace process possible. It was a change that had begun before the Gulf War. The lack of Arab support during the Lebanese War in 1983 was a bitter pill for the Palestinians to swallow. They had to contend not only with the Israelis but also with the Syrians, who forcibly ejected them from the Tripoli district. Not a single Arab country offered any real help. In the eyes of the Palestinians, the PLO had been abandoned by the Arab regimes. With the PLO leadership and followers dispersed in far-flung lands – Tunisia, Sudan, Yemen, Iraq – the Palestinians living on the West Bank and in Gaza began increasingly to place their fate in their own hands, instead of relying on the PLO leadership. This attitude inevitably gave rise to the *intifada*, which was initiated and directed by the local Palestinians on the scene, and not by the distant PLO leadership, which for a time became almost irrelevant. The local inhabitants of the West Bank and Gaza have been much more realistic than the Palestinians; they have a better knowledge of how to deal with Israel and what can be attained from her. They knew only too well that the stones and rocks of the *intifada* by themselves would not lead to the destruction of the Jewish state, and that only by political negotiations could they hope to attain their goal of a Palestinian state. The sorry state of the PLO leadership after the Lebanese War, on the one hand, and the new self-confidence of the local Palestinians after the outbreak of the *intifada*, on the other, led the PLO to adopt the policy – which previously had been anathema to it – of political negotiations and compromise with Israel.

At the same time, the internal situation inside Israel had also undergone a metamorphosis. The Israelis began to realize that there was no going back to the *status quo ante* of the pre-*intifada* days. The vast majority of Israelis were sick and tired of the 'Occupied Territories', and of the Palestinians. Voices both from the left and the right of the political spectrum were increasingly heard calling for the need for separation of the Israeli and the Palestinian peoples. The Likud concept of one 'Greater Israel', one political unit embracing both peoples, was being undermined by the call for separation. The growing disillusionment with the political concepts of the Likud with regard to the Territories was one of the factors which brought about the victory of the Labour Party in the elections of 1992, and which enabled the newly-elected Government to pursue dramatically different policies from those of its predecessor.

Thus the three concentric circles of interrelationships, which moulded and shaped the Arab–Israeli conflict over the years, all underwent dramatic changes which, for the first time, made the prospect of peace between Arab and Israeli a real possibility.

However, these changes in themselves were not sufficient to mount a successful peace process. A half a century or more of hostility and warfare leaves deep scars that cannot heal easily. Suspicion, hatreds, prejudices, stereotypes and sheer ignorance of each other, have been characteristic of both camps. On the Arab side, the reasons for this attitude are particularly complex. For 50 years the identity of Arabism had been inextricably bound up with enmity for Israel. Lines had been etched very sharply between 'them' and 'us'. The old feelings of enmity toward 'them' have lived on, nurtured by orthodox Islamic circles on the one hand, and by Arabist intellectuals on the other. Moreover, a systematic process of demonization of Israel had taken place, while in Israel a similar process occurred with regards to the Palestinians in general, and the PLO and its leaders in particular. Peace activists, Abie Nathan, for example, went to prison for daring to ignore the national consensus and the law that was passed forbidding any contact with the PLO.

Under such circumstances, the changes in the three circles of inter-relationships were not enough to bring about an automatic blossoming of a peace process. The only possible way to bridge the chasm that separated the two peoples was by means of ultra-secret contacts, led at first by well-meaning intermediaries, and later by Arabs and Israelis whose determination to make peace was stronger than the taboos their respective societies had placed on having such contacts.

Secret meetings between Arabs and Jews seeking to overcome the enmity between the two peoples had, indeed, taken place from the very beginnings of the Zionist Movement. Long before the Second World War, Ben Gurion was holding secret talks with Palestinians and other Arab leaders, offering, in return for Arab consent to Jewish immigration and settlement, Jewish help in the attainment of full Arab independence. After the overthrow of King Farouk, Ben Gurion expressed the hope that the new regime in Egypt might be more forthcoming in accepting the State of Israel. A secret emissary was subsequently sent to Egypt on behalf of President Eisenhower in 1956 to try to arrange a meeting between Nasser and Ben Gurion, or some other Israeli representative, and later, in 1962, Ben Gurion made another attempt to arrange a meeting with Nasser, this time through the mediation of President Tito of Yugoslavia. Nothing came of these efforts, or of the many other feelers that were put out in the 1950s and 1960s. Reuven Shiloah, Eliyahu Sasson and Josh Palmon were particularly active in trying to find ways, at the very least, to soften the hostility of Israel's Arab neighbours. In a variant of secret diplomacy, the Mossad at times used its secret channels to friendly intelligence services in a bid to sound out the possibilities of developing discreet political contacts with Arab countries. At the same time, an ongoing relationship was developed with Jordan, through dozens of secret meetings, first with King Abdullah, and later with King Hussein and Crown Prince Hassan.

Yet all this activity was to no avail, because the Arab–Israeli conflict was governed by a set of interrelationships which negated any possibility of reaching a peaceful solution to the conflict. History had to take its full course. Conditions had to be suitable. The disintegration of the Soviet Union, the Gulf War, the demise of the PLO following its expulsion from Lebanon and its disastrous backing of Saddam Hussein, the *intifada*, and the rise to power of the Labour Party in Israel in 1992, all following on President Sadat's courageous peace with Israel, provided such suitable conditions. The stage had been set for secret diplomacy to take its course. Both Sweden and Norway stepped into the breach, and the end result was the Oslo Accords, which set the tone for Israeli–Palestinian reconciliation, and for the peace process to take root.

We must ask ourselves why the secret diplomacy of Oslo was so successful, while the parallel negotiations being conducted at the same time between Israelis and Palestinians in Washington were such an abject failure. It must be said at the outset that Oslo was a very special, almost unique case, for in this media-era of the post-Cold War period, diplomacy has become increasingly overt, even transparent. In the age of CNN there are very few secrets left in diplomacy. The Washington negotiations conducted by Dr Elyakim Rubinstein were so public that, in the words of Shimon Peres, they resembled a permanent press conference. With the media pouncing on every idea raised, there was no possibility in Washington to undertake intellectual exercises, to float ideas which had not yet received the full backing of those responsible, to create a meeting of minds, because every word uttered could be leaked to the press with concomitant repercussions. The advantage of Oslo was twofold: the official talks between responsible officials were preceded by a pre-negotiation period in which non-governmental persons – members of research institutes – sought to create accepted formulas to enable official negotiations to begin; these were conducted in the utmost secrecy, which enabled the participants to reach agreement without first having to explain themselves to their public back at home.

The lesson to be learned from Oslo is that the greater the complexity and the sensitivity of the subject at hand, the more secrecy has to be maintained during the critical phases of negotiations. The Camp David negotiations between Menachem Begin and President Sadat, and the Oslo Declaration of Principles are the models which must be followed if comprehensive peace is to be achieved in the Middle East. It worked between Israelis and Egyptians; it worked with Palestinians. As the time of writing [the summer of 1997] we have yet to see if it will work with the Syrians.

9

Peace at Home and Peace among Neighbours*

CARMI GILLON

In June 1967, a few days after the liberation of Jerusalem, the gates of the Old City were opened, allowing people from all over the country to come and visit the Old City. My grandmother, the late Hannah Frumkin, had waited for this day in anxious expectation like many other Jews, but more so as a former resident of the Old City going back to visit her childhood home. I accompanied her on that visit and she, finding her way with the greatest of ease through the Old City she remembered so well, brought us to the courtyard where her family had lived: the 'Lily Courtyard'. There she met her former neighbours from the el-Husseini family. Their reunion was very moving, filled with memories and stories of years gone by, but utterly lacking in any sense of real friendship. In fact, this was the first and last time these two families would meet. Up to the summer of 1967, as a child growing up in Jerusalem, just a stone's throw from the border in the nearby Mamilla Quarter, the conflict between the Arabs and us seemed to me to be no more than a neighbourhood quarrel, since there was a clearly defined border separating the Jews in West Jerusalem from the Arabs in the East, a border symbolized for us by the Jordanian Legionnaires we could see manning the Old City walls. There were other Arabs, 'good Arabs', like those living in the village of Abu Ghosh on the western approaches to Jerusalem, where we sampled Middle Eastern delicacies at the Nirvan restaurant situated just above what was then the main highway to Jerusalem. It was during that visit to the Old City with my grandmother, that I understood for the first time that the conflict between the Arabs and us was not a dispute between neighbouring states or even neighbouring peoples, but rather a conflict in our own – common – backyard. The thought of Haj Amin el-Husseini[1] and my grandfather sharing the same courtyard toilet has percolated through my

---

*Trans. David Zinder.

consciousness over the years, until it developed into the realization that the paramount problem facing the State of Israel was to work towards achieving peace at home with the Palestinians, and that the conflicts between us and our neighbouring countries were of secondary importance. Moreover, it became clear to me that domestic peace is much more difficult to achieve than any other.

I became aware of this many years later, when I found myself participating in the process aimed at resolving the conflict between us and our neighbour to the east – Jordan. The difference between these two processes – between the Jordanians and us and the Palestinians and us – was enormous.

IT ALL BEGINS WITH TERMINOLOGY

While we were negotiating with the Jordanians on the details of our agreement the subject at hand was a peace treaty, and the process of achieving it was referred to as 'a peace process'. While we were negotiating with the Palestinians there were instead specific subjects under consideration: the 'Oslo Accords', or the 'Cairo Agreement', or the 'Taba Agreement' – never a peace agreement. The process for achieving these agreements with the Palestinians was referred to as 'the political process'.

AND CONTINUES WITH ATMOSPHERE

The negotiations with the Jordanians may be characterized as being suffused with goodwill and marked by a determination to reach a mutually beneficial agreement. They were also attended by a large measure of creative thinking, to ensure that no minor hitches would mar the overall atmosphere of mutual trust. The atmosphere in the negotiations with the Palestinians, on the other hand, and the deliberations that preceded each meeting were dominated by an atmosphere of mutual arm-bending. It was clear to all involved that there was a great need to reach a political solution, but no one was willing to define the outlines of such an agreement as a 'peace agreement'. It was reality – not goodwill – that bred the need, and the atmosphere at these talks could only be described as one of deepseated mutual suspicion.

TRUST VERSUS SUSPICION

The history of the Israeli–Jordanian conflict over the years has been the history of 'fair-play' wars – two armies facing off against each other and waging war. And while each side fervently believed in the justice of its cause, the wars they fought were not waged by people who hated each other. Even after their soldiers' blood had been shed in battle, the commander of a Jordanian tank battalion (or an Egyptian or a Syrian) and the commander of an Israeli tank battalion could still shake hands over a 'fair fight'.

The history of the Israeli–Palestinian conflict is the chronicle of wars 'played unfairly'. On the one side are the Palestinians continuing to live under Israeli control of virtually every aspect of their daily existence, and on the other side the Israelis who mourn the loss of wives and children blown up in buses in Jerusalem or Tel Aviv. This war has nothing to do with 'fair play'. This is a war fuelled by Palestinian hatred of the 'Zionist conqueror', and Israeli hatred of an opponent who repeatedly resorts to terrorist atrocities.

THE ESSENCE

The most difficult dispute with the Jordanians was over territory and water. Whenever territorial disagreements began moving in the direction of a crisis, in the back of our minds we knew that there was always the option of mediation, as was the case, for example, in the negotiations with the Egyptians over Taba, and even there, ultimately, no mediation was necessary.[2] Water is a movable commodity, particularly as the Israeli–Jordanian border is such a long one, and eventually a solution was found for this issue as well. All of the essential problems were solved, and all that was needed was for the two negotiating teams to flesh out, as broadly and as deeply as possible, the substance of the framework agreements. In contrast, during the negotiations with the Palestinians, it was virtually impossible to find even one point, however trivial, that did not turn into a major point of controversy. So much was this so, that negotiators in fact proceeded with both hands tied behind their backs, since they could not make a move, on even the most minute clause in the complex and tortuous agreements eventually signed with the Palestinians, without the approval of the political echelons. What this meant, in effect, was that the agreements worked out at the negotiating table were not a framework to be fleshed out with substance, but rather a mosaic put together piece by piece, clause by clause, with the two negotiating teams halting the process again and again at each point along the way in order to check their bearings. This was the nature of the negotiations carried out by separate teams simultaneously on three different aspects of the situation, at three different levels: the team dealing with security issues; the team dealing with economic issues; and the team dealing with confidence-building measures. At the same time, the extensive interdependence of all three aspects had a direct bearing on the rate of progress along each track. Overall, the issue of security was given absolutely top priority as the foundation upon which all the other agreements would be built.

THE TEST

In both types of negotiations mentioned above – with neighbours and with states – the participants knew that the results of their efforts would be put to the test within a very short time, and the negotiations and their possible results aroused high expectations among the peoples of both nations. Like the peace accord with Egypt, the agreement with Jordan was assessed along a broad spectrum, marked by a vision of eternal peace at the one end of the scale and war at the other, with a broad middle ground for testing the results. The needle gauging this spectrum can move abruptly from a state of war at the far end of the scale, through stages of a 'cold' peace, to political crises, the severing of diplomatic ties, etc., while at the other end of the scale, the passage of a single tourist bus from one side of the border to the other can have the effect of warming up a cold peace. And what is most important is that there are still borders and armies and various early-warning systems with which this peace is secured. The peace with the Palestinians, on the other hand, is tested along a very narrow band, large sections of which are not even controlled by the two negotiating sides. A routine closure of the West Bank on Israel's Independence Day is enough to create a crisis on the Palestinian side, and a lone Arab knife-wielder is enough to cause a crisis on the Israeli side. The needle of peace has so little room to manoeuvre on such a narrow spectrum of possibilities that a discourteous remark by junior officers from either side immediately leads to the conclusion – however short-lived – that 'there's no one to talk to on the other side'. This test of relations also suffers from the lack of a clearly demarcated border that can be either a border of peace or a border of war. This problem of actual demarcation lines on the ground has been partially solved in the Gaza Strip (though we must not forget the Israeli settlements that have remained in what is known as the Katif Bloc of the Gaza Strip), but in Judea and Samaria, and particularly in Jerusalem, the two populations are physically integrated. With our neighbours across the border we can decide either to enjoy the fruits of peace, or live in conflict and war, paying the heavy price of armed conflict every few years. With a partner living under the same roof, living in conflict means endless warfare. The first and most important contribution of the political process to this state of affairs is to bring into sharp focus the fundamental impossibility of the situation.

Settling the conflict between Israel and the Palestinians can be likened to settling the differences between a husband and wife who loathe each other, and are endlessly suspicious of each other's every move, but who, at the same time, are forced to reach an accommodation for the sake of the children. Neighbours can choose to quarrel or make up and be friends again. A married couple who have developed a deep-seated hatred toward each other cannot quickly find their way back to any form of friendship. They can declare – with or without the help of mediators – that they have attained a modicum of domestic peace, but they will have to undergo an extended process before this domestic ceasefire turns into a genuine peace rather than a shaky patchwork of agreements. The Israelis and the Palestinians are like that warring couple. Comparing the political process with the Palestinians to the political processes under way with our neighbours is fundamentally erroneous, since these two sets of relationships are different in kind. By the same token, just as peace inside the home must take precedence over peace-making with neighbours outside, so there would be a fundamental error involved if the need to reach comprehensive agreements with the Palestinians was not given top priority.

PEACE AT HOME TAKES PRECEDENCE OVER PEACE WITH NEIGHBOURS

All the agreements that Israel signed with its immediate neighbours, Jordan and Egypt, as well as with more distant Muslim countries such as Morocco, Tunisia, Qatar and Oman, are profoundly influenced by, and I would even say dependent upon, domestic peace, i.e. the political process with the Palestinians.

When the Netanyahu Government chose to delay the signing of the Hebron Agreement, and opened the Hashmonaim tunnel near the Western Wall, leading to bloody clashes between the two sides, there was instant political reaction in the countries mentioned above. The Prime Minister of Israel and his policies came under virulent attack in Egypt, and the largely positive dynamic that had developed between Israel and Jordan, and between Israel and the other Arab countries that had established contacts with Israel, was immediately frozen.

The Americans, as indefatigable mediators, invested all their efforts, and rightly so, in overcoming the crisis between Israel and the Palestinians, paying little attention to other issues of Middle Eastern diplomacy, chiefly the suspension of the political process between Israel and Syria.

Much has been written about the reservations of President Mubarak of Egypt and King Hussein of Jordan with regard to Yasser Arafat. Nevertheless, it was they, of all people, the undisputed rulers of independent states, who grovelled in the dust at Arafat's feet, allowing him to dictate their political agenda. When the negotiations over Hebron were about to be concluded, it was Mubarak who understood that his influence in the eyes of the Americans would be measured by the degree of his ability to influence Arafat. He used this influence to pressure the United States to advance certain Egyptian vital interests.

The President of Syria, Hafez el-Assad, alternately heated up and cooled down the Syrian border with Israel and the Lebanese front, and as soon as the Hebron Agreement was signed, quickly sent out conciliatory messages as part of his preparations for renewing negotiations with Israel.

In this situation there is only one real winner, and that is Arafat. In his wildest dreams he could not have believed that less than two years after his historic entry to Gaza he – and only he – would determine the face of the New Middle East, following the conclusion of the Camp David process.

King Hussein, Arafat's erstwhile enemy, and one of his greatest detractors, saw that public opinion in his own country was turning against him personally, and against the warm relations he was trying to cultivate with Israel. The King found the earliest opportunity to go to Gaza to persuade Arafat to sign an agreement with Netanyahu.

Despite American pressure, Mubarak and his closest adviser, Foreign Minister Amru Mussa, gave Arafat strong backing when he decided to delay signing any agreements with Israel in order to extract further promises, with specific dates, for the continuation of Israeli redeployment.

Dennis Ross is working in one direction – persuading Arafat to go ahead with the peace process and at the same time trying to wrest additional concessions from Netanyahu. Meanwhile, the donor nations[3] are sending funds directly to the Palestinian Authority without consulting Israel, as they did at the beginning of the political process when every dollar earmarked for the Palestinian Authority went through Shimon Peres' office.

The conclusion from the above is crystal clear. Until such time as Israel manages to make peace at home it will not be able to make peace with its neighbours.

So far as the Arabs are concerned, Israel exists on territory that is not claimed by anyone except the Palestinians. Recognition of Israel's existence, not to mention establishing peaceful relations with it, is entirely dependent on the acquiescence of the Palestinians, and until such time as they give the Arab countries the official stamp of approval for Israel's existence, there is no chance for truly peaceful relations between Israel and its neighbours. This is not a radically new conclusion and has been well known to Israeli leaders and clearly understood by them for years.

The practical conclusion from the above is that Israel must, first and foremost, invest all its efforts in achieving a permanent settlement with the Palestinians. This is the main, and I dare say, the only objective facing any government that seeks to achieve any kind of peace with its neighbours.

Without detracting one iota from the importance of the agreements reached with Jordan and the other Arab countries, we must reiterate and emphasize that a settlement with the Palestinians is the *sine qua non* for the achievement of new agreements and the continued implementation of those already signed.

Israel will reap the fruits of peace with all that this implies, particularly in the economic sphere, only after it succeeds in achieving domestic peace with the Palestinians. And the measure of warmth emanating from the contact between Netanyahu and Arafat will determine the degree of warmth that will prevail between Israel and the rest of the Arab countries in the region.

NOTES

1. *Translator's note*: The former *Mufti* – religious leader – of the Arab community in Palestine prior to the establishment of the state.
2. *Translator's note*: 'Taba' was the name given to a small salient in Sinai, on the Red Sea just south of the port city of Eilat, that was hotly contested by both Israel and Egypt during the last stage of the negotiations on Israel's withdrawal from the Sinai Peninsula. Sadat made it a matter of principle to regain 'every inch of Egyptian territory', and Prime Minister Yitzhak Shamir insisted – until he was proven wrong – that the area of Taba belonged, historically, to Mandatory Palestine, and therefore was not Egyptian territory that had to be returned.
3. *Translator's note*: A group of European nations which, with the first implementation of the Oslo Accords, agreed to donate funds to the Palestinian Authority in order to help set up its civil administration by funding specific large-scale civil projects.

10

On the Right of Deniability and the Obligation to Loyalty*

EFRAIM HALEVY

INTRODUCTION

My only meeting with the late Reuven Shiloah, the first head of the Mossad, took place in his office at the Foreign Ministry in Jerusalem. It was in the late 1950s; he was the political adviser to Foreign Minister Golda Me'ir. Shiloah had been a trusted adviser to the first Prime Minister of Israel, David Ben Gurion. After resigning from his post as head of the Mossad, he moved directly into the diplomatic service, was appointed Minister at the Israeli Embassy in Washington, and then filled a number of positions at the Foreign Ministry until his untimely death. He was, I believe, the first Mossad official who made the move from the intelligence community to the diplomatic service. During our meeting I hardly gave this fact a thought, and it never occurred to me to ask him about the move from the hidden world of espionage to the visible world of diplomacy. At that time I had no idea that I would follow a similar course – a 35-year commitment to the Mossad, in which I rose to the position of deputy head, followed by a career in diplomacy as Israel's Ambassador to the European Union.

My meeting with Reuven Shiloah focused on Israel's relations with Europe, in the wake of the first steps toward unification – the creation of a Common Market and the development of free trade between its members. At that time I wrote and edited the 'Monthly Review' published by the Chief Education Officer of the Israel Defence Forces (IDF).[1] The idea behind this publication was to give IDF officers a periodic review of a variety of

---

* Trans. David Zinder.

Author's note: This article was written one year before the 'Mashal Affair' (a bungled attempt by the Mossad to assassinate a high-ranking member of the Hezbullah, in Amman in September 1997), which soured Jordanian–Israeli relations.

Israeli, regional and international topics, and I believed then that the overall European complex was an area that should be of interest to Israeli Army officers. At that time Shiloah was in charge of developing Israeli policy *vis-à-vis* Europe in its first stages of unification. Looking ahead, he foresaw that Israel would have to make tremendous efforts in order to put its relations with Europe on a healthy and permanent basis. As he saw it, the Europeans' guilty conscience about their attitude toward the Jews and the Holocaust would, in the near future, give way to a desire for 'normalization'. Consequently, in order to justify and nourish a true relationship with the gradually unifying Europe, genuine common interests between Israel and the European countries would have to be identified and cultivated.

Not long after this meeting – in April 1961 – I published the last of my monthly reviews, under the heading 'Competing on the Road to Unification', and left my position at the Chief Education Officer's headquarters in order to begin working at the Institution for Intelligence and Special Duties – the Mossad.[2]

As we have noted, Reuven Shiloah was the first Mossad official to move from the organization into diplomatic service. Over the years, a number of other ex-Mossad officials have been taken into the foreign service: Hanan Bar-On (who eventually became Deputy Director-General of the Foreign Ministry); Yitzhak Ben Ari (Ambassador to Copenhagen and Bonn); Avner Idan (Minister in Washington, and later in Bonn, and Ambassador in Stockholm) – these are but a few of those who took this route.

I never spoke to any of my colleagues about the substantive and subjective aspects of such a move. How does one deal with the transition from a code of conduct characterized by an obsessive flight from publicity, exposure and the media, to activities in which public exposure is a primary tool? How does an intelligence officer who has made a habit of using covert methods of persuasion accustom himself to the use of conventional and totally open forms of leverage?

These are just a few of the many issues worthy of attention and discussion, but they are not the main focus of this article.

My appointment to the post of Israeli Ambassador to the European Union was preceded by sharp controversy between the Prime Minister, the late Yitzhak Rabin, and Foreign Minister Shimon Peres. This dispute was accompanied by a chorus of background noises, and over a number of months much was said and written about it that led me to consider a number of issues, the significance of which, as I see it, goes far beyond my own personal case. As I shall show later, at some point these concerns merged with my own private case, and it is conceivable that this joining together in my mind of the general issue and my particular case created in me the need, and perhaps the ability, to define problems which many of my elders and betters had preferred to ignore for well over a generation.

FUNCTIONING UNDER CONDITIONS OF ANARCHY

Espionage and intelligence have been a part of the human condition for as long as warfare. Intelligence, and the process of information-gathering that lies at its core, has always been a vital part of any military campaign. The Bible is replete with examples of such operations. One of the most noted is Moses' dispatching of the 12 spies to Canaan before the People of Israel entered the Promised Land. This was a dangerous mission, but a decision was made to choose only men from the highest ranks of leadership for the task. Numbers 13:2–3 has the story: 'Send thou men, that they may spy out the land of Canaan, which I give unto the children of Israel; of every tribe of their fathers shall ye send a man, every one a prince among them. And Moses sent them ... .' The 'Natziv' of Volozhin (one of the great rabbis of the nineteenth century, and among the first rabbis to call for the revival of Jewish nationalism) wrote about these verses in his commentary on the Torah, *Ha-amek Davar* ('Delve Deep'):

> He who is a prince and great among the people of Israel and knows the tactics of warfare, he shall go and not the layman, even though it is possible that the layman is familiar with a greater number of military tactics and is well versed in the matter. Be that as it may, the commandment was to take from among the great ones of Israel, who know how to reconnoiter and weigh the matter at hand; also so that their reports will be more closely heeded, and it is from matters such as these that we must learn for all our worldly deeds.[3]

For thousands of years nations have justified their need to deal in espionage and intelligence, the execution of which always demanded the selection of the very best people from among the military and political echelons of the nation. The domestic legitimacy for these activities has always been confronted by total opposition on the international plane. When Joseph's brothers came to him in Egypt to ask for food to take back to drought-ridden and starving Canaan, Joseph took them to his house and accused them of being spies (see Genesis 42:11–16). From the commentaries on these verses, it is absolutely clear that in those days the punishment for spying was death.

This sweeping de-legitimization of intelligence work is all the more bizarre when it is compared to the waging of war that intelligence is designed to serve. From the very earliest stages of human civilization, different cultures around the world have felt the need to formulate rules of warfare. On the face of it, this is almost an oxymoron: how is it possible to give the killing of human beings 'legal/judicial' approval. After all, the act of killing is irreversible; it is the worst, the cruellest thing that can be perpetrated on an individual on the face of the earth. Nevertheless, very early on, it became clear that without fashioning rules to govern the conduct of war, there was a real danger that anarchy would engulf the entire world. Over the generations, the rules of war proliferated and became more and more sophisticated. Legal experts and scholars embarked on a project of national – and later international – codification of the conduct of war. There are even precedents for 'international tribunals' for war-crimes. International treaties deal with various important aspects of this issue in ever-growing detail.

The more progress is made on broadening and deepening the legal aspects of warfare, the stranger the continued reluctance to include intelligence within legal parameters. And yet, intelligence work is universal. Superpowers and nations of widely different international importance have created long-range intelligence-gathering agencies to collect information on their opponents. Regimes of all kinds – from the worst dictatorships to the most enlightened democracies – deal in this business. While it is true that the development of new technologies has brought about major improvements in methods of information-gathering, nevertheless the human aspect of this activity – HUMINT, human intelligence – has retained its place as the 'prime mover' in the profession.

For every brilliantly successful intelligence operation there is, of course, a matching painful failure. Modern history is full of stories about intelligence-related 'affairs' that have caused grave damage to international relations and created deeply embarrassing situations for nations, heads of state, governments and a range of prominent people. And yet, despite all this, to the best of my knowledge, no country has ever made any attempt to introduce order into the field of intelligence, either legally or administratively. There are no conventional 'understandings' in the field, not to mention any attempts on the part of legal systems to risk entering this minefield armed with manuals on jurisprudence.

This state of affairs becomes all the more pressing and volatile in direct proportion to the need of governments and society to deal openly with the fallout of intelligence activity. After all, the lack of rules and legislation touches not only on what has always been defined as a vital interest in the overall defence strategies of a country, but also on the activities of intelligence officers working on behalf of their governments all over the world. We are not referring to individual actions, which, as we all know, the powers-that-be continually try to circumscribe with mandatory legislation. We are referring only to the clearly defined domain of public actions, so how is it possible that civil law steers clear of even the outermost boundaries of this activity?

It is no accident that the attempts to formulate a GSS law, regulating the activities of the General Security Services in Israel, have encountered such difficulties. And if these attempts have run into so many obstacles, it is no wonder that attempts to create a legal framework for intelligence operations abroad have been ten times more difficult.

This issue bears special significance in Israel. From the day the State was established, indeed even before it became a sovereign state, intelligence-gathering abroad was given the highest priority on the national agenda. The leaders of the country at that time, presumably like those in power today, felt that one of the only ways to balance the superiority in numbers and resources of Arab countries both near and far from Israel's borders was to ensure the continuous flow of solid and reliable intelligence about the opponents' capabilities and intentions, and the parameters of their economic, military and social frameworks. Without good intelligence of this kind, Israel would have needed to have maintained a standing army of a magnitude that the country and its economy could not support. What is more, devoting such enormous resources to defence needs would no doubt have had a disastrous – perhaps even fatal – effect on the quality of life in Israel, a country which, after all, was not conceived as a latter-day version of Sparta.

It transpires, then, that the availability of good intelligence is a vital ingredient not only for Israel's physical survival, but for its cultural and social fortitude as well. How strange then that an intelligence officer working abroad can be left – by the people who sent him on his mission – totally unprotected and at the mercy of those enemies whose secrets he was sent to uncover.

ANONYMITY: THE AUTHORITY AND THE PERMISSION

For many years, the 'long arms' of the intelligence services of the great powers and lesser nations were never subject to public scrutiny of any kind. During the Cold War, the two superpowers, the United States and the Soviet Union, openly admitted the actual existence of the CIA and the KGB, but the laws and regulatory procedures that governed them were not applicable to most of their tasks or areas of authority. They most certainly did not touch on the area of resources and *modus operandi*. In most other countries in the world, the very existence of such intelligence bodies was not revealed to the public at large.

Over the years it had become a tradition to deny the existence of these organizations, not to mention the fact that a strict ban has been imposed on divulging the names of all those involved in the intelligence work, including the heads of the services. Since the organizations lacked any legal structure there were those who demanded that recruitment to their ranks be based on volunteers. However, it is neither just, fitting nor proper for such missions in the service of one's country to be performed on a voluntary basis, and as a result this whole area has remained unregulated and unresolved to this day.

The provision of legal status for intelligence operations carried out beyond a country's borders raises inherent difficulties in three discrete areas:

(1) international law – relations between nations;
(2) internal law;
(3) foreign relations.

Sticklers would add a fourth area – public ethics – which raises problems that are exceedingly difficult to solve.

With no reciprocal arrangements between countries to regulate these activities, there is clearly a matter of principle involved in ordering the execution of intelligence operations in another country. If there is no internationally accepted legal basis for this kind of activity, and if it is impossible to devise a legal concept that allows it, does it not follow that national governments are forbidden to carry out such actions in the sovereign territory of another state?

The closer we look at domestic legal systems of individual countries, the more difficulties this issue raises in the area of international law. If this kind of activity is forbidden by international law, and if there is no legislation on the national level allowing it, does the head of an organization or a military commander have the right to order a subordinate to carry out activities beyond his nation's borders in the sovereign territory of another country?

And this leads us to yet another question. What is the degree of legality of any order given to a subordinate to carry out a mission in a foreign country? Is it legal at all? And, if so, what is its legal basis?

In our modern world, intensive legislative efforts are underway to enact laws aimed at protecting citizens' right to privacy. This has become one of the most important issues on the agenda of many enlightened nations. Is an order given to a civil servant to infiltrate someone else's private domain and remove his most closely-guarded secrets, ethically valid? How can such orders tally, for example, with a country's signing of international treaties aimed at regulating far-reaching mutual safeguards for individual privacy?

These questions are not unique to Israel. They are equally applicable to every country grappling with such issues, including the largest of the world's democracies.

To the best of my knowledge, the legal world has not addressed these issues, choosing rather, deliberately and consciously to avoid them. And just as the legal world has remained silent on these issues, so too have generations of political leaders everywhere. Whenever a 'spy scandal' has occurred, the people involved have been tried and given harsh sentences. Negotiations for their release, or for their exchange in return for others, have always been conducted secretly, with countries and governments preferring to reach *ad hoc* agreements on each individual case according to the specific interests of the parties involved. And let us be very precise here: we are speaking of an intelligence officer who is a fully-fledged civil servant of his country. We are not dealing with an agent who is a bone fide citizen of a country where he is being 'run' by a case officer. When caught, such agents are regarded as traitors to their country, and this is not at issue in this article.

The extent to which the legal world has avoided dealing with the area of intelligence may be illuminated by a case that occurred a few years ago. A number of Israel's finest fighters were sent abroad on a mission to rescue Jews. At the same time, word reached the authorities that a non-Israeli, residing in Israel, was not pleased with some of the rescue operations, and intended to make public certain information that could have endangered the lives of the men sent abroad. There were those who thought that this was a case where the state was not only entitled but obliged to take legal action to prevent this man from carrying out his intentions and endangering the lives of our people abroad. An appeal was made to the Attorney-General to take steps to prevent the publication of the potentially damaging information. The Attorney-General replied that he had no legal recourse in this matter. He rejected the claim that since the fighters had gone out on their mission with official authorization and permission, and on orders that had been personally approved by the Prime Minister, he could not absolve himself of responsibility for their safety, and indeed that the safety of all those sent on missions abroad rested squarely on his shoulders. The Attorney-General did not hold himself responsible for fighters 'of this kind'. Since these men were fighters who had not been legally inducted into the army, and did not operate according to the rules of military procedure, it followed that in the Attorney-General's opinion, the state was not legally responsible in any way for its unnamed emissaries abroad.

What was surprising at that time was not only the Attorney-General's categorical ruling, but the fact that he did not require any time at all to study the problem with which he had been presented. He quickly handed down his decision, and then showed no further interest – either professionally or personally as a concerned Israeli citizen – in seeking alternative ways of preventing the danger facing a group of Israelis engaged in state business. In the days and weeks that followed many efforts were made to circumscribe and minimize the threat, and these efforts, using means that fell within the limits of the law, were ultimately successful.

The Attorney-General did not show the slightest interest in the eventual outcome of the issue that had been brought before him, and we are talking about a person who, it is generally believed, symbolizes not only the rule of law but the best tradition of public ethics.

THE PRINCIPLE OF DENIABILITY

From here there is but a short step to a hard-and-fast rule political leaders have adopted through generations concerning everything related to the world of espionage and intelligence – the principle of 'deniability'.

This principle has taken root first of all because a country is not expected to take responsibility for intelligence work carried out on foreign soil, and secondly because it is also generally understood and accepted that in cases such as these the agent's home country denies any knowledge of the act itself and of the person who supposedly committed it. Some countries have taken this denial to extremes, so that even after it has been made perfectly clear that the act in question could not have been perpetrated under any circumstances by an individual acting on his own, and that it could only be the work of an organization or a state, the country responsible has refused to admit having anything to do with the affair. What is more, the agent sent to carry out the mission has been ordered by his country to deny any connection with his dispatchers; he has been obliged – as an inseparable part of the execution of a mission – to support his Government's denial of any connection to him or his activities.

As a result the operative has faced his captors/prosecutors stripped of any form of protection, without the least measure of publicly-acknowledged state defence, with neither instructions, regulations nor international charters that he could invoke in his defence. In those instances where a country has decided to come to the aid of one of its intelligence soldiers it has done so indirectly, covertly, concealing any indication of its involvement from the public eye. But in general, intelligence personnel have usually been left to face their fate on their own.

In most cases governments have preferred to let the country spied upon complete all the legal procedures involved in the indictment, verdict and sentencing of the operative, and only afterwards to begin seeking covert ways for his extraction, release or exchange, etc. Negotiations leading up to the resolution of these problems have invariably been handled by unofficial mediators: prominent lawyers, or well-connected contacts. Only on rare occasions have such negotiations been conducted through diplomatic channels, or by official – and visible – representatives of the country involved. Countries will go as far as that in order to put as great a distance as possible between themselves and these 'affairs'.

The principle of deniability has often been stretched to the limit. Two Israeli espionage scandals (one well-known, the other less so) are worth noting in this context. The first was the so-called 'Lavon Affair' of the 1950s (named after Defence Minister Pinhas Lavon and later known simply as 'The Affair'), when a group of Jews were caught in Cairo and accused of sabotage and espionage. Two members of the group were sentenced to death and executed, while the others were sentenced to very long prison terms. Israel and Egypt were then in a state of war and the prisoners of 'The Affair' had neither the status nor the rights of prisoners of war. Israel never openly took responsibility for the lives and fate of these men and women in Egypt, and all the efforts made to prevent their execution or reduce their prison terms were made indirectly through intermediaries.

This group was trained and run by IDF Intelligence Branch, and its members operated under IDF orders. A bitter debate raged at the time between Defence Minister Pinhas Lavon and the head of Intelligence Branch, Colonel Benyamin Gibli, on the question: 'Who gave the order?' (to activate the sabotage cell). There was no question, however, about the fact that the order had in fact been given and that it had originated in Israel. Less germane to this issue, but worth noting, is that to the best of my knowledge, no one has ever examined the legality of the order, its plausibility, or indeed any other legal aspect of the issuing of the order itself. In all the countless articles, speeches, books and statements that have dealt with 'The Affair' over the years, not a single lawyer – well-known or obscure – has ever tackled this question.

Be that as it may, in October 1956, two years after 'The Affair', the Sinai Campaign was launched and, as we all recall, the Egyptian Army was badly mauled. A large number of Egyptian soldiers were taken prisoner, and when the fighting was over the two countries naturally had to deal with an exchange of prisoners. The Prime Minister and Minister of Defence at the time was David Ben Gurion, and Moshe Dayan was Chief-of-Staff. The bare fact of the matter is that when all was said and done, the prisoners of 'The Affair' were not included in any of the exchanges, and were left languishing in Egyptian jails. Their release was never stipulated as a condition for an exchange of POWs. They were not 'captured soldiers' but 'convicted spies', and the country's leaders did not feel obliged to make the release of these emissaries of the state a condition for terminating the final stage of the Sinai Campaign. Many years later, the prisoners of 'The Affair' were released and brought back to Israel, where – in secret – they were given a heroes' welcome. They were inducted into the army retroactively, given military rank and provided with all the benefits concomitant with their new status. During the entire period of their imprisonment no one in Israel had ever suggested inducting them into the army and thus turning them into bone fide POWs – an internationally recognized status that would have ensured them certain privileges which although limited would have been, under the circumstances, highly significant.

It is not hard to imagine what would have happened in Israel if the Government had decided to forgo the return of even a single IDF soldier captured by the Egyptians during the Sinai Campaign. It is highly unlikely that the ministers would have been allowed to maintain 'business as usual'. The same did not apply, however, to soldiers 'of a different stripe' – the members of the espionage ring of 'The Affair'. The efforts, such as they were, that were made by the state to secure their release did not even remotely resemble the efforts invested in ensuring the return of Israeli POWs, and public sentiment in Israel for 'our spies', and public actions taken on their behalf, were but a pale shadow of the actions taken to secure the release of imprisoned military personnel.

Nearly 20 years later, at the end of the Yom Kippur War in 1973, negotiations were held once again between Egypt and Israel on the exchange of prisoners of war. Unlike the situation in the Sinai Campaign, this time the Egyptians were holding a large number of Israeli soldiers, and the negotiations for their release were lengthy, complicated and tortuous. Enormous public pressure was brought to bear in an effort to speed up the process, and its intensity was in direct proportion to the depth of the trauma inflicted on the country by that war. Apart from the Israeli soldiers taken in battle, the Egyptians were also holding an Israeli citizen who had been caught spying in Yemen, and was handed over to Egypt before the war broke out. This time, Israel demanded outright that he be included in the group of Israeli POWs to be exchanged, and be returned to Israel together with the captive soldiers. The Egyptians strongly opposed the demand. As far as they were concerned the Israeli was a spy, and thus not eligible for any of the privileges accorded to soldiers captured in battle.

The head of the Mossad at that time took a firm stand on this issue, demanding the agent's inclusion, for this purpose, among the Israeli POWs to be released. He even engaged in a head-on conflict over the matter with the Minister of Defence, Moshe Dayan. The Egyptians refused to budge, and the release of the Israeli prisoners was delayed. Naturally, pressure grew inside Israel to conclude the exchange of prisoners, and Prime Minister Golda Me'ir found herself under heavy cross-fire – from the Minister of Defence on the one side and the head of the Mossad on the other.

As the pressure mounted, the Government finally decided to back down and not make the intelligence officer's release a condition for the overall exchange of prisoners. Ultimately, the 'spy' was brought back to Israel, but separately from the other IDF prisoners of war. He was 'different', and was treated accordingly by both his captors and his dispatchers. These two cases underscore the fact that the issue of political responsibility for agents of the state has remained vague and unresolved. And this very vagueness is of particular and vital importance.

If, as is accepted today, one of the primary tasks of the long arm of intelligence is to provide the political echelons with the means for carrying out special missions which the leaders are then able to disown, the cover of deniability relates directly to those cases when an operative is caught red-handed. What is the point of the principle of deniability if the political echelons must retract their denial the moment the operative-emissary is caught during or following the act itself? Deniability is required *only* when something goes wrong and the act is revealed to the opposite side and/or the public at large.

The concept of deniability raises a number of issues and questions. Is the agent who embarks on a 'deniable' mission abroad obliged to understand that within the framework of the agreement he has made with his dispatchers he accepts that the rule of deniability will apply to any situation in which he may find himself?

Does the leader of a country have the legal and – more pertinently – the moral authority to send an agent on a mission while at the same time divesting himself of even partial responsibility for the fate of the operative should he or she be caught? Is the leader's authority firmly anchored in some form of legislation? Is the legality of his decision subject to scrutiny in a court of law? Is it valid? Is it fair?

We arrive here at a demarcation line of the greatest possible significance to the ethical fortitude of Israeli society. Is there any danger that the political echelons' accepted right of deniability in external affairs might be applied to internal affairs as well?

We should be clear about what is at stake here. If the right of deniability is a necessary condition, or even perhaps a necessary aspect, of the actual mission, does not this right also apply to necessary acts of the political estab-lishment toward field operatives even *after* an agent has completed his mission and returned to live in the country as a regular citizen? In other words, if an agent is tried, or imprisoned, or degraded while on a mission abroad, can there be any justification for the fact that the political echelons continue to disown him, and even stigmatize him, years *after* his mission has been completed?

This is but a small step away from a sweeping denunciation of all Mossad operatives whoever they are, and from either partly or completely dis-qualifying them as candidates for jobs requiring an 'unblemished' record. This, in an attempt to uphold the political echelons' 'innocence' and their ability to conduct international relationships according to the codes of behaviour that have been agreed upon – at least formally – between nations. Do the political echelons have the right to demand this kind of sacrifice from their subordinates? Should all this be included under the heading of 'built-in hazards of the profession'?

FROM THE PRINCIPLE OF DENIABILITY TO THE OBLIGATION TO LOYALTY

Two years ago, a protracted process of negotiation between Israel and Jordan was concluded, and on 26 October 1996 a peace treaty was signed at a moving ceremony at Ein Evrona in the Arava desert. In his address at the ceremony, and subsequently in a second address in which he presented the treaty to the Knesset, the late Prime Minister, Yitzhak Rabin decided to mention me by name as one whom he felt deserved special praise for his part in the chain of events leading up to that moment.

It was my great privilege to be involved in these events as a representative of a succession of Prime Ministers, and it was my especial privilege to serve under Yitzhak Rabin when our paths crossed at various times during 25 years of our professional relationship. On a number of occasions, during the years preceding the signing of the peace treaty, I passed through the town of Shuneh in Jordan, the same town where the heads of the Jewish Yishuv in Palestine had met with King Abdullah, King Hussein's grandfather, on the eve of Israel's War of Independence. Among the participants in those meetings was the late Reuven Shiloah, and it often occurred to me that there was an inherent symbolism in what I was doing nearly half a century later, and in the fact that I was travelling along the same roads taken by those first emissaries of the state to Jordan.

After the signing of the peace treaty the question arose of appointing the first ambassador to Jordan. I met with the Prime Minister and he asked me to consider accepting the post. He also told me that the Jordanians regarded me as most fitting, and would willingly accept me in that position. I told the Prime Minister that if that was his wish then it was mine as well.

The Prime Minister made it clear to me that he could not make this decision on his own, and that it was by no means guaranteed that I would be appointed. He promised, for his part, to do whatever he could to make it come about. From that moment on and for a number of months afterwards, a personal and public campaign sprang up surrounding the issue of the appointment, at the end of which the Prime Minister notified me that he had been unable to secure my appointment. At the time I did not respond to many of the manifestations of this campaign, and the time is not yet right for me to revive this matter today and take issue with one allegation or another.

One issue, however, does deserve mention in this article, and that is the claim that my past record as an intelligence officer automatically excluded me from the appointment to Jordan or, indeed, to any ambassadorial post. This appeared in the Israeli press, based on quotes from Israeli sources, together with the additional information that it was also the reason for the Jordanians' reluctance to accept my appointment. This news item was totally without any foundation in fact, since Jordanian government officials had indicated the exact opposite to the highest echelons in the Israeli Government, to the Prime Minister and the Foreign Minister. Despite this, not a single Israeli official made any effort to deny the erroneous report or publicly set the record straight. One Israeli daily published an editorial on the subject, under the heading that a *worthy* candidate for the position should be found, and the article made it very clear that a person 'such as myself' did not fill the bill. As I saw it, this added a new dimension to the principle of deniability, and consequently I requested a meeting with the Prime Minister.

Like all the previous meetings we had held on the subject of my appointment, this meeting with the Prime Minister was a private one with only the two of us present, and he allotted me a relatively long period of time. I told the Prime Minister that I had come to him in connection with articles touching on only one aspect of my possible appointment as ambassador to Jordan – an aspect which, in my opinion, he could not allow to go unanswered: the claim that my past as an intelligence officer rendered me unfit to be a candidate for the position.

I told Prime Minister Rabin that he knew as well as I did that the Jordanians had no such reservations about my appointment, and the very fact that such a claim had been made by Israelis was an extremely serious matter. What was at stake here was not the fact of my personal disqualification, but the sweeping discreditation of all Mossad employees who were 'infected', so to speak, by this 'disability' the moment they began working in secret government service. The leader of a country did indeed have the right of deniability towards his agents while they operated abroad, and he was entitled to expect that every intelligence officer would accept and honour this right, otherwise there would be little justification for his mission in the first place. However, it was my opinion that the leader did not have the right to disown an intelligence officer once he had completed his mission. On the contrary, the right of deniability entailed the obligation of loyalty on the part of the leader toward his subordinates. If this held true in relation to the chain of command in the military, it was true seven-fold in the domain of intelligence, especially because it was so closely connected to the sweeping principle of deniability that all intelligence officers accept as part of their work in the clandestine world.

As I saw it, this obligation applies to a country's leader both during and after his term of office. Moreover, in my opinion, it was the leader's obligation to stand proud and firmly to oppose anyone who makes such claims, which were tantamount to a profound and permanent disgracing of anyone entering the shadowy world of the secret services. Neither the profession of intelligence nor the people who labour in its service are debased or worthy of contempt. On the contrary, they are the stuff that world leaders are made of, presidents and prime ministers in the United States and in Israel, and elsewhere, members of parliament and heads of vital sectors in the economy, scholars in Israel and in the most outstanding of universities in the free world.

All this raised a number of questions, but three in particular need to be addressed. Firstly, what right did anyone have to disqualify a person for a diplomatic appointment just because in the past he had served as an intelligence officer? Secondly, did a country's leader have the right to demand that intelligence officers uphold the principle of deniability if he himself disowned this officer in the eyes of the very society in whose defence he was sent on missions of state? Finally, did not the leader pull the rug out from under his own right to send intelligence officers out on missions of any kind if he acquiesced to the value system that came to light in this case?

I told the Prime Minister that I did not want to serve as ambassador to Jordan if he did not want me to. 'My desire to serve as ambassador to Jordan is there as long – and only as long – as you wish it too', I stated.

The Prime Minister listened to what I had to say without interrupting me once. At the end he said he would talk to the Foreign Minister again on the issue. I did not request an alternate appointment instead of the embassy in Jordan, but a few days later I was asked to come to see the Prime Minister, and he proposed, on behalf of himself and the Foreign Minister, that I be appointed Israeli Ambassador to the European Union in Brussels. Eventually, the Foreign Minister, who had been so strongly opposed to the Jordanian posting, pushed through the approval of my appointment in Europe, and personally supported it against all those who came out against it for one reason or another.

I would like to believe that both the stand I took on this issue and its ultimate outcome have made a significant contribution to bolstering the equation of 'the right of deniability and the obligation to loyalty' in intelligence affairs, and their mutual dependency. If this does indeed prove to be the case, I will have been amply rewarded.

NOTES

1. From its inception the Israeli Army has been an educational tool for the purposes of immigrant absorption, teaching the Hebrew language, providing secondary education, and addressing the ethical standards. The Education Corps is the branch of the IDF that deals with these issues.
2. *Translator's note*: Institution in Hebrew is *'mossad'*, hence the name of the intelligence organization.
3. Quoted in 'Ha-Hayal ve-Ha-hossen' (The Soldier and the Strength) in Yehoshua Hagar-Lau, *Army and Warfare in Ha-amek Davar, and Meshekh Hokhma* (Israel: Hayeshiva Hgvoha Or-Etzion, 1979). I have a personal interest in this quote as I am a fifth-generation descendant of 'Ha-Natziv' of Volozhin.

Part Three

Intelligence for Peace in Global Strategy

11

The American Intelligence Community

R. JAMES WOOLSEY

The American intelligence community consists principally of three sub-stantial networks around the world that are capable of collecting intelligence – from electronic signals, imagery and espionage – and the infrastructure that is necessary to analyse and disseminate their product. There are other collection networks that make important contributions as well, such as that for open sources and that for measurement and signatures intelligence (MASINT), but it is helpful to focus on the three first-mentioned, since it is they that drive the cost and the structure of the community, as well as much of the controversy about it.

At the height of the Cold War these three networks were extensive enough to give the United States a world-wide presence to conduct these three types of collection. Today, as a result of substantial reductions in the size of the US intelligence community, these three networks are capable of something slightly less ambitious. The phrase 'world-wide reach' probably best characterizes it. That is, each network is smaller than it once was, but each has been restructured so that with some notice and time for redirection the United States can have the ability to collect intelligence from virtually anywhere in the world with one or more of the networks. Increasingly, these three networks are interdependent – spies tip off satellites, and satellites tip off spies.

The intelligence community has been reduced in size in recent years at a pace about double that of the domestic side of the US Government. Indeed, along with the Department of Defense, of which much of the intelligence community is also a part, intelligence has been the government pace-setter in size reduction – close to a 25 per cent personnel reduction will take place during the 1990s. Budgets, although they have stayed roughly level in nominal terms in recent years, have shown substantial reductions in real terms (i.e.

*Adapted from Foreword *National Security Studies Quarterly*, Vol. 1, No. 3 (18 October 1995). R. James Woolsey was Director of Central Intelligence from 1993 to 1995.

taking account of inflation). These combined reductions in personnel and in real resources will mean that during the 1990s, the number of American reconnaissance satellites is being cut nearly in half, the number of National Security Agency (NSA) electronic intercept facilities is also being heavily cut, and the CIA's overseas presence is seeing substantial reductions both in the number of locations and in the number of intelligence officers at each one. It is vitally important that all three of these networks, and the capability to analyse and disseminate intelligence, continue to be modernized and their flexibility increased as the community's size shrinks.

As far as the organization of the intelligence community is concerned, this is a subject for which the ratio of verbiage to positive action is often very high in the United States – in part because politicians and journalists often want to have something public to say about intelligence, and organizational matters are comparatively easy to discuss without running into classification problems. Intelligence reorganization is also a subject in which there is a serious risk that the ratio of activity to improved effectiveness will be similarly high. In short, one can do a lot of reorganizational wheel-spinning for very little positive effect. There is always the risk, indeed, that the output of reorganization will be negative, as disruption replaces useful work. Reorganizers should adhere to the Hippocratic Oath: first of all, do no harm. Normally, in intelligence, the pay-off from ensuring that very talented people are involved and that they are motivated to do their best is much much higher that the pay-off of moving organizational boxes around.

In the US intelligence community the networks responsible for signals collection and for espionage are generally well designed and well managed by, respectively, the NSA and the CIA, under the overall authority of the Director of Central Intelligence. The network for collecting visual intelligence needed clearer central management, particularly in the acquisition of its airborne reconnaissance platforms and sensors, and an important step in that direction was taken in 1994, with the creation of a central office in the Department of Defense (DoD) for this purpose.

The DoD office has moved forward decisively to develop a series of new unmanned aerial vehicles (UAVs) for intelligence collection, but only after there was an aggressive effort (in 1993) that successfully demonstrated the value of long-endurance UAVs equipped with modern sensors and communications for the timely collection and dissemination of imagery. The development and use of UAVs had been slighted in the United States for years for a number of bureaucratic reasons. By equipping an innovative long-endurance airframe, designed by Abraham Karem (former designer for Israeli Aircraft Industries) with advanced sensors and communications, and by drawing on some of the operational lessons learned by Israeli operators of UAVs over the years, a successful demonstration was achieved – one that at last moved the US Government toward recognition and the systematic use of these extremely useful, and relatively inexpensive, intelligence collection systems.

Effective and timely imagery dissemination has been a problem for some years inside the US Department of Defense. As the 1991 Gulf War showed, this has principally been a difficulty at lower echelons of command. During the Gulf War, imagery reached Allied Headquarters in Riyadh quickly, but dissemination out to the battlefield commanders was plagued by delays, bureaucracy and incompatible and inadequate equipment. Most American commanders at, say, the division-commander level, thus contrasted slow-arriving imagery (virtually useless in the very fast-moving 1991 ground war) with rapidly-arriving and highly useful signals intelligence managed by NSA. Many have thus urged that a strengthened hand for a central imagery organization within the US intelligence community might be useful in helping imagery dissemination catch up with the dissemination of signals intelligence. It is not yet clear whether the newly-created National Imagery and Mapping Agency (NIMA) will be able to bring this about or not.

A great deal of nonsense has been written in recent years about the alleged failure of the CIA, and of US intelligence in general, to predict the end of the Cold War and the collapse of the Soviet Empire. The actual record has been set out in some detail recently in two careful and thoughtful publications. In the prestigious US quarterly *The National Interest* (Fall, 1995), Bruce Berkowitz and Jeffery Richelson's article 'The CIA Vindicated: The Soviet Collapse Was Predicted', examines many of the CIA's estimates and assessments about the Soviet Union that were not previously available to the public – many of them have recently been declassified pursuant to orders issued by my predecessor, Bob Gates, and myself. Berkowitz and Richelson's assessment is supported by the even more detailed recent monograph by Douglas MacEachin, published in May 1996 by the Center for the Study of Intelligence: 'CIA Assessments of the Soviet Union: The Record Versus the Charges'.

Although some economic figures produced by the CIA about the Soviet Union and Eastern Europe (chiefly aggregate estimates of Gross National Product) were badly off base, as were the GNP assessments made by most leading Western academics, these mistakes should not substantially diminish the value of other CIA work during the Cold War – generally ranging from good to excellent – on virtually all other Soviet issues, including many aspects of the Soviet economy. The public record is now available for anyone who wishes to look at the matter objectively.

A further major controversy concerning the US intelligence community has been the allegation that the community has not begun adapting itself to deal with the issues of the post-Cold War era until the last year or so. There is even less of an objective case for this proposition than for the notion that the CIA misassessed developments in the Soviet Union. The proliferation of weapons of mass destruction, terrorism, rogue states, and other such post-Cold War issues have for some years been given substantial prominence by my predecessors and by the superb professionals of the intelligence community, and this redirection was continued vigorously in 1993 and 1994 – it is not an invention of the last year or two.

At the same time we must all realize that just because the Cold War has ended does not mean that we can now afford to ignore Russia and China. The stresses inside the Russian military, the effectiveness of Russian custody of fissionable material, their advanced weapon technology, which may be increasingly sold to other countries, and the complex and troubling partnerships between Russian business, organized crime and the power ministries, including Russian Intelligence, are all important subjects on which the United States needs to continue to collect intelligence. Similarly, China is a source of advanced weaponry and some technology relevant to weapons of mass destruction for nations in the Middle East and elsewhere. And the use of nationalism as a substitute for discredited communism is on the rise in China. The peace of East Asia, and of other parts of the world, in years to come may depend heavily on how well we understand many aspects of Chinese society and the Chinese Government.

There are two main reasons why some have not understood how thoroughly and continuously the intelligence community has been adapted to the post-Cold War world for a number or years.

In the first place, because the three networks with world-wide reach – electronic intercepts, reconnaissance satellites and espionage – existed during the Cold War and continue to exist (albeit in changed form) some critics appear to believe that this indicates an unwillingness by the intelligence community to adapt to the new era. The reality is that these three networks must continue to exist and exhibit at least a world-wide reach if the United States is to continue to be a world power. We cannot afford to close any one of them down, as the then Secretary of State, Henry Stimson, closed down the State Department's code-breaking in the 1920s, remarking that 'gentlemen don't read one another's mail'.

If the United States, for example, shut down the CIA, as Senator Moynihan has proposed, the virtual destruction of our ability to conduct espionage would make us essentially blind and deaf to the plans and activities of terrorists and the proliferators of nuclear, chemical and bacteriological weapons around the world. Secretary Stimson and the rest of the world were lucky that in the interwar years the US Navy and British Intelligence were both being less than gentlemanly with respect to Japanese and German 'mail', and the codes that protected them. Without the British and the US Navy code-breaking, at many crucial turning points the Second World War could have gone in very different directions. The victories in the Battle of Britain, at El Alamein and at Midway, for example, owe a huge debt to intelligence. If we, as a nation, make a Stimson-like mistake by closing down a vital intelligence capability, then the next time we need a crucial item of intelligence there may well be no one to cover for us.

A second reason for the false assumption that the intelligence community has not been adapting to the post-Cold War era is that some confuse the fundamental design of these three collection networks with the tasking of them. These three networks, and the infrastructure to analyse, produce and disseminate intelligence, are principally designed to obtain the information needed to avoid or manage major crises, and to support our military forces. In short, they are largely designed to learn about such things as the proliferation of weapons of mass destruction, terrorism and the plans and activities of rogue states, and to help American and allied military forces fight effectively. But because they must continually be in existence in order to be able to fulfil these functions, they are often available in peacetime for other purposes with very little added effort or cost. A reconnaissance satellite, for example, can be tasked to map poppy and cocaine fields. A CIA case officer can recruit sources to learn about efforts by another country to bribe its way to a contract to the disadvantage of American business. If the nation decides that it does not want to use the intelligence community to learn about such matters, then the community can easily stop collecting intelligence about them, but very few resources will be saved. There is no way to cancel a portion of a satellite and save the cost of that share of it that does poppy and cocaine mapping.

A final note: in democratic countries with guaranteed freedom of speech it is possible to do great harm to citizens' confidence in important parts of their government by making irresponsible charges against government agencies. Intelligence is especially vulnerable to this. Because so much has to be kept secret to protect intelligence sources and methods it is sometimes impossible to give public answers to false charges either thoroughly or promptly.

In the long run there are three antidotes that can help counteract the weakening of public support for the difficult task of maintaining the intelligence that is vital to the protection of free nations. Each antidote is important, but each is only occasionally and partially effective. First, those who manage intelligence must be acutely conscious of their duty to see to it that their agencies follow the rule of law. Second, the intelligence produced must be the professionals' honest, best assessment – with never a hint that Intelligence Assessments have been adjusted to make a policy look good or to please a policy-maker. Finally, when the passage of time or a change in circumstances make it possible for some previously protected facts about intelligence to be publicly discussed, then some of the aspects of the difficult choices and risks of the craft of intelligence may be shared with the public. But in democratic nations, providing sound intelligence and maintaining public support for those who fulfil this vital function will always be the most difficult, and the most thankless, job in government.

12

Intelligence, Security and Peace

ADMIRAL FULVIO MARTINI

It is difficult for a foreigner, even if he is an insider, to address an Israeli audience on the subject of intelligence, security and peace. This is because the Israeli people live in a particularly troubled area, where the concepts of peace and security are seen from a different perspective than they are by those who live in other countries.

During its short life Israel has fought many wars – too many wars – and has experienced the perception of a continuous, impending threat, unparalleled in the recent history of other countries (except during the First and Second World Wars).

In my capacity as a member of Italian Intelligence, I have had the privilege of working with Israel, and for Israel, over a period of several years. My generation is that of the Cold War, since I retired from active duty during the days of the collapse of the Soviet Empire. In retrospect, I feel able to say that throughout my professional life I contributed to the best of my ability to the building and maintenance of a framework of security.

Yet, I never deluded myself that the fall of the Soviet Empire and the crumbling of the communist system would bring the world to a lasting and perfect peace. World history is made up of confrontations, struggles, bids for hegemony, different and conflicting ideologies. Therefore, there will never be the serenity, peace and sense of security to which a certain part, or rather a substantial part, of mankind constantly aspires.

But let us return to our subject. What, we may ask, is intelligence? In answering this, we may say that intelligence is a tool used by governments, by the leaders of a community, of a people, of a human group; it is the tool which enables one to know what lies around the corner or beyond the hill. For continental peoples – by this I mean non-seafarers – it is a sort of reconnoitring around their territory; for marine peoples it is something more.

When Joshua sent explorers to the land of Canaan and the town of Jericho, his purpose was, essentially, to know who it was he would be facing, whom he had to contend with. And since then, as now, confrontations often ended in armed clashes, he also wanted to learn about these strangers' weak points. However, the real thing – i.e. modern intelligence – was born with the great maritime and trading powers.

It must be said that for these powers the concept of intelligence was associated not only with security and peace but also with aspects the nature and scope of which went beyond the limited purposes of self-defence. For instance, the Venetians – who were the first to set up a modern intelligence service – used intelligence not so much as a tool for their security but more as a tool for knowing how to act on both the commercial and the diplomatic levels. In other words, it was a matter of collecting information about the places where trade was more profitable and where it was easier to send their ships on missions of exploration or, possibly, military conquest. These aims remained unchanged even when this type of activity was, so to speak, exported by British agents, Dutch agents, etc., and I am convinced that, at least initially, intelligence was more useful to the British East India Company than to the Government of Great Britain.

Later, the evolving world situation reached a stage where intelligence became a fundamental element in military strategy, since knowledge of the enemy's strength and intentions clearly put one of the contenders in a superior position. Subsequently, there was an increasing need for acquiring as much information as possible on economic, industrial, social resources, which, together with the armed forces of a state, make up the composite picture of a country's offensive/defensive capabilities.

At the same time, a search was started for newer and more subtle means of acquiring such information. This last step led to electronics: intelligence became also a technical matter, and we switched from Mata Hari to satellites. Concurrently, intelligence, aimed at enhancing security and peaceful coexistence between peoples, gained a higher profile.

As regards Israel, it is self-evident that without an effective intelligence organization the birth and survival of the state would have been much more difficult – perhaps even impossible. Israel, however, had the good fortune to belong in the Western world, and to enjoy the friendship and solidarity of the Atlantic Alliance. For this reason, when foreigners – and I count myself among these, since although I am a friend I am nevertheless a foreigner to Israel – were operating on a certain side of the barricade, they always had the feeling that they were fighting not only for Israel, but also for their own country.

For instance, in the case of Italy (as in many others), we confronted people who were not specifically hostile to Italy, but often sided with the Soviet bloc in order to stand against Israel. Consequently, we had a double incentive: to lend a hand to Israel, our friend and ally, and to oppose a common enemy, i.e. the Warsaw Pact coalition.

In those years, the world was split in two. But, in all honesty, as I have already mentioned, the end of the Cold War did not bring about the end of all international problems, and it would have been naïve to have expected it to have done so. Indeed, as regards the intelligence services of the Western world, I would say that the disappearance of the Big Enemy has produced a time of crisis and instigated a search for a new identity.

This obviously does not apply to the Mossad, which, in its particular situation and particular area of operation, has no need at all to look for a *raison d'être*. But there is no doubt that many Western services, large and small, are still undergoing critical times.

I left my position as head of the main Italian Intelligence and security service, Servizio Informazione e Secureza Militare (SISMI), toward the end of February 1991, that is, when the Gulf crisis was already heading towards a favourable military solution for the United Nations and the American forces. In December 1990, in a sort of testament to my station heads and a number of senior officers in the service, I had said that the end of the Cold War would entail a reappraisal, or a retargeting of the work of the intelligence services.

I do not believe that I am endowed with the gift of prophecy, but it was clear that the services had to take stock of the new state of affairs that had come about due to the disintegration of the former balance of power created by the two major blocs. The services now had to adjust to different realities and objectives, and retrain their staff for other tasks.

War was not imminent, but the rivalry between conservative powers and developing powers – the 'haves' and the 'have-nots', I believed, was to become fiercer and more bitter. For instance, there would be problems of proliferation, of economic espionage, of financial struggles, which would replace the clash of armoured divisions. There would also be other problems: the danger from organized crime was increasing, and even though the threat of Middle Eastern terrorism was on the decline, a new terrorism would emerge.

In this connection, I would like to recall what happened in the 1960s and 1970s, when for the first time the intelligence services had to cope with a new reality: the reality of terrorism of Middle Eastern origin (well let's say mostly, if not completely, of Middle Eastern origin).

In that period, terrorism became a factor in the Cold War. And as a result, while for Commanders-in-Chief and General Staffs in Western countries –

except Israel of course – the Cold War had been a war played mostly on paper – the Orange Forces against the Blue Forces, the Blue Forces against the Pink ones, etc. – this was not strictly the case for the intelligence services. While for the military the Cold War had remained mostly a lukewarm affair, for the intelligence services, at least in some cases, it had been very hot.

At any rate, in the 1960s and 1970s, and in the 1980s as well – say, until the fall of the Berlin Wall – terrorism became a problem of previously unknown magnitude.

In earlier times too there had been acts of terror, but these belonged to a brand of anarchical terrorism in which individuals or small groups assassinated other individuals. (Such an act was the spark that ignited the First World War.) It is true to say, though, that the phenomenon was never so complex, widespread and violent as it was in the period following the Second World War. Terrorism based on nationalistic roots developed among the Basques or the Irish, as well as large-scale Middle Eastern terrorism of Palestinian origin. Clearly, this last fitted better than the others in the context of the Cold War.

The new terrorism made use of the ploys and techniques successfully tested by nationalist guerrillas in the Second World War, as well using improvements in the manufacture and development of explosives and personal weapons. Moreover, it took advantage of the dramatic expansion of commercial air transport, and the freedom of movement from one country to another. As a result, intelligence, which had been born as a tool for gaining knowledge of the enemy's plans, capabilities, etc., was given an additional task of fighting terrorism – a battle which bore no resemblance to war between countries, but was rather a new and unique kind of warfare.

It was no longer just a fight against the KGB, or the PLO as such; a galaxy of terrorist groups emerged that carried out their operations by every means possible, and could be confronted at the national level by the security agencies, but when they carried their actions across international borders this necessitated the involvement of the intelligence services as well. Thus the need arose for international cooperation, and for more – and closer – ties between services operating on the same side of this struggle.

I participated personally in this fight, and can boast of operations carried out with positive results by Italian Intelligence. In addition, this was an area in which both the old SID (the precursor to SISMI) and the new SISMI made a strong contribution that was greatly appreciated by the West.

Italy's proximity to the Arab world, and its intimate acquaintance with Arabism, gave us a good operational edge. Moreover (as I have said on other occasions) I count Italy's political weakness, or, if you prefer, its lack of 'imperialist' aims, a valuable asset for Italian Intelligence. Unlike the other colonial powers who had colonies in the Mediterranean and in Africa, Italy had a good reputation in these regions and its representatives were always welcome there.

There is no doubt that intelligence has direct links with security, and that the detection of potential terrorist operations on its own territory, or in the territory of an ally or friendly country, is always a plus for an intelligence service. Yet anti-terrorist activity called for a new *modus operandi* and a completely different approach to the problem as compared to the conventional tradecraft of intelligence, which, until then, operated mostly in the political–military field.

It is certainly not up to me to lecture the Israelis on the complexities and difficulties of the fight against terrorism, and the role played in it by the secret services. It is certainly unnecessary to explain to Israel, the first target of such terrorism, how all this has affected our lives, and the price, not least in psychological terms, that we have had to pay for coping with the problem. It is a very complex and unusual problem. And the fight against it has compelled us to adjust to new guidelines and new procedures quite unlike anything we might consider as our traditional job.

The latest developments in the Middle East caused the downgrading of the international dimension of this type of terrorism, which has now, unfortunately, become an internal issue relating to the Middle Eastern area and Occupied Territories.

Yet this does not mean that the intelligence services can lower their guard *vis-à-vis* this type of threat, because there is now a new form of international terrorism rearing its ugly head, and that is the terrorism that springs from Islamic fundamentalism. Equally violent, but perhaps more radical, this new terrorism seems even more unmanageable – and therefore more dangerous – than the Middle Eastern terrorism of essentially Palestinian origin. It is a phenomenon with a thousand different facets, bound to, I might say, a complex psychological matrix, where a deliberate will for self-sacrifice is compounded by other factors such as a deeply rooted pride in Islam's ancient history, long-suppressed revanchist aspirations, raging religious zealotry and hatred born of poverty and social problems.

The terrorism of the 1960s and 1970s and Islamic fundamentalist terrorism have a tragic feature in common: more often than not they strike out at defenceless people. Aiming to sow terror and insecurity in the civilian population, terrorists attack public transport, sparing neither women nor children. It is this aspect of their actions that makes them both hateful and especially terrifying.

Remaining in this perspective of intelligence, security and peace, I would like to mention yet another activity which the intelligence services may, on occasion, be required to perform, and that is to come to the rescue of official diplomacy.

Diplomacy has at its disposal a range of operating techniques and options. However, at times, official diplomacy has difficulty overcoming certain rules and regulations – or formal procedures of any kind – which the services can overcome or bypass. This is especially true when dealing with the services of countries where democracy is applied along different patterns than in the West, which, as a result, enjoy greater powers within their respective countries, being scarcely controlled by both public opinion and Parliament.

Among the most significant (and rather frequent) occasions I was referring to, I may mention, for example, a crisis breaking out for any serious cause in a country which – due to political, strategic, economic reasons – makes it an object of interest for several other states.

In my personal experience, I had once to handle this type of situation in the North African region. Without going into details, let me say that on this occasion the Italian Intelligence Service (SISMI) – under my direction – made a skilful use of its knowledge of the region and the goodwill it enjoyed there to establish contacts and negotiate with all those involved, to a successful outcome.

Obviously, in any such case the objectives of the various parties concerned are never the same; it is a sort of 'a security blanket', with each one pulling the blanket his way, and there are of course winners and losers. On this subject, and on a personal level, I think it is fair to say of SISMI during my term of office that the service was actually able to solve by proxy-diplomacy a number of problems of the type mentioned above, in the best interests of my country and also those of the majority of the parties concerned.

It is clear by now that those who considered that the end of the Cold War meant the retirement of the intelligence service were indulging in a dangerous brand of wishful thinking. The collapse of the Soviet Empire has, for instance stepped up the risk of proliferation of nuclear, biological and chemical (NBC) mass-destruction weapons in such countries as Iran, Iraq, and Libya. Moreover, because of the general volatility of the international situation, the intelligence services will have to assume more tasks in addition to their traditional responsibilities for collecting information and fighting so-called conventional terrorism. At world level new forms of threats are emerging: cybernetic terrorism, capable of disrupting a country's communications, transport and finances; biochemical terrorism, with its potential for horror; and the danger of alliances between terrorism and crime.

This is the reason why matching intelligence resources to the task is a problem which must be confronted and discussed at the appropriate government levels, and why all countries must do their share in building up an increasingly strong security system. This security should give, if not to each individual then at least to large segments of mankind, the standard of serenity and peace that all men are entitled to obtain in life.

13

Eavesdropping on Radical Islam*

EMMANUEL SIVAN

It is by now well established that the Islamic resurgence is not a throwback to the Middle Ages but a complex and sophisticated response to the challenge of modernity. The resurgence embraces some (but not all) of modernity's aspects and is certainly adept at using its instruments, 'from the Kalachnikov to the tape recorder', as the saying goes.

Indeed, audiotapes offer a unique means to learn how Islamists actually go about spreading their message and how they discuss a variety of topics within their own ranks, for internal consumption. Perhaps the most interesting of these topics is their attitude toward democracy. The attentive listener learns that when speaking frankly among themselves, Islamists have strong views on this subject.

ISLAM'S CASSETTE TAPES

Muslim preachers are wont to complain that the world has become one global village (*qarya l'lamiya*), where CNN and Hollywood dictate the agenda and where Islam is marginalized.[1] But these preachers themselves have carved out a formidable media niche in the realm of the audiotape filled with the message of the Islamists.

Since Ayatollah Khomeini's movement in Iran in the mid 1970s, the cassette has played a crucial role in the spread, survival and success of fundamentalist Islamic movements. Tapes have such an important role because in the absence of a Comintern-style hierarchical structure, they constitute a resilient web that holds together a plethora of local movements and groups, operating mostly within national borders. The constant flow of

*This article is an edited version of that which first appeared in *M.E. Quarterly*, March 1995, and draws on research for a project conducted for the Twentieth Century Fund. Emmanuel Sivan teaches history at the Hebrew University in Jerusalem.

tapes in the area from Afghanistan to Morocco knits like-minded Muslims into a larger whole. Indeed, the tapes even flow into Europe and North America – and the other way, too, from France to the Maghrib, from the United States to the Middle East.

The following analysis draws on recordings by about 30 Arabic-language preachers whose audiotapes shop-owners all over the Middle East judge to be most popular. All these activists–performers have passed, then, a market test of impact. The speakers are neither theologians and jurists splitting hairs in erudite treatises, nor journalists writing for external consumption. They run the whole gamut from proponents of reform to revolutionaries. The 30 speakers, it should be stressed, are often not just preachers. Some are veritable media stars (Ahmad al-Quattan, 'Umar 'Abd al-Kafi, and especially 'Abd al-Hamid Kishk, the most popular preacher in the Yusuf al-Qardawi, Nasir ad-Din al-Albani). Others are major thinkers ('Abd as-Salam Yasin, Muhammad Qutb, Yusuf al-Qardawi, Nasir ad-Din al-Albani). They also include top leaders of fundamentalist Muslim organizations (the Front Islamique du Salut, Hamas, Islamic Jihad, Muslim Brethren). A famous martyr of the Afghanistan war (Abdullah 'Azzam) is still widely listened to.

Audiotapes are cheap to produce and even cheaper to copy; in Egypt, for instance, they cost three pounds, or one dollar. (Videotapes costing four to six times as much as audiotapes are still far less diffused.) Their simple mode of reproduction leaves much of the distribution and usage to autonomous initiatives. They are easily marketed through mosques, booksellers and various other shops.

The tapes mostly contain sermons delivered in mosques on Fridays or on religious holidays, and follow a similar pattern: the speaker quotes the Qur'an or the Hadith (sayings and actions of Muhammad) as well as their major commentators, mostly medieval but also modern. He endeavours further to probe their meaning with the help of examples from contemporary politics, references to everyday life, folk proverbs and funny and salty stories. He weaves all this into moral vituperation or exhortation. The sermon serves as both an exercise in indoctrination and a form of entertainment.

Alternatively, the cassettes record a *dars* (lesson), usually delivered by the preacher just before the Friday prayer or, not necessarily in the mosque, on a weekday evening. The *dars* is geared systematically to teach articles of faith or chapters of law. The interaction with the audience is greater and the informality higher in this setting. Here the audience may pose questions, ask for legal guidance, even challenge the speaker's interpretation. The speaker resorts to a homely style, often in the colloquial language, picking examples from daily life. One can hear the audience laugh, cry, jeer and talk back.

For close, sustained, checkable argument there is no substitute for print, but for direct exchange the oral electronic medium has advantages. It permits the uncovering of emotional layers – the performer's as well as the listeners' – that underlie the readily accessible, rationally constructed arguments.

Audiotapes provide a privileged conduit to listen in on what is actually being said inside the movements of the Islamists. In most cases, the tape is recorded before an audience. As the target audience is the movement's adherents and supporters, the tapes indicate to what the audience is susceptible, in the name of what it is mobilized. In the tapes one can listen to the movements' activists speaking directly to rank and file; and, if lucky, one may even hear the latter talking back.

It is these listeners to whom the preacher must be attuned, and they often take an active part in the sermon through interjections and questions. This opens a tiny window through which to peer into that great unknown: the mood and preoccupation of the rank and file of Islamic movements who attend such gatherings.

What, then, do the cassettes tell about Islamist views of democracy?

GUILT BY ASSOCIATION

The preachers approach democracy with suspicion because of its Western origin, indicated by its Greek etymology and the development of democratic theory during the Age of Enlightenment, notably by Jean-Jacques Rousseau, that 'arch-enemy of Religion'.[2] An Egyptian sheikh, Ahmad al-Mahalawi, half-jokingly suggests that pagan Egypt may have been the originator of the democratic idea, for didn't Pharaoh offer unto Moses, according to the Qur'an, 'to conduct a sort of referendum among the Jews so as to find out whether they actually want to leave Egypt?'[3] Nowadays, democracy is the touchstone of that New World Order 'created by George Ibn Bosh and Mister Zift Baker'[4] to contain Islam.

No doubt many Muslims (or, rather, 'Muslims in name only') clamour for democracy, but that is, says the Jordanian Yusuf al-'Azm, the end product of the 'inferiority complex of those of us who are infatuated with Western culture. For isn't democracy one of those "imported ideas" they are so eager to embrace, ideas which also include nationalism, secularism, socialism?'[5]

Of course, many *ulema* (men of religion) argue that democracy is compatible with Islam, indeed, that it has an exact Islamic equivalent, the legal concept of *shura* (consultation).[6] But, retorts the blind Egyptian sheikh 'Umar 'Abd ar-Rahman (presently in a New York jail awaiting trial), that is

false Islam. It points to the 'shameful predilection of our religious establishment towards apologetics; they wish to endow Islam with a face-lift, lest
they be accused of being reactionary'.[7] Or it could be that these pseudo-
Muslims are motivated by fear of (or subservience to) the 'powers-that-be.'
'In our times', sniggers Kishk, 'Men of religion slavishly do the bidding of
the powers-that-be, with an excess of zeal; they even contribute what they
have not been asked for. If the ruler says that socialism is a great idea, the
ulema sing the praises of socialism for hours on end. If the ruler declares
himself in favor of democracy, the *ulema* deliver set speeches about Prophet
Muhammad as an accomplished democrat.'[8] What else could you expect of
such people whom the preachers call 'scoundrel *ulema*', '*ulema* of the palaces',
or 'those hypocrites'?[9]

GOD'S SOVEREIGNTY

Such preliminary suspicions about democracy, based upon its origin,
sponsors and supporters, are just tell-tale indicators, a sort of guilt by
association. The tapes' sermons probe further. What is the essence of
democracy? The answer is unanimous: the sovereignty of the people means
ultimate power to man, and not to God as enjoined by the Qur'an and Sunna.
Man is a frail, fallible, easily tempted creature; how, then, could one even
think of thus empowering him?

Ahmad al-Quattan explains: 'When the Communist bloc collapsed, the
governance of the people was declared victorious, yet that is tantamount to
governance predicated upon such human faults and blemishes as egotism,
sloth, greed, obtuseness, domination, and oppression.'[10] Such a pessimistic
view of human nature – deeply ingrained in the living Muslim tradition –
leads to a view of religion as a means of purification and regimentation.[11] It
likewise explains the evils that plague the Western countries, where democracy reigns supreme.

In itself, majority rule has little appeal to the preachers. For them, it is the
quality, not the quantity, of the sovereignty-holders that counts. Further,
Islamic activists – much like fundamentalists in Judaism, Christianity and
Hinduism – thrive upon the notion that they constitute an enclave of the
virtuous, a band of the elect and the pure-hearted, the last defenders of a
once glorious, now besieged religion. The virtuous few represent the only
glimmer of hope.

A frequently quoted Hadith confirms this outlook. The Prophet
Muhammad allegedly said that after his death the *umma* (community of
Muslim believers) would be torn asunder and split into 73 factions, all but

one addicted to false beliefs. The latter group will persist in fighting for the True Faith until Judgement Day; it alone will inherit the earth. If one follows this Hadith, how can an 'impure majority' dominated by 'factions of false beliefs' have the makings of a virtuous regime?

THE WESTERN MODEL

The West shows what democracy really leads to, says the Palestinian 'Abd al-'Aziz Dweik:

> Look closely at what is dubbed the American model, and what do you see? Drugs, alcohol, drunken driving, sex on television, pornographic films ... AIDS which is caused by the spread of homosexuality ... women and men kissing in public, and growing poverty due to economic policies geared exclusively to serve the well off ... Their very technology is saturated with eroticism, and that is what they export to Egypt in the form of movies and television serials.[12]

'Electoral rights do exist there, yet they are a sheer formality', mocks a Saudi sheikh, 'for to be elected you need money, lots of it. And once elected you are beholden to the interests of the rich and neglect the downtrodden.' 'They do have a degree of liberty', concurs an Algerian, 'but at what price? The rat race, no time for one's family, for things spiritual, and in their stead – addiction to entertainment.'[13]

This is also the prevailing view with regard to Western Europe, 'that same Europe where, many of our countrymen think, all is so much better.' So says the now-imprisoned Front Islamique du Salut (FIS) leader, 'Ali Belhadj, who also concedes that man-made laws have brought some equity and justice in France, Italy, and the United States. Being man-made, however, these laws might be easily abrogated or amended for the worse. For the Westerners have no moral guidance, no sense of measure. 'The Europeans do not respect human rights alone but go further and defend animal rights in the manner of that tart Brigitte Bardot. They even defend vegetation rights like those of trees in public parks', he adds to the loud laughter of his listeners. 'Indeed they equate liberty and permissiveness, notably in sexual matters. And this is what they call syphilization (civilization)', he notes with sarcasm.[14]

Democracy, and man-made laws in general, correlate closely with consumer culture. They go hand in hand, says the Egyptian Wajdi Ghunayim, 'with the reign of décolleté and moda (fashion), with language suffused with advertising loan-words, such as chic, delicat, senso, relaxe'.[15] Their common denominator is the appeal to the bestial instincts of human nature, let loose in the name of 'doing one's own thing'. Authentically Islamic behaviour precludes hedonism and is the obverse of bestiality. Yet such behaviour is quite rare in the nominally Muslim world. For bestiality consists in being subjugated by one's passions, whims and pleasures rather than controlling them. And it is of little import – much like in the case of drunken driving – whether people do this deliberately or not. The cumulative consequences for society are destructive.[16]

Moreover, hypocritical as ever, the West does not practise abroad what it holds so dear at home. Examples abound, but three will suffice: French colonial rule in Algeria, the US invasion of Panama and Europe's indifference to the fate of the Bosnian Muslims.

DEMOCRATIC EXPERIENCE IN THE MIDDLE EAST

Westerners pay little attention to the self-proclaimed 'democratic' nature of such regimes as Gamal Abdel Nasser's in Egypt and Hafiz al-Assad's in Syria, seeing these, rather, as thinly veiled despotisms. But for Islamists the Middle Eastern experience with 'democracy' leads them to draw some harsh conclusions about the utility of democratic ideals for the region.

These regimes, says the Saudi sheikh Safar al-Hawali 'conferred sovereignty upon forces inimical to God – the forces of unbridled desires'. Everywhere in the area the quest for democracy ended up with military regimes dominated by 'riff-raff and barbarians'. He goes on: 'What did Syria get from the struggle for democracy? The reign of that "Crusader" party, the Ba'ath; a party hell-bent upon subverting Islam in the name of Arab blood kinship.' The Sudan set upon a Western-type parliamentary course only to veer into General Ja'far an-Numayri's tyranny, a carbon copy of the Libyan and Iraqi regimes. And the litany goes on: in South Yemen, all powers were ultimately conferred upon the Presidential Council, which used them to impose 'Leninist laws'. Even in Habib Bourghiba's Tunisia, though less prone to violence, popular sovereignty signified presidential veto power.[17]

Sheikh Kishk recounts horror stories about his time in jail during the rule of Gamal Abdel Nasser, 'that great paragon of the people's rule'. Massive torture accompanied adulation of the Ra'is (President) as if he were God. This modern Pharaoh's attitude toward Islam was illustrated by the case of a Muslim activist brought before the notorious People's Court. The judge forced him to recite the first Sura (chapter) of the Qur'an – but backwards, from finish to start. 'Of what avail were to Nasser all his palaces and lavish resorts, all his bodyguards and henchmen? Like other despots who had eaten up the money of orphans and widows, oppressing the believers, he was ephemeral.'[18] But the Egyptian people paid a heavy price, and to this very day reel under its weight.

Nor did the situation in Egypt improve much in the quarter century since Nasser's death. Sheikh Salah Abu Isma'il, who served in the People's Assembly (Parliament) under Anwar Sadat, entertains an appreciative audience with stories about the security services running one of their stooges as a candidate against him. Not only did they conduct a smear campaign but on election day many of the sheikh's supporters found their names absent from the voting rolls. He also criticizes the work of the Parliament in which he once sat:

> And what man-made laws did they pass in this parliament? A law letting off the hook an adulterer who killed the aggrieved husband, allegedly in self-defense; and another law which required the license for a newspaper to be renewed after the death of the owner – a deft means to restrict the freedom of expression. Parliament didn't apply this principle, however, to the renewal of the license for a bar, which could automatically pass to the legal heir.[19]

The regimes of Sadat and Husni Mubarak were not tyrannies and, it is admitted, did permit a measure of party activity. Yet the Egyptian Government is far from committed to liberty. To the extent that freedom was expanded it was essentially freedom from moral constraints. Kishk blames the regime for the flourishing trade on Pyramids Street in Cairo – that epitome of the open-door economic policy, 'awash in alcohol, gambling, night clubs, and loose women'. And all this so as the better to serve tourism and 'that great ideal' of economic growth by all means.[20] For Belhadj, the October 1992 earthquake in Cairo signalled divine admonition to Egyptians to change course. 'Let's observe how low did public morality stoop: people do not give to charity any more, nor do they respect property which we entrusted to them. Males obey females, filial loyalty disappears when children get married. Men drink wine, clad in silk. They associate with musicians and belly dancers.' A particular cause for worry is the decline of the institution of marriage: 'Both men and women tend not to marry and rely upon servants and maids who help at home.'[21]

Belhadj describes Algeria under the National Liberation Front (FLN) as a combination of Nasser's and Sadat's formulas: despotic single-ruler, single party, ever-present security services, moral laxity in the *nomenclatura*, permissive laws in order to attract tourists, and foreign technology.

Kuwait, 'the sole parliamentary regime in the Gulf', is, due to its unearned oil wealth, an upscale version of the former two countries. According to Sheikh Qattan, Kuwaiti parents send their sons to private schools where foreigners, 'usually atheists', teach, and where they are introduced to rock music and drugs. They send their daughters to finishing schools abroad and let male members of the household have access to pornographic and Marxist books. Christian Filipino nannies raise smaller children and are the object of licentious exploits by their employers. This multitude of sins, sexual and financial, accounts for God's retribution visited upon Kuwait via the Iraqi occupation. But nothing much has subsequently changed, Qattan ruefully noted in 1993.[22]

'ARTISTIC ROT'

In the cultural sphere as well, Islamists choose to take Middle Eastern despots at their word when they claim to be democrats. They conclude that Arab-style democracy produces an 'artistic rot'[23] that is avidly consumed all over the Middle East. By artistic rot, the Islamists mean cultural artifacts designed to satisfy hedonism and individualism, which dominate the growing Arab communications market, pushed by technological progress and facilitated by the rapid evolution of the media. Immoral fare is offered to the masses – in the name of the democratic principle of freedom of choice – through films, television soap operas, songs, popular magazines, and the like. 'Muslims are indifferent to the death of thousands of *jihad* fighters in Afghanistan, while the whole of the land of Arabism is in deep mourning over the death of one song star', scoffs a Palestinian Hamas leader.[24] Marketing Arab-language artifacts is easier now and becoming more so every day, but their contents are almost to a fault un-Islamic, nay, anti-Islamic. The heroes of movie and television become icons, which attract tepid Muslims and none-too-sophisticated believers into the orbit of secularism and profanation. Life-styles of the rich and famous artists provide vicarious gratification for the underemployed, unemployed and badly housed youth of Arab countries. The loose mores of Egyptian and Algerian stars (sex, alcohol, drugs, family violence) laid bare in the media for all to hear and see serve not as cautionary tales of immorality but as titillating idiosyncrasies, as emblems of creativity and experimentation.

Revealing their fears, the Islamic militants detect the hand of the security services of the Egyptian pseudo-democracy in the performance and marketing of licentious songs, for these lull disgruntled youth and lead them astray. Activists also discern the fingerprints of a Hollywood-based, 'Judeo-

Masonic' conspiracy to de-Islamize the Middle East with the help of movies, soap operas and shampoo ads.[25]

ESTABLISHING A MORAL ORDER

Judged by its origins, nature and consequences, democracy deserves to be categorically condemned. What, then, is to be done?

The preachers are unanimous: the sole solution is to normatively regulate sin-prone humans through divine regimentation, that is, by applying to the letter the Shari'a, the Sacred Law of Islam. 'Sovereignty to the Qur'an, not to parliament' (*as-siyada li'l-Qur'an la li'l-barlaman*) runs their common adage. Muslims may not run their affairs as they please. They must obey the Shari'a as interpreted by *Ahl al-Hall wa'l-'Aqd* (those who untie and fasten, that is, forbid and enjoin; eminent authorities in matters of jurisprudence). Membership in this select group is determined by learning, virtue and devotion to the application of the Shari'a. Given their age-old opportunism, few *ulema* qualify for membership. It is *Ahl al-Hall wa'l-'Aqd*, not Parliament or the High Court, who should pass judgement upon the compatibility of existing laws and clarify moot points in the Shari'a and apply it to new issues.

Most preachers look askance at the option of 'codifying the Shari'a', namely passing new laws that lay it out in modern terms, for the institution that legislates might later amend such laws, even abrogate them. An Islamic government may initiate a law in order to fill a gap where the Shari'a is silent or ambiguous, but not otherwise. The legislature might, for instance, render interest-taking licit by providing legal loopholes. Existing laws only should be subject to review in terms of compatibility with the Shari'a.[26]

True, application of the Sacred Law may seem harsh; yet it is just and effective. To illustrate this point, Sheikh Kishk quotes an interview with a professional thief broadcast over Egyptian radio. The thief admitted that he had been trained as a welder and used to earn his living in that trade. 'Why then did he switch to stealing? Did he have no choice? He can indulge in whim whereas we have pity on him. God decreed that a thief's hand must be cut off. Should we have more mercy upon him than does the Creator?' Belhadj recites a similar story, stressing that where this Qur'anic injunction is implemented (in countries as divergent as Iran and Saudi Arabia), criminal acts against property are less frequent. 'This goes to prove that, contrary to what our enemies say, we are not extremist but reasonable, rational people who call for the restoration of the Islamic way of life as a solution to social problems.[27]

And what about the executive authority? Here the *shura* (the Islamic principle of 'consultation') concept is the panacea. Rejecting the *talfiqi* (apologetic, eclectic) gloss presented by time-serving (and modernistic) *ulema*, the preachers examine the historical evidence. They establish that the *shura* was implemented only in early Islam. It was the *Ahl al-Hall* that elected the first four Rightly-guided Caliphs, and provided them with moral and legal guidance during their incumbency. Consultation of the community-at-large – gauging the people's concerns – was optional and came second.

This form of government was spectacularly effective. One only has to remember how successful the Islamic state was in the Golden Age, winning battles from Spain to India and starting a glorious new civilization. 'The most competent people were thereby picked, morality reigned supreme in politics, Islam spread the world over.'[28] Kishk recounts edifying stories about these halcyon days, and remarks, to his audience's derisive laughter: 'All this happened despite the fact that the Muslims knew nothing about such wonders as democracy and socialism.'[29] And this is indeed the model to follow.

Constraints upon the ruler in this order should be those set by the sacred Law. The ruler is duty bound to consult with the Ahl al-Hall wa'l-'Aqd, but this consultation refers merely to points of detail in the application of the law and to matters not covered by it. All matters laid out explicitly by the law are beyond the purview of interpretation and consultation. This is all the more so with regard to Shari'a principles, which sets limits that neither rulers nor *ulema* may transgress. They likewise set the terms within the precinct of which any consultation must be conducted.

EXPLOIT DEMOCRACY?

Democracy may be a purveyor of moral dissolution and weakness. Yet the fact remains that resurgent Islam is usually unable to impose itself as a system of government through revolution or *coup d'état*. Its educational efforts have success but will pay off only in the long term. In the meantime, the situation appears to be getting worse as morality goes downhill and the market economy, which appeals to greed and instant gratification, surges. Violent action against regimes usually provokes ruthless repression.

Should the Islamists, then, have recourse to the much maligned electoral process when available? Despite the preachers' reservations with regard to 'rule by the ignorant majority', they answer with a resounding 'yes'. They may despise democracy but they are ready to exploit it in the pursuit of power.

Realities have a way of shaping positions. Hence the appearance of catch-phrases as launched in Algeria, 'Islamic state through the will of the people' (*dawla Islamiya bi-iradat ash-sha'b*). FIS leader, Rabah Kbir, now in exile in Germany, elaborated upon this slogan (in a sermon recorded in Oran in October 1991), but was ambiguous over whether it means a plurality of parties would be maintained under an Islamic state. he was likewise opaque about accepting the principles of alternating governments. 'God may deploy stratagems of deception against his enemies', he remarked.[30]

Other speakers are more forthright. Sheikh 'Abd ar-Rahman declares that it is sinful to sit alongside apostates in a parliament that does not abide by the Shari'a. Political parties would be a factor furthering dissension within the *umma* (nation), as evidenced by their fissiparous effect in the West.[31] Salah Abu Isma'il, who sat in one such parliament, holds that the Egyptian regime's slogan, 'In the name of God and in the name of the People' (*bismilla wa-bismi'sh-ha'b*) is totally oxymoronic. Yet he refuses to be drawn into a discussion of the Islamists in power.[32]

FREE SPEECH AND MINORITIES

The electronic preachers do not make general statements about intellectual and cultural pluralism, the sinews of democracy, but their chance comments on the subject give an idea of where they stand. Belhadj laid down a principle in early 1991, before the first round of the elections, that 'no anti-Muslim ideas may be aired in public' in the future Islamic state.[33] Kishk, in a sermon recorded in the early 1980s, fulminated against Mahmud Muhammad Taha, a Sudanese scholar and thinker whom he called a *dajjal* (imposter, Anti-Christ), on the grounds that his 'ideas woo hundreds of thousands [*sic*] in his native country.' Kishk feared, lest Egypt might also be contaminated by Taha's theories: to wit, that the authentic revelation was that of the Prophet's Meccan period; when Muhammad moved to Medina (in 622), he was transformed into a politician and had to make compromises; consequently, norms and precepts laid down there are not binding.[34] (Taha paid a heavy price for his iconoclastic approach to the holy texts: in 1985, the Sudanese dictator Numayri executed him for apostasy.)

A decade later, the same Kishk launched a venomous attack upon another alleged apostate, the Indo-British novelist Salman Rushdie, whom he depicted as the last link in a long chain of 'false Muslim conspirators'. That chain included, among others, Kemal Attaturk (said to have been a Jew masquerading as a Muslim, the better to subvert Islam) and, long before him, medieval Jewish 'false converts' to Islam, such as Ka'b al-Akhbar. Ghunayim tars Rushdie as 'an atheist' for claiming that the Prophet received revelations from Satan and that his wives whored around. Ghunayim is equally vituperative against those Muslim intellectuals (such as Naguib Mahfouz and Yusuf Idris) who defended Rushdie.[35]

The question of Christmas in Muslim lands provides more insights into the preachers' attitudes toward pluralism. They agree that the Christians cannot become fully-fledged members of the polity, due, above all, to the fact that they are nonbelievers, but also due to their role during the last century or so as conduits for 'cancerous' Western ideas (such as nationalism). The principle of equality before the law is not applicable here; they would enjoy *dhimmi* status, the legal category offered to monotheistic non–Muslims living in an Islamic state. This assures them of security of life, limb and property, but disbars them from military service and positions of authority (judges, ministers, top civil servants, and so forth). They may neither proselytize nor conduct religious activity in the public sphere.

The preachers' tone is unambiguous. Listen, for instance, to Sheikh Mahalawi:

> Before this Friday sermon, an official of the Religious Endowments Ministry came and gave me a paper containing instructions to preach on Islamic tolerance towards *dhimmis*. I protested against such dictates but I'll readily tackle the subject. Verily, Islam is, and has always been, tolerant with regard to *dhimmis*, yet on the condition that they know their place.

In contemporary Egypt, 'the Copts do not fulfil this condition and the state gives them free rein.' If Egypt has anti-Coptic riots,

> Which I [Mahalawi] do not condone but understand, this is in part because of the government's criminal negligence; has it not permitted them to build new churches, though there are more than enough of them in a country where over 90 per cent of the inhabitants are Muslims; has the regime not let them parade their religious affiliation in public (for example, crosses on car stickers and dresses), which is a sheer provocation to Muslims? Have our rulers not let the Copts store arms in churches and set up summer training camps?

The paragon of this 'Christian arrogance' is the UN Secretary-General Boutros Boutros-Ghali (whose sins include the Camp David Accords and the Bosnian tragedy).[36]

For Sheikh Kishk, such arrogance is personified by Pope Shenouda III, that 'American agent', and his assertive politics.[37] Kishk also delves into the past, claiming that there were no Christians among the political prisoners in 1955, 1965, 1974 and 1977, only true believers (namely the Muslim Brethren and its radical offshoots). Instead, many a Copt served on the staff of the military prisons. When Kishk was arrested in 1965, a Coptic prison doctor mocked him: 'How come you have pains in your joints if you can do the gymnastics of prayer?' Earlier crimes soon come to the preachers' minds: Coptic and Syrian collaboration with imperialism, their subversion of the Ottoman Empire (through Arab nationalism and missionary work), and their aid to the crusaders.

Ultimately, the sheikhs reach back to the original discord: Muhammad's disputation with fellow monotheists, where it is evident, according to Qattan, that the 'Christians are in a pretty bad way, though not as bad as the Jews'. To prove his point, both he and the Egyptian Muhammad Hasan sort out the Qur'anic polemics against Christianity: the spuriousness of the Trinity, the Resurrection, the Second Coming. The Crucifixion was a punishment meted out to Jesus because his disciples attributed divinity to him.[38]

Hasan hastens to draw what for him is the logical conclusion: as non-believers but monotheists, Christians are entitled to forbearance but should live on sufferance and pay the poll tax as a sign of their second-class status. In this he is joined by Sheikh As'ad Bayyumi at-Tamimi, leader of the Palestinian group Islamic Jihad: 'We are not against the Christians; they will have their rights according to the Pact of 'Umar', a reference to the seventh-century edict setting out the *dhimmi* status. Maronites who have transgressed the pact will receive their retribution from the Hetzbullah.[39]

Or listen to another popular cassette (and television) star, who occupies a grey zone between dyed-in-the-wool fundamentalist and conservative, Sheikh 'Umar 'Abd al-Kafi. How should one greet Coptic neighbours and fellow workers? He is asked in his Cairo mosque. 'Never be the first to greet', he advises, 'and when you do greet, just use the perfunctory "good morning", and not a more effusive salutation.[40] And above all, never, never go out of your way and give them your good wishes on their holidays, especially those related to the false beliefs such as Christ's Resurrection [i.e. Easter].' The point is clear: keep sociability to a minimum. In a meeting with a group of women, he answered in the negative a question by a student sharing a dormitory room with a Coptic girl on whether she can undress before the Copt at night. Says 'Abd al-Kafi: 'This is *haram* [forbidden], for it would be tantamount to male gaze being set upon you; it is an affront to your chastity.'[41]

Cairo cassette-shop owners attest to the popularity of tapes that claim to expose the 'secrets of the Coptic Church' (moral turpitude, conspiracies with foreign agents and missionaries); the sources for the stories are recent converts to Islam. And on a more strident note, 'Abd ar-Rahman seems to have rendered licit in a *fatwa* (religious opinion) the robbing of Coptic jewellers in Upper Egypt to finance the operations of armed Islamic bands. He may have also legitimized the killing of 'Coptic zealots'.[42]

Even in Algeria, where a minuscule number of Christians live, Belhadj finds time for theological polemics on Christology. In his typically pithy style, he concludes that in the future Islamic Algeria, their status will be in conformity with fourteenth-century treatise on *dhimmis* by Ibn Qayyim al-Jawaziya, a most restrictive interpretation of the rights of non-Muslims.[43]

CONCLUSION

No quarter for democracy: this is the verdict of the 30 most popular Sunni Islamist preachers. No quarter for pluralism, liberty and equality before the law either, unless subordinated to and constrained by the Shari'a. Their multitude of fans seem to concur.

Westerners debating the question of Islam and democracy would do well to listen to these voices, representing as they do the hegemonic discourse in the Islamist movement. When Islamists talk to each other rather than for external consumption, the talk is clearly and unambiguously anti-democratic. And so would be their behaviour should they seize power.

WHO'S WHO OF ISLAMIC PREACHERS ON CASSETTES

Jamal 'Abd al-Hadi: Egyptian historian and preacher.

'Umar 'Abd al-Kafi: Egyptian television preacher.

'Umar 'Abd ar-Rahman: Egyptian sheikh currently awaiting trial in connection with the World Trade Center bombing.

Salah Abu Isma'il: Egyptian Muslim Brother and former member of People's Assembly.

Nasir ad-Din al-Albani: Syrian scholar living in Saudi Arabia.

Hasan Ayub: Egyptian popular preacher.

Yusuf al-'Azm: Jordanian leader of the Muslim Brethren.

'Abdullah 'Azzam: Palestinian volunteer in Afghanistan, assassinated in Pakistan in 1989.

'Ali Belhadj: Algerian leader of FIS, now under house arrest.

Hamid al-Bitawi: Palestinian pro-Hamas preacher.

'Abd al-'Aziz Dweik: Palestinian pro-Hamas preacher.

Wajdi Ghunayim: Egyptian popular preacher.

Muhammad Hasan: Egyptian popular preacher.

Safar al-Hawali: Saudi theologian arrested in September 1994 for leading an alleged plot.

'Isam al-Iryan: Egyptian Muslim Brother, chairman of the Physicians' Association.

Harb Jabir: Palestinian Hamas leader.

Bassam Jarrar: Palestinian Hamas leader.

Rabah Kbir: Algerian leader of FIS, now in exile in Germany.

'Abd al-Hamid Kishk: Egyptian most popular Islamic preacher.

Ahmad al-Mahalawi: Egyptian popular preacher.

Fawzi al-Mahdi: Egyptian popular preacher and Coptic convert to Islam.

'Abd al-Basit Muhammad: Algerian secretary of FIS in the Oran region.

Ahmad Nawfal: Jordanian of Palestinian origin, leader of Jordanian Muslim Brethren.

Yusuf al-Qardawi: Egyptian thinker, now living in Qatar.

Ahmad al-Qattan: Kuwaiti preacher.

Muhammad Qutb: Egyptian thinker, now living in Saudi Arabia.

Ra'd Salah: Israeli Arab, mayor of Umm al-Fahm and leader of the Islamic movement in Israel.

As'ad Bayyumi at-Tamimi: Palestinian leader of the Islamic *Jihad*.

Fathi Yakan: Lebanese thinker, leader of Jama'at Islamiya.

'Abd as-Salam Yasin: Moroccan major thinker, under house arrest.

'Abd al-Majid Zindani: Yemeni leader

NOTES

1. Safar al-Hawali, *al-Aqabat al-Sab' l'il-Tawba*; idem, *Muqawwimat al-Mujtama' al-Muslim*; Hamid al-Bitawi, *Humum wa-Ma'asi al-Muslim al-Yawm*; 'Abd al-Hamid Kishk, no. 402.
2. Safar al-Hawali, *Qir'at min ad-Dasatir al-Arabiya*; Abdullah 'Azzam, *al-Ghiba*.
3. Ahmad al-Mahalawi, *al-Fina at-Ta'ifiya fi Misr*.
4. Ahmad Nawfal, *Utruhat*. '*Ibn Bosh*' can be translated as 'son of the rabble'; '*zift*' as 'annoying'.
5. Yusuf al-'Azm, *Aqlam Arabiyat al-Huruf Ajnabiyat al-Wala'*.
6. For examples, see John O. Voll and John L. Esposito, 'Islam's Democratic Essence', *Middle East Quarterly*, Sept. 1994, pp. 3–11.
7. 'Umar 'Abd ar-Rahman, *Shubuhat Hawla'l-Jihad*.
8. 'Abd al-Hamid Kishk, no. 314.
9. 'Umar 'Abd ar-Rahman, *Ulema al-Az'ar*. See also Harb Jabir, *La Ilah illah-llah wa Atharha fi'n-Nafs*; 'Abd as-Salam Yasin, nos 3, 30.
10. Ahmad al-Qattan, *Huquq al-Insan*.
11. 'Azzam, *al-Ghiba*; idem, *al-Hubb fi-llah*; 'Abd al Hamid Kishk, no. 37; 'Ali Belhadj, no. 9.
12. 'Abd al-'Aziz Dweik, *al-Mihal al-Amriki*; Ra'id Salah, *al-Quds wa-Makka*; Muhammad Qutb, *Dawr al-Mar'a*; Nawfal, *Utruhat*.

13. Safar al-Hawali, *Muqawwima*; Ahmad al-Qattan, *al-Afan al-Fanni*, no. 3.
14. 'Ali Belhadj, nos 5, 45.
15. Wadji Ghunayim, *Suluk al-Khatib*; idem, *Hijaz al-Mar'a al-Muslima*; Hasan Ayub, *Fi-l Mar'a*; Yusuf al-Qardawi, *Khutba fi-l Mar'a*.
16. Ahmad al-Qattan, *Tarbiyat al-Abna'*, no. 3.
17. Hawali, *Qira'at*.
18. 'Abd al-Hamid Kishk, no 395.
19. Salah Abu Isma'il, *al-Mukhattat al-Isti'mariya*.
20. 'Abd al-Hamid Kishk, *ath-Thalitha al-Kabira*; idem, *az-Zilzal*.
21. 'Ali Belhadj, *al-Amr bi'l-Ma'ruf*, no. 7/1.
22. Ahmad al-Qattan, *al-Fasad fi-Kuwayt*; idem, *Tarbiyat al-Abna'*, no. 5; idem, *Khutbat al-Mu'tamar al-Islami*.
23. Qattan, *Afan Fanni*.
24. Bassam Jarrar, *al-Quds wa'l-Aqsa*.
25. Qattan, *Afan Fanni*, no. 3; 'Azzam, *Aqlam*.
26. Nasir ad-Din al-Albani, *al-Amr bi-l-Ma'aruf* (4 cassettes); 'Ali Belhadj, nos 7/1, 7/6, 19, 42; Jamal 'Abd al Hadj, *Akhta' fi't-Ta'rikh*; 'Abd al Basit Muhammad, *Khutba*; Yasin, *al-Manhaj an-Nabawi* (series, 9 Cassettes).
27. Kishk, no. 395; 'Ali Belhadj, *at-Ta'a*; idem, no. 9.
28. 'Abd al-Hadj, *Akhta*.
29. 'Abd al-Hamid Kishk, nos 515/516.
30. Rabah Kbir, *Khutba*.
31. 'Abd ar-Rahman. *Shubuhat*; Isam al-Iryan, *al-Amal at-Tulabi al-Islami*.
32. Abu Isma'il, *Mukhattatat*. See also Hawali, *Qira'at*; 'Ali Belhadj, *Silsilat al-Jihad*, no. 2; idem, nos 7/6, 45.
33. Belhadj, no. 9.
34. 'Abd al-Hamid Kishk, no. 373; idem, *al-Radd'ala Rushdi*; Ghunayim, *'Uqubat*; see also 'Umar 'Abd al-Kafi, *Salman Rushdi*.
35. Mahalawi, *al-Fina*.
36. Ibid.
37. 'Abd al-Hamid Kishk, nos 410, 422.
38. Ahmad al-Qattan, *al-Tasammum fi Filastin*; idem, *Mujadala ma'a Nasrani*; Muhammad Hasan, *Salb al-Masih*.
39. Hasan, *Salb al Masih*; As'ad Bayyumi at-Tamimi, *Khutba*.
40. By the latter, 'Abd al-Kafi means *As-salamu 'alaykum*, a salutation reserved by many pious Muslims only for fellow Muslims.
41. 'Abd al-Kafi, *al-A'yad*; idem, *Dars li-l-Nisa'*. Same ruling on undressing in Ghunayim, *Hijab al-Mar'a*.
42. *I'tirafat Qasis* (anon., 3 cassettes); Fawzi al-Mahdi, *Kuntu Nasraniya*; 'Umar 'Abd ar-Rahman, *Tafsir Surat al-Kahf*.
43. 'Ali Belhadj, nos 15, 19, 38.

14

The Islamic Republic of Iran – a Warning Report[*]

A FORMER IRANIAN GOVERNMENT OFFICIAL

Once again new incarnations of the champions of despair and death are actively engaged in whittling away the achievements of the advocates of peace and well-being in Israel and the Arab World. Muslim criminals, chiefly the organizations known as Hamas and Hetzbullah, existing solely on sufferance of Iran and Syria, are making every effort to derail the peace process initiated by the courageous actions of the late Egyptian President, Anwar Sadat, and subsequently embraced by Menachem Begin, Yitzhak Rabin and King Hussein of Jordan.

It is clear to all that the Syrian President, Hafez el-Assad – like the so-called Arab 'Rejectionist Front' of the 1960s and 1970s – has never truly cared about the welfare of the Shi'ite community in Lebanon, nor has he been truly moved by the sight of Lebanese mothers clutching their children to their breasts and fleeing to safety. Hetzbullah and Hamas, as well as the Shi'ite and the Sunni communities of Lebanon and the West Bank, have been nothing more than pawns in Assad's endless and sinister games aimed at achieving hegemony for him over the entire Arab world.

The Lebanese, as well as the people of other problem-plagued Muslim nations, are all desperately seeking ways for their nations once again to become areas of trade and peace rather than areas of murderous warfare under the banner of Islam. However, the realization of this long-sought dream will only be possible if the *velayat-e-faghih* – the clerical leaders who also double as political leaders – are deposed, and their activities as murderers in the name of Islam are stopped.

Clearly, religious zealotry, particularly in its self-righteous form, poses the greatest danger to peace and security in the Middle East, and indeed, in all

---

[*] This article was written by a senior member of the Iranian establishment during the time of the Shah, who preferred to remain anonymous for various reasons.

other parts of the world as well. When I talk to people who find fault with the operations launched by the Israeli Army during Shimon Peres' term of office as Prime Minister, operations aimed at countering the excesses of the Hetzbullah terrorists in Lebanon, I always pose a simple question: What would you do if you happened to be the leader of a nation whose northern borders and all the inhabitants living along them, including women and children, were the target of indiscriminate bombing by agents of a third country located some 3,000 miles away?

In the long run, it is the Palestinians who have the most to lose from these murderous games played by the religious leaders of Hamas and Hetzbullah. Given what looks like a no-win situation, Israel will pull back to what I call 'Israel proper', or 'Fortress Israel', and will continue to survive as it has done during the many cycles of conflict in the past. If this scenario does indeed come to pass, then the Palestinian people will be robbed of their best chance for independence and statehood.

Earlier in this article, I mentioned the 'Rejectionist Front' of the late 1960s and 1970s. There were countries like Iraq, Libya and Syria, who, with the exception of Syria, had no common border with Israel. Both Libya and Iraq hardly played any role at all in the three major armed conflicts that took place between the Jewish state and its Arab adversaries. However, Iraq, Libya, and later, Syria, all devoted a sizable proportion of their national resources to fostering acts of terror against Israel in the international arena. In the 1990s, the countries that until then had belonged to the Rejectionist Front, were replaced by various terrorist organizations that took over the name of 'Rejectionist Front'. Among these rogue organizations, the main protagonists are Hamas, Hetzbullah, Islamic Jihad, and the Popular Front for the Liberation of Palestine.

As a pariah state in the international arena, Iran is the main force behind these organizations, supporting them with hardware such as Katyusha rockets, detonator timers, a variety of deadly explosives, as well as humanitarian aid such as medicine, food and money. According to reliable news reports, Iran spends a whopping half a billion dollars annually to sponsor acts of terrorism perpetrated by the 'Rejectionist Front' organizations. The chief beneficiary of Iran's help – which is dispatched to Lebanon by means of numerous flights of 747 Jumbo jets carrying weapons and ammunition – is Hetzbullah and, to a lesser degree, Hamas.

Attacks carried out by Hamas and Hetzbullah against targets inside Israel are coordinated and approved by high-ranking Iranian officials in meetings held in the Iranian Embassy in Damascus. It is highly unlikely that meetings such as these take place without representatives from Syria's intelligence apparatus. And even assuming there is no such representation, it is widely believed that the Syrians – like many other interested parties – have, in all probability, planted listening devices in the Iranian Embassy in Damascus, so that they are well-informed about terrorist operations planned by Hamas and Hetzbullah in the West Bank and Lebanon.

The most amazing aspect of this scenario is the fact that Iran, in its capacity as a rogue country, has been permitted by the international community to engage in large-scale acts of terror inside Israel and the surrounding countries, and to sabotage, successfully to date at least, all the prospects for a lasting peace between Syria and Israel. This in itself is vivid proof of the extent to which the perverted leaders of an oil-rich country like Iran are able to block the road to peace and prosperity for millions of people in other nations. The ultimate motives underlying Iran's continuing efforts to sabotage the peace process and the chances for a prosperous future for Arabs and Israelis alike, are a subject of conjecture by many leaders of public opinion.

There is no question about the fact that for over 40 years Iran has been actively involved in Lebanese politics. However, prior to the establishment of the world's only theocracy in Iran in 1979, the policies of the Shah of Iran toward Lebanon were confined to supporting the Lebanese Shi'ite community, and using it as leverage against the ever-increasing influence of the Palestinians – who had their own reasons for regarding the monarchy in Iran with contempt.

The Shah's limited, and mostly – though not exclusively – humanitarian, aid to Lebanon was handled and put into effect by the Iranian Foreign Intelligence service, which was a separate entity from what is commonly known as the SAVAK (although technically they both belonged to the same organization). As is the case with regard to many national intelligence services, Iranian Foreign Intelligence conducted a form of foreign policy in a number of countries around the world which, for a variety of reasons, were beyond the domain of the Iranian Foreign Ministry. Among the countries dealt with in this manner by Iran were Israel and South Africa (neither of which had full diplomatic relations with Iran), as well as the Iranian support for the Shi'ite community of Lebanon.

Before discussing the fascinating story of the cooperation between the Iranian and Israeli Intelligence services in Lebanon, it is important to discuss briefly the development of this cooperation between Iran and the Jewish State. Contrary to the smokescreen of politically motivated slogans and declarations emanating from both countries, Iran and Israel, more than any other two countries in the world, are bound together by a host of historical and geopolitical forces.

Ever since its establishment in 1948, and throughout its turbulent history of several full-scale wars with its Arab neighbours, Israel, as a geographically isolated nation, has made many efforts to develop friendly ties with a number of non-Arab countries in the Middle East and its periphery. Prominent among these were Iran, Turkey, South Africa and a number of black and North African nations. None of these countries, however, can match Iran in terms of its natural alignment with Israel.

Israeli relations with Iran have been guided throughout by forces of mutual historical interests and common destinies. The reality behind Iranian–Israeli ties are best described perhaps by Lord Palmerston's oft-quoted phrase: 'There are no permanent friends or permanent enemies; there are only permanent interests.'

One factor which is common to both Iran and Israel is their deep-rooted distrust of their Arab neighbours, and, indeed, of the Arab world as a whole. This is a historical fact that cannot be altered by any peace treaties signed between Israel and some of her Arab neighbours, nor by the current populist policies of the Islamic Republic of Iran epitomized by its support of mass demonstrations shouting 'Death to Zionism' or 'Death to America'. Indeed, systems of government come and go in Iran, leaving in their wake a tapestry of tumult and change in the nation's domestic and foreign policies, yet one factor remains unchanged both under the Shah and under the present Islamic regime: their common suspicion of the Arab world. This is the central thread that weaves together the destinies of Iran and Israel.

In the subsequent sections of this chapter, I will attempt to dissect the reasons and forces that drove Iran toward a policy of profound belligerency and intransigence *vis-à-vis* Israel and the West in the Middle Eastern arena. To begin with I would like to discuss the fundamental differences between Iran as a responsible member of the international community during the reign of the Shah, and its present status as a pseudo-revolutionary rogue state actively engaged in espousing and supporting acts of terror both within and beyond its own national boundaries. I have no doubt that this is a source of immeasurable chagrin and regret, both for the Democratic Party in the United States and the Labour Party in Britain, both of whose administrations were responsible for the reckless policies that led to the downfall of the Shah's regime in February 1979. My contentions here have absolutely nothing to do with the speculative stories and conspiracy theories that characterize the mentality of the majority of Iranians and others as to the reasons behind the overthrow of one of the West's staunchest allies in the Middle East. The scope and purpose of this chapter precludes a lengthy dissertation on my part on the developments and events that brought about the fall of the Peacock

Throne and the establishment of a dictatorial theocracy. Nevertheless, I have no intention of disregarding the highly sensitive developments that brought about a change for the worse in the life of the Middle East, through state sponsorship of an ongoing campaign of terror and death that seems to have no end in sight.

As an intelligence adviser to the Shah's regime, I observed with pain and disbelief the muddled thinking and faulty evaluations by the CIA under Stansfield Turner concerning the true state of affairs in Iran at that time. It is clear that under pressure from the enemies of the Shah in the United States Congress (Democratic senators, all openly opposed to the Shah because of what they believed – justifiably – was his support of the Republicans in both congressional and presidential elections), Jimmy Carter's administration arrived at the conclusion that replacing the monarchy in Iran with elements of Dr Mohammed Mossadegh's defunct National Front, would better serve American interests in a world still in the throes of the Cold War. I will not go into details concerning the *modus operandi* of CIA agents and the tactics they employed to remove the Shah from the political arena of the Middle East. Suffice it to say that had it not been for the hostile attitude of the American Intelligence community toward the Shah's regime, many of the disastrous events that occurred in the Middle East following the changing of the guard in Iran would not have occurred. Among these events we can count the Soviet invasion of Afghanistan in 1980; Iraq's prolonged military conflict with Iran, which left behind an orgy of death that claimed the lives of one million men who fell in the battlefields; Iraq's invasion of Kuwait in 1991 and the ensuing Gulf War (operation 'Desert Storm'); and the drastic changes in the religious–political infrastructure of Lebanon – a direct result of the ascendancy of the clerics in Iran – that gave birth to such militant groups as Hamas, Hetzbullah and the Islamic Jihad. Of particular importance to this study is the story of Hetzbullah in Lebanon.

One of the effective countermeasures that helped to check the excesses of Middle East terrorism in the 1970s was a network of intelligence cooperation between Israel and two non-Arab nations in the Middle East – Iran and Turkey. While Israel and Turkey have maintained their bilateral cooperation in many fields of covert cooperation, Iran is no longer a member of what was then known as TRIDENT. Ever since its inception, the Islamic Republic of Iran has adopted a policy of attacking anything that is in any way related to Israel. However, this policy of Iranian hostility towards Israel is both ironic and ludicrous since Iran considers the entire Arab world – with the exception of Syria – as its arch-enemy. This is tantamount to saying that with virtually no friends in the Arab world in general, and an unfriendly attitude toward Yasser Arafat and the Palestinians in particular, Iran continues – against the wishes of the Arab nations – to adhere to the now-obsolete slogan calling for 'the destruction of Israel'.

Outside the framework of TRIDENT, and chiefly through bilateral contacts between the top brass of the two nations' intelligence services, a great deal was achieved in the general campaign against subversion and acts of terrorism in the Middle East in the 1970s. Of particular importance, in this connection, is the two nations' spectacular cooperation in support of the Kurdish movement for autonomy within the boundaries of Iraq, and its side effect of sabotaging the offensive capabilities of the Iraqi regime of Saddam Hussein.

The heads of Israeli Intelligence made frequent visits to the mountain-top headquarters of Mulla Mustapha Barazani's fighters at Haji Omran, deep inside Iraqi territory. In some cases these visits took on the nature of daredevil adventures, fraught with real dangers. On a number of instances, the head of Israeli Intelligence, and his party of Israeli agents, escorted by armed elements of the Iranian Intelligence service, came under heavy Iraqi aerial bombardment. On at least one occasion, the rescue operation that was mounted to save teams involved in such cross-border operations was nothing short of miraculous.

The peace agreement signed by the Shah of Iran with Saddam Hussein during an Islamic conference in Algiers in 1974 was undoubtedly one of the greatest mistakes of his monarchy. The Shah's hasty peace with the Iraqis, at the expense of the aspirations of the Kurdish people, was concluded without any formal or informal consultations with the Israelis or the Americans, who had generously supported the Kurdish cause for almost 20 years.

The war stories related by the Iraqi military delegations dispatched to Teheran for peace talks, as well as their spontaneous expressions of joy and gratitude following the declaration of a ceasefire by the Kurds, made it very clear to what extent the armed conflict with the Kurds had rendered the Iraqi Army incapable, under any circumstances, of embarking on a second military adventure of any kind. Seven years after the signing of the Algiers peace agreement, which provided Iraq with the opportunity to build up its armed forces, the armies of Saddam Hussein crossed into Iran in an invasion that eventually left nearly a million soldiers dead, and almost the same number wounded and disabled. Ten years after its invasion of Iran, Iraq set out to realize yet another chapter of its expansionist dreams by invading and conquering Kuwait, an oil-rich Persian Gulf sheikhdom. Nearly a quarter of a million Iraqi soldiers lost their lives in the counter-attack of forces that became known as 'Desert Storm', a campaign which effectively destroyed Iraq's military potential and put an end to Saddam's expansionist fantasies.

I wonder if it would have been possible for Iraq to fight these two major wars had it not been for the Shah's ill-conceived desire for peace with a man like Saddam Hussein, whose sole mission in the world seems to be to drive millions of people to misery and deprivation.

Prior to the changes that overtook Iran in 1979, Israeli and Iranian Intelligence services ran a series of large-scale operations in those Middle Eastern countries that devoted vast resources to terrorism and subversion. For reasons best known to myself, I prefer not to divulge any details of these operations.

Israel and Iran also embarked upon a series of intelligence operations of a humanitarian nature. Of special significance in this series of joint operations was one whose main aim was to provide an escape route for a large number of Iraqi Jews who lived in fear under a regime of persecution against religious and ethnic minorities that was particularly blatant in relation to the Jewish community. To achieve the objectives of this operation, a number of Iraqis were recruited to serve as agents, with the help of the pooled resources of the Iranian and the Israeli Intelligence services. Establishing contact with the Jews living in different urban centres in Iraq had to be carried out with the utmost care. There was, indeed, no room for error. For over three decades the entire Iraqi population has been living under the watchful eyes of agents of the Iraqi Intelligence known as *Amnol-Aam*, the *Estekhabarat*. The slightest mistake in the planning and execution of the operation would have blown the cover of the entire effort, undoubtedly endangering the lives and livelihood of both the agents and the Jewish families whose only desire was to live in a land where they could practise their faith without fear of persecution.

After careful preparation, it was decided that the Jewish families who were to be brought out of Iraq, would dress up in traditional Kurdish garb in order to enable them to travel incognito between their cities and villages and the areas under Kurdish control. The families and their belongings were all turned over to agents of the Iranian–Israeli intelligence apparatus, who arranged to fly them out to Teheran. After a brief period of rest there, they were sent to Israel aboard El Al planes. Whereas on the surface there may be some similarity between the rescue of the Iraqi Jews and the rescue of the Ethiopian Jews years later, in fact there was a huge difference between these two operations. Mengisto Haile Mariam, the Marxist ruler of Ethiopia, was in constant contact with agents of the Israeli Intelligence services, and, indeed, Israel even maintained a small station of operations in Ethiopia. The state of affairs in Iraq was entirely different.

Under Mengisto Haile Mariam, Ethiopia was the protégé and staunch client of the Soviet Union in the Horn of Africa. During the darkest days of the deteriorating relations between Ethiopia and the West, a joint plan was drawn up by top personnel in the Iranian and Israeli Intelligence services to approach the Ethiopian leader with the purpose of moving him away from his affiliation to the Soviet camp. Israel's station chief in Teheran at that time was an intelligent hard-working agent known by his code-name 'Nassim' ('breeze' in Persian). Nassim's assignment was to explore and, if possible, reverse, Ethiopia's ever-increasing involvement with the Soviet Union. At an unusual meeting which Nassim managed to arrange with the Ethiopian leader in Addis Ababa, the Israeli agent reminded Mengisto of the time when the leader was an NCO in the Ethiopian Army of Emperor Haile Selassi, and in charge of the army's automobile pool. Nassim asked Mengisto, 'How on earth did you end up a Marxist?' To which the Ethiopian leader answered, 'I know nothing about Marxism, and the only reason that forced me to seek help from the Soviets is fear of Somalia (Ethiopia's neighbour), and the military hardware it is receiving from the United States.' The Israeli Intelligence officer pursued the issue further, and asked Mengisto, 'Do you think there may be ways to mend the fences between Ethiopia and the West by a new approach to the issue of military aid?' To which the Ethiopian leader said, 'Sure. Have the Americans deliver 54 tanks to my army, and I promise to kick the Russians out of Ethiopia overnight.'

Iran had pledged to pay whatever it might cost to get Ethiopia back into the Western camp. The year was 1974, and Gerald Ford was President of the United States. Immediately upon Nassim's return from his historic visit to the Horn of Africa, the United States was contacted via the special channels of the CIA. Every single member of the analytical departments of both the Israeli and the Iranian Intelligence services was convinced that in a very short time Ethiopia would be released from the tentacles of international communism. However, much to the astonishment of Iran and Israel, the Americans turned down this simple and inexpensive way of kicking the Russians out of the Horn of Africa. It was only after the collapse of the Soviet Empire in the early 1990s that Ethiopia once again normalized its relations with the West.

Not many of the joint operations launched by the intelligence services of Iran and Israel reached a cul de sac like the Ethiopian venture. In the majority of their joint operations, above and beyond what I described earlier concerning Iraq, the two countries had spectacular successes in their operations against terrorism and violence in the region.

Many observers speak of Israel's promotion of Hamas in the 1980s – as a counterweight against the PLO – in terms of a 'misguided' or 'ill-conceived' effort. These observers, however, forget the fact that at that time, the state of affairs in Israel and in the Arab world was totally different than it is today. These same observers forget (or perhaps, given the classified nature of much of this information, simply do not know) that Israel, together with Iran, bolstered the defensive and offensive capabilities of the Shi'ite community in Southern Lebanon, with a view to rendering ineffective Palestinian terrorist operations launched against Israel from this area close to Israel's northern border.

The joint military and humanitarian aid provided to the Shi'ite Muslims of Southern Lebanon by Israel and Iran produced only limited results – a failure due chiefly to corruption among the recipients of this aid (such as the Khalil family, and the Iranian ambassador to Lebanon), who pocketed the bulk of the aid. Indeed, the principal reason for the deep-rooted hatred felt by the Shi'ite Muslims in Lebanon toward the outside world (and Israel, in this respect, is only a scapegoat, a convenient target) is the fact that they have had to put up with decades of injustice and negligence which were forced upon them by their own corrupt leaders. What is more, for many years they were treated in their own country as second-class citizens by the Christian minority and the Sunni Muslims, both of whom relegated the Shi'ites to a marginal position in the local political hierarchy, leaving them only the relatively unimportant position of the Speakership in the Lebanese Parliament.

Moussa Sadre, an Iranian Muslim cleric from the holy city of Qum, some 124 kilometres south of Teheran, was an exception among Shi'ite leaders, who, for the most part, seemed bent on seeking their own personal benefits with little or no regard for either legal or moral boundaries. Sadre assumed the leadership of the Shi'ite community of Lebanon in the early 1960s, and quickly set about improving the plight of his followers by aligning himself both with the Shah's government in Iran, and with any other regime in the region which expressed a willingness to help the downtrodden Shi'ites in Lebanon.

Moussa Sadre was determined to keep the Shi'ites away from any alignments with political organizations whose sole aim, as it turned out, was the exploitation of the Shi'ites for their own short-term purposes, with no long-term benefits of any kind for their people.

Sadre's plans for improving the living conditions of the Shi'ites were dealt a serious, though not fatal, blow when an uninformed Shah turned against him as a direct result of plots hatched by an incredibly corrupt Iranian ambassador to Lebanon, and by Kazem Khalil, whose son was the Lebanese ambassador to Teheran. All of these events took place between 1971 and 1979, when Iran was about to fall prey to a host of other conspiracies against it, stage-managed by a number of Western powers.

The clerics who took over power from the National Front, against the wishes of the United States, had for a long time harboured dreams of manipulating the Shi'ite community of Lebanon for their own purposes. Moussa Sadre, as an honest and moderate leader of the Lebanese Shi'ites, was an obstacle to the realization of these dreams, and consequently plots were hatched to remove him from the political scene in Lebanon. I firmly believe that Muammar Ghaddafi did not, by any means, act alone in the ruthless assassination of Moussa Sadre. The train of events and the extraordinary developments that brought about the bloodbath in Lebanon which followed Sadre's murder, bear witness to the fact that Ghaddafi did not have much to gain by eliminating the spiritual leader of the Shi'ite community of Lebanon.

Moussa Chamran was an Iranian dissident during the Shah's reign. Together with a number of other Iranians, Chamran had received paramilitary training in Palestinian camps, mainly in Libya. He later became the Chairman of the Joint Chiefs-of-Staff of the Iranian armed forces under Ayatollah Khomeini. In 1971, seven years before the Islamic revolution, Chamran, with the approval of Moussa Sadre, had devoted himself to training a group of armed bodyguards in order to provide Sadre with protective security. This was the nucleus of an initially innocuous organization which, in the wake of Moussa Sadre's assassination, took on several different names, and eventually emerged as the Hetzbullah.

From the very beginning, Iran's fundamentalist regime has pursued a highly active and calculated role in an effort to manipulate the Lebanese Shi'ite militia to help further subversive Iranian aims in the region. Iran continues to this day to pursue this policy relentlessly, despite the fact that the entire world is now eagerly looking for a formula which will finally bring about a firm and lasting peace in the Middle East.

Most of the leading men and women of ideas in the world are, indeed, baffled by the West's low-key response, especially that of Iran's trading partners in Western Europe, to the ever-widening circles of subversion endorsed by the Islamic regime in order to derail the peace process through its support for a host of terrorist organizations operating in the area. The United States is almost totally isolated in its vehement anti-Iranian rhetoric and actions, as opposed to Japan, France, Germany and, to a lesser extent, Britain, which cynically pursue their own advantages by disregarding the trade restrictions imposed on Iran by the United States. In this manner, through trade relations and economic cooperation, they actually contribute to the perpetuation of a pariah regime. Indeed, in the absence of a military solution that might tame the extremist policies of the Iranian regime, economic sanctions, if carried out rigorously, could be of great value in checking the excesses of Iran's intractable foreign policy. In 1951 all the British had to do to destabilize the nationalist regime led by Dr Mohammad Mossadegh, was to station two warships in the mouth of the Bab el-Mandab in the Indian Ocean, thus effectively blockading Iranian exports of oil to other countries. As a result, Iran's financial reserves disappeared, and for a period of six months the Government was unable to pay its employees, both civilian and military. This situation, directly brought about by the British embargo, led to widespread public discontent, to the extent that one year later, in 1953, the CIA succeeded in provoking the military and some segments of the civilian population to stage a revolt against the Mossadegh Government and replace it with a pro-Western administration.

The dramatic changes that have taken place in the fabric of world affairs over the past few years, and major ethical considerations, might make it difficult, if not altogether impossible, to re-enact the same scenario now, on the threshold of the twenty-first century. However, the highly effective weapon of a world-wide embargo on Iranian oil, as the only means of exerting pressure on the clerical regime in Iran, should not, in any way, be under-estimated. To offset the huge impact of a world without Iranian oil, and to prevent public discontent in the West following a dramatic hike in the price of gasoline at the filling stations, the world's leading economists must devote time and energy to working out satisfactory alternatives to Iranian oil exports. In the Persian Gulf area, Saudi Arabia might be persuaded to increase its daily output; help could also come from the looming re-entry of Iraq into the international oil markets. Since Iraq is committed by the provisions of the 1991 ceasefire to spend oil revenues under strict United Nations super-vision, it is unlikely that it could spend these potential oil revenues on the production of weapons of mass destruction. A closely supervised re-entry of Iraq into the international oil market could, in all probability, ease the difficulties that might arise from a total embargo on Iranian oil.

An international naval blockade of Iran, with or without the blessing of the United Nations, aimed at depriving this pariah country of its petrodollars, remains, apparently, the only way the international community can check the excesses of a regime which is the main source of inspiration and financial backing to terrorist organizations and countries dedicated to state-sponsored terrorism. There is absolutely no doubt that any change in the Iranian regime, or in the implementation of its extremist doctrines, could have a tremendous impact on those organizations and countries involved in international terrorism with Iranian help and encouragement. Faced with a Middle East without Iran and its vast investment of petrodollars in terrorism and acts of subversion, Syria, with its secular system of government, would lack the necessary resources single-handedly to support and finance the Hetzbullah, the Hamas, or the Islamic Jihad. The greater part of Syria's bargaining power in its on-again off-again peace talks with Israel is based on the activities of the Hetzbullah, which is the creation of the Islamic Republic of Iran. This is not to say that in the event of a peace agreement between Israel and Syria, and without Iranian support, the Hetzbullah will cease to exist. The so-called 'Party of God' still enjoys a degree of support in the Shi'ite community in Lebanon. However, deprived of its financial and inspirational support from Iran, the Hetzbullah is likely to lose much of its clout as an effective paramilitary organization.

Iran's negative influence on the peace process between Israel and Syria is not the only reason that warrants the creation of a united front by the Western powers for the purpose of destabilizing the Islamic Republic of Iran. The Iranian Intelligence services, together with the Revolutionary Guards, are actively involved in perpetrating terrorist conspiracies covering extensive areas of the globe, ranging from the Middle East to North Africa, the Balkans, Western Europe and even such unlikely regions as Argentina in South America. Iran supports, both ideologically and financially, the terrorist training camps in Sudan. It also supplies Hetzbullah, Hamas and the Islamic Jihad with small arms, explosives and money, not only to sabotage the prospects of peace in the Middle East, but also to create turbulence and instability in moderate Arab countries. The fundamentalist clerics of Iran are the source of support, of all kinds, to Shi'ite and various dissident groups in Saudi Arabia and other Persian Gulf states, particularly the United Arab Emirates and Bahrain. And the list of evil policies pursued by Iran is not limited to all we have mentioned above. The intelligence services of the Islamic Republic of Iran have been, and still are, systematically involved in a campaign of murder and terror directed against Iranian members of dissident groups in other countries. Interpol has recorded well over 500 murders committed by agents of Iranian Intelligence in Turkey, England, France, Italy and the United States since the emergence of the fundamentalist Islamic regime in Iran in 1979. Almost all the Western countries, on whose soil these ruthless killings have been perpetrated, have looked the other way and allowed the terrorism of the Iranian clerics to continue with impunity. For obvious reasons, it seems that Western Europeans place much greater emphasis on economic gains by means of trade with Iran than on the ideals of freedom and human dignity which they claim to espouse as the foundations of European culture.

Inside Iran itself, not a day passes without some innocent person being put to death by the authorities. Reports by human rights organizations, such as Amnesty International and the United Nations' Human Rights Commission, are replete with harrowing stories about large numbers of Iranian dissidents who have been put to death by firing squads on trumped-up charges of drug trafficking. In mid April 1996, the Revolutionary Guards threw a 19-year-old boy to his death from the balcony of an 18-storey apartment building in the western section of Teheran. Apparently the boy was celebrating his nineteenth birthday with a number of friends and classmates, and his only crime was that the neighbours in the building complained about the music the youngsters were playing at the party. Almost all the wire services, as well as the BBC, covered this heinous act of the Iranian regime. Following this summary execution, 20 boys and girls, friends of the victim, were arrested and imprisoned without charge. Their crime? Disappointed when local media refused to send a correspondent to cover the story, the victim's friends contacted news services inside and outside Iran, hoping to be able to show the world a small example of the criminal behaviour of the Islamic Republic toward its own citizens. This was, indeed, a minor story compared with other appalling crimes committed repeatedly by agents of Iranian Intelligence and disciplinary forces.

It is now common knowledge that the fundamentalist regime of Iran has embarked upon a feverish campaign to develop home-grown weapons of mass destruction. Reports provided by spy satellites speak of intensive, massive construction efforts being made by the Iranian to dig tunnels and cavities deep inside the southern mountain ranges, in the vicinity of the Gulf of Oman and the Persian Gulf. There is little doubt that Iran's intentions in digging these tunnels is to hide, and safeguard from aerial attacks, weapons of mass destruction such as improved versions of the Scud missiles (now mostly manufactured and altered in Iran, thanks to technological help from North Korea, China and Russia), as well as chemical and biological warheads. Iran has already acquired all the technological know-how it needs to manufacture inside Iran all its requirements of small arms and the outdated but still effective Katyusha rockets. Iran has also amassed an impressive array of military hardware, purchased from China, North Korea, Russia and some East European countries badly in need of Iran's petrodollars.

No sane country would spend such phenomenal sums of money on armaments if it didn't entertain certain nightmarish dreams of armed conflicts. At the present moment, Iran does not seem to be in any imminent danger of another invasion like the one launched across its borders by Iraq. In the aftermath of the Gulf War, the Iraqi Army is still in total disarray. With its air force paralysed following massive losses of aircraft during the War, and the declaration of its northern and southern sectors as 'safe havens' and 'no-fly zones', Iraq is likely to enter the twenty-first century without the military stamina to venture another armed conflict with a country the size and strength of Iran.

This being the case, who, then, are Iran's enemies? What kinds of threats to its existence does Iran intend to neutralize by means of such weaponry as

Russian submarines and Scud missiles, Chinese Silkworm missiles and biological weapons of mass destruction? What are the reasons behind the amazing similarities between the arms build-up in Iran and Libya?

To answer these vexing questions, one must take into account the fact that Iran, ever since the fundamentalist clerics seized power, has proven its steadfast interest in fomenting crises and diplomatic problems for the West, chiefly the United States. Once we understand this premise, we can easily come to the conclusion that there is every indication that Iran is likely to involve itself in a military adventure aimed at disrupting the vital flow of oil to Western Europe, the United States and Japan, by making navigation unsafe in the extremely vulnerable waterways of the Persian Gulf. In the absence of a United States naval presence, Iran even has the capability of disrupting safe navigation in the nearby Gulf of Aden and Bab el-Mandab.

What is most amazing in all this is the absence of any response from the West *vis-à-vis* this bleak prospect. There are many opinion-makers who believe that an eventual confrontation with Iran is inevitable. However, it seems as though the West, led by the United States, seems to be more concerned with the little mischiefs perpetrated by Ghaddafi than with the frightening long-range ambitions of a regime that has effectively taken Western civilization hostage by trampling on the rights of others. Postponing an effective and serious confrontation with this Iranian threat, not necessarily by military means, will only serve to exacerbate the situation by increasing the dimensions of the potential threat posed by Iran to the vital interests of the community of nations.

The hounding of the Shah by Western media in the 1970s, which expressed itself in stories that often bordered on the ghoulish, together with the ill-conceived policies of the Carter Administration, effectively paved the way for the ascendancy of the Mullahs in Iran. I can only hope, at this point, that Western print and electronic media, as well as human rights organizations and, of course, the Western powers led by the United States, will demonstrate the same missionary zeal with which they overthrew the Shah to let the Iranian theocrats realize that, should they continue their relentless pursuit of evil in the name of Islam, their days as the masters of Iran are numbered.

15

Russian Intelligence: The Jewish Connection and the Challenges of Peace

A SENIOR ISRAELI INTELLIGENCE OFFICER

HISTORICAL BACKGROUND

The first professional and organized form of intelligence system in Russia was created during the reign of Ivan the Terrible. Its creation was part of sweeping reforms introduced by the Tsar in order to consolidate his hold over the country, and to reap the greatest possible political and economic benefits from his rule.

What he created was an intelligence system that functioned mainly as a highly organized and – in the terms of those times – a very efficient secret police force. This system remained more or less unchanged until the time of Peter the Great, who introduced improvements into the system as part of his move toward modernization and greater exposure of Russia to the West.

It was in the days of Peter the Great that Russia spread throughout Europe an intelligence network which functioned along the lines we know today. In each of the important European countries he placed what was called in Russian a *rezident*, a term used to this day in intelligence circles to denote the head of a local bureau. His duties were to gather information on military, political, economic and diplomatic activities, and report on them directly to the Head of State. At that time, this was part and parcel of the duties of ambassadors everywhere. In fact, every Russian ambassador in the West was an intelligence agent, who carried out intelligence operations on instructions from his government, and in the service of his government's policies.

It was during that same period in the eighteenth century, that, for the first, time Military Intelligence was separated from Political Intelligence. The former operated then as it does today, within the framework of the Russian General Staff.

*Trans. David Zinder.

At the time, this system was regarded as one of the best of its kind. It included a section (added during the time of Catherine the Great after the failure of the Pugachev coup) that had no counterpart in the West: a political Secret Police force whose function it was to operate against dissidents opposed to the Empress' regime. Thus from the time of Catherine the Great in the nineteenth century, the Russian Intelligence system comprised a foreign intelligence network based on operational branches set up in the various countries, military intelligence directly subordinate to the General Staff, and a political Secret Police force.

Some of the finest minds in Russia served the intelligence services of those days. Among them, for example, was the renowned geographer Prezhavelski, who used his frequent trips abroad as a cover for missions on behalf of his employer – Military Intelligence. Another such example was the famous writer, Turgenyev, who was one of the better Russian Intelligence agents. These and others joined voluntarily to serve the Russian Intelligence system.

Bismarck, who was Prussian Ambassador to Russia during 1852–62, made special mention in his memoirs of the high professional standard of the Russian counter-intelligence service which oversaw all the foreign missions in Moscow.

It was in the field of the secret service – the political police – designed to monitor activities carried out by opponents of the Government, that the Russian Intelligence system reached its highest level. The main impetus for its creation came, as we have noted, after the Pugachev rebellion. In 1814 Tsar Nicholas I established a special unit in the Tsar's office called Tartaya Opravlenia – the Third Directorate, that was directly responsible for the activities of the political detective system.

In a manner reminiscent of what has happened there during the past ten years, Russia underwent a period of extensive liberalization towards the end of the last century, during which time the Third Directorate was abolished, though the Secret Police remained intact. As the one department was abolished, a different department was created in the Gendarmski Opravlenia, called Akherna. This is a well-known phenomenon in intelligence circles, when, in the course of a move toward liberalization, two new services are created to take the place of one that has been terminated. These are usually designed to compete among themselves for the best results.

According to a report written by the French Ministry of the Interior in 1903, the Russians succeeded in deploying a widespread intelligence system – through the services of Military Intelligence, the Third Directorate and the Akherna. The French report noted, too, that the first branches of Russian Intelligence in the United States had been set up, and have been functioning there ever since. Russian Military Intelligence was not far behind in its development, and consequently, shortly before the outbreak of the First World War, Russia had the largest and most advanced intelligence system in the world. Generations of Russian leaders maintained the firm belief that a strong country requires a strong intelligence system so as to retain its position of strength in the international arena. This has been a guiding principle of Russian policy up to the present day.

All this raises the obvious question: if their intelligence was so good, how are we to explain the success of the 1917 Revolution in toppling the House of Romanov? The fact is that, according to all accounts, the various branches of the Russian Intelligence system of the time were actually very effective in their counter-revolutionary operations, and succeeded in identifying the various subversive movements, and Secret Police agents penetrated those that were regarded as potentially dangerous to the regime. It was not the intelligence system that collapsed in 1917, rather it was the regime and its system of government that collapsed.

THE CONCEPT OF INTELLIGENCE AND CHARACTERISTICS
OF THE SERVICES

Anyone involved in Intelligence is well aware of the various professional problems one finds in the field. One of the main problems is the way in which the political echelons view and treat intelligence. In other words, the extent to which the political echelons rely on intelligence, and use the available intelligence systems on a regular basis.

Historically speaking, it could be said that the political power culture in Russia is based on a strong reliance on intelligence systems, regarding them as a highly important element in its survival, security and the development of its policies. This attitude is more pronounced in Russia than in the democratically-based West – even among the less democratic Western countries.

Ever since the eighteenth century, Russian political systems have relied extensively on intelligence, and effectively integrated it into their policy-making processes. Today, the Russian Intelligence concept is based on the understanding that intelligence must serve the country's national security. The concept of 'national security' is the constant variable, i.e. what is included in it and what is not at any given point in time. In today's Russia, national security is a very broad concept, and includes political, diplomatic, social, economic, military, ecological and scientific matters, as well as the safeguarding of the intellectual and spiritual values of the nation.

The Russian Intelligence systems are supposed to serve national security, and those national interests that constitute national security are the guiding force behind the intelligence services' activities. These include foreign interests outside Russia as well. In these cases a special service is assigned to each such area, and charged with a single objective: finding solutions solely for the issues involved in its area of responsibility.

In Russia there is no such thing as 'the intelligence community'. What does exist is the concept of many different 'special services', custom-made to deliver solutions for a particular aspect of a larger issue of national security, or for the issue itself in its entirety.

The second characteristic of the Russian intelligence system is that it conceives of the world as being composed of two opposing systems: Russian and Western. Thus the world and its conflicts are understood as a perpetual power struggle between the two. Cooperation does exist between the two systems, but their relationship also involves a large measure of mutual sabre-rattling. There is no ideal balance, but rather a constant struggle between two sides, and the nature of their cooperation is the result both of their absolute military strength, and their power relative to each other.

The Russians have reached the conclusion that today, more than at any time in the past, a major factor in the relative power of any country is its scientific/technological potential. This potential, they believe, far out-strips that of traditional power-factors. The future, so the thinking goes, belongs to those who know how to develop and realize their intellectual/technological/scientific potential. The Russians still set great store by their military systems, but their significance, relative to their scientific/intellectual potential, is dropping steadily in their esteem. According to the Russian concept, the growth of a modern country's power is based, for the most part, on development in the areas of economy, science and technology, and any major power intent on making progress and retaining a position of strength must maintain an edge over other countries in these fields in order to do so.

Today Russia sees itself as a society that is making every effort to transform itself from an industrial society to a technological/scientific one. This transformation is virtually the sole condition for entering the twenty-first century and retaining the status of a major power. On the other hand, the Russians also feel that should a major internal crisis occur inside Russia itself, the countries surrounding it will exploit its temporary weakness and take action against the ailing power.

The Russians also believe that the military confrontations that have erupted in various areas of the country have not been caused by military circumstances of any kind, but stem rather from social and economic problems. The events in Nagorno-Karabakh were the outcome of socioeconomic problems, specifically related to large-scale unemployment, that were channelled into violence and warfare.

The reasons for the war in Chechnya were not purely economic, but were rather linked to black market profiteering. This caused the outbreak of violence that turned into a war which claimed the lives of over 100,000 soldiers and civilians.

These two examples underline the Russian concept of 'national security' and its broad range of applications. It is in the service of this 'national security' that the intelligence services carry out their duties. By definition, each special service functions on behalf of state interests and security, both domestically and abroad. Their aim is to provide the head of state with reliable and objective information on their area of responsibility. As they see it, this information is of vital importance to the leaders of the state in order for them to make their policy decisions.

The special services are a breed apart from the other governmental systems, in that they employ unconventional means, and include covert activities, while at the same time benefiting from eased restrictions that allow them to recruit operatives from other organizations and to function under the cover of other official bodies.

According to the Russians, in a modern society the concept of 'national security' is constantly expanding, as is the domain of 'national interests' and their number. The upshot of all this in practical terms is that the number of secret services and the extent of their responsibilities multiply in direct proportion to the expansion of state interests. And indeed, this is the situation today – the number of intelligence services functioning in Russia is greater than ever before, and they operate in a great many areas – far more than the KGB did in its heyday.

Another aspect that has always characterized all of Russia's intelligence services is their direct subordination to the head of the country's political system – the head of state. Authority over these services has never been delegated to a particular minister or, indeed, to the government as a whole. Consequently, the head of the KGB was, in fact, the second most powerful man in the country. This was the case while the Soviet Union still existed in its previous form. At that time, it was assumed that the mere existence of so many secret services, secret police units and detective forces, would be sufficient to ensure the continuity of power in the Soviet Union. And in fact, it was these secret service bodies that enabled the regime to last as long as it did. The Communist regime in Russia did not collapse because of inept or insufficient intelligence. The collapse of Communist Russia was a replay of the story of 1917 – the collapse of a massive political structure despite the continued efficacy of its intelligence apparatus. The KGB submitted precise and professionally astute assessments, and made the right operational moves, but the political echelon failed in its reading of the situation. It either did not know how to exploit the intelligence material submitted by the services, or refused to do so, and, through political weakness, brought about the collapse of the superpower and its disintegration into so many different countries. And all this despite the existence of one of the best intelligence services in the world.

Another of the dominant characteristics of the Russian Intelligence services is their centralized control. Up until the 1990s, with the breakdown of the Soviet Union and the consequent dismantling of the KGB, all Russian Intelligence services were concentrated under one administrative roof. This guaranteed a higher degree of efficiency and better cooperation and integration of service functions than almost anywhere in the West. It ensured tighter control over the services by the political echelons, and prevented any possible danger to the regime from the intelligence apparatus itself. During the entire Soviet era up to 1994, ten reform programmes were carried out in the intelligence system, five of which took place during 1991–94, causing serious damage to the system in the process. The other five reforms took place over an extended period – from the Revolution in 1917 to 1991.

The intelligence organization in Russia was a dual, two-headed, system, serving the country on the one hand and the party on the other. Employees of the organization had to be adept at working in both fields. Thus, for example, Khruschev was deposed only after the head of the KGB gave his support to the men who eventually ousted him.

For the outside observer, the danger of a rampant politicization of intelligence in this kind of system rears its head all too clearly. However, Russian organizational culture has always functioned in a dual framework – state and ideology, under the direct control of the head of the governmental–ideological system.

Before it was dismantled in 1991 the KGB numbered 420,000 employees. In this respect, we must take into account that the Soviet Union was an international superpower with the longest borders in the world and far-flung global interests. And yet, despite the fact that the Soviet Union has been replaced by a much smaller Russia, there are more people now working in the various organizations that replaced the defunct KGB, than there were at the height of its power. The service that gained the most from the demise of the KGB was the Foreign Intelligence service – the SBR. The head of this organization, who had previously been the head of one directorate within a larger system, was promoted to the position of head of a large organization responsible solely to the President. All the other components remained more or less unchanged, and, periodically, questions are raised about possible reforms to reduce their number.

When East German super-spy Marcus Wolf was asked to comment on the relative merits of unification or separation in the intelligence organizations, he suggested that there should be a single unified system to prevent unnecessary complications. But he believed that on the operational level, each unit should remain totally autonomous.

From all the above, and based on historical precedents and the Russian concept of intelligence, we can say that despite the great changes that have occurred in Russia over the past three years – changes in leadership and functions – the professional traditions of the Russian Intelligence services have remained virtually intact.

In the same way as the intelligence services of the Soviet Union managed to absorb, internalize, and improve on the intelligence systems of Tsarist Russia, so present-day Russia has preserved the intelligence traditions of its immediate predecessors. To this we might add that despite all its problems, the Russian regime surpasses those of the West and Israel in its understanding of how to rely upon and use the fruits of intelligence activities to the best possible advantage.

THE QUESTION OF THE PRESS

An issue that surfaces from time to time, but has never been described in any great detail, is the use Russian Intelligence services have made of journalists in the past and present, and will no doubt continue to do in the future. According to available data, some 50 per cent of the Soviet Union's undercover agents have used journalism as their cover. What is more, some 50 per cent of all those recruited by Russian Intelligence services in other countries were journalists. Journalists have easy and 'kosher' access to sources of information, to political systems and to many sectors of the population. The Russians understood this well, took advantage of it in the past and, as far as we know, are still exploiting it today. Another aspect of the use Russia has made of the news media is an area in which the Russians are *nonpareil* – disinformation. Journalists who worked for them managed to introduce information into the press that was aimed at influencing political and diplomatic processes. They did this more or less blatantly, depending on the circumstances, and in a most professional manner. The fact is that overall, they placed great store by the benefits that could be reaped from such operations and, in all likelihood, will continue to employ this tactic in the future as well.

There was an unusual example of this use of disinformation by the Russians at the beginning of the 1990s. At that time, the Government introduced a new policy to prevent the drain of capital from Russia. The KGB developed and put into action a plan to use its agents to disseminate news items throughout the West indicating that Russian businessmen involved in smuggling capital out of Russian and into the West were in fact connected to the KGB, the underworld and the Mafia. The entire operation was superbly orchestrated, and repercussions of this unusual disinformation campaign still resurface from time to time in the media.

RUSSIAN INTELLIGENCE AND THE JEWS

Under Tsarist rule, Jews were totally excluded from any kind of intelligence activity. The first time Jews were included in the recruitment efforts of the intelligence services, and actually participated in operational activities, was when the intelligence services combed the anti-Tsarist revolutionary movements for potential agents.

After the 1917 October Revolution, the Jews became the most significant national minority inside the new Russian Intelligence services. The reasons for this were, on the one hand, their absolute loyalty to the new Communist regime following their cruel oppression under the Tsars, and, on the other, their inherent quickness of mind and intellectual flexibility. Thus it happened that in the first years after the Revolution, a large number of Jews – a much larger percentage than their relative proportion in the population – were enlisted into the Soviet Intelligence services. Jews were recruited both by the Foreign Intelligence services and the internal security services. The infamous *gulags*, or work-camps, were conceived and put into effect, for the most part, by Jewish officers. Russian Intelligence also sought out Jewish recruits in target countries because of their command of languages, their independence from, or lack of loyalty to, their countries of residence, and their ideological affinity to communist thinking. The first wave of recruitment was based primarily on ideology, and extensive intelligence reports have been found which were written by Jewish agents working for Soviet Intelligence. This honeymoon between Soviet Intelligence and the Jews came to an end after the Second World War. Even during the war with the Nazis, a policy was introduced to block the advancement of Jews in the intelligence services, and to cease recruiting Jews altogether. Nevertheless, and in spite this policy, even after the war, Jews could be found in many key professional positions in the services.

As late as the 1990s, there were still a number of high-ranking KGB officers, up to the rank of general, who were of Jewish descent. The present Foreign Minister of Russia, and former head of Foreign Intelligence – the SBR – Yevgenyi Primakov, is Jewish. He was born Yevgenyi Kirschblatt in Kiev. The former head of the KGB and, briefly, Chairman of the Communist party, Yuri Andropov, was descended, on his mother's side, from a Jewish family from the Caucasus.

While the Jews were an important factor in the Soviet and Russian Intelligence services, they also, for a while, became a target of these services. Up until the Second World War the Russians paid little attention to the Jews. After the war, and particularly after the establishment of the State of Israel, Soviet interest increased, particularly regarding those Jews who found their way to the scientific, technological and social elites of the Soviet Union, and in relation to the newly-established Jewish state that had aligned itself with the West. The Russian position was not based on anti-Semitism as such, but on the fact that this group had become a factor that demanded the attention of the security services. The Russian Intelligence services had always maintained an ideological department. Prior to the Second World War it was called 'Z Department'. After the war it was incorporated into the Second Directorate, which was responsible for counter-intelligence. In 1967, a directorate designed to combat nationalist and ideological subversion was re-established, and it included a separate Jewish Department. The person who set up this department eventually rose to become Deputy Chief of the KGB, a fact which underscores the quality and status of the personnel dealing with Jewish/Israeli affairs. In retrospect, the Russians understood that had they in 1948 allowed the emigration of 10,000–20,000 Jews who were in any way connected to Zionism or to Israel, they might have been able to nip in the bud the later development of Zionist activities in the Soviet Union, and would have prevented foreign elements from inciting Jews inside and outside the Soviet Union to take action against the regime. The Russians made a crucial error when they underestimated the relative strength of the Jewish people inside Russia, and did not deal with – and deport – the hard core that later developed into the Zionist movement in that country. To this day the intelligence services and the leadership in Russia have consistently misread the inherent strength of the national aspirations of its Jewish minority. At the same time, efforts – however flawed – made by the State of Israel, and the struggle of the Jews themselves, brought about a solution to the problem in a manner that was consistent with Zionist goals, and a far cry from designs of the Russian regime.

The Russians regarded the Jews' Zionist activities as dangerous because they turned the Jews into well-organized groups, fired by ideology and motivation that were not in keeping with official government policies, thus creating a dual loyalty. The Russians saw these developments as dangerous from the point of view of intelligence as well, fearing that the Jews might be used by foreign espionage services for purposes of intelligence-gathering. As a result, Jews were targeted in the same way as other minorities (e.g. the Chinese, the Germans, etc.) whose homeland was outside the Soviet Union.

CONCLUSION

It may be clearly stated that the tradition of Russian Intelligence today, is the outcome of operational patterns determined even before the 1917 Revolution. Over the years, changes have been made and improvements introduced, but nevertheless, these patterns have remained essentially the same.

Right from the outset, the Russians developed their secret police in order to uncover, penetrate and prevent activities by opponents of the regime. In Russian culture, the intelligence services have always been regarded as serving national security. Their form, size and numbers are determined in direct relation to the definition of national security at any given point in time. Today, on the face of it – at least by Western standards – the overall volume of intelligence activity in the world, and the concomitant number of its targets, have both been reduced. This, however, is not the case in Russia. Indeed, in Russia, the concept of 'national security' has expanded, and includes all political, diplomatic, military, economic, technological and social activities. As involvement in issues of national security expands, the various intelligence bodies reorganize themselves to cover that particular area, and provide the decision-makers with the best and most reliable information that can be of any help to them.

In all the upheavals that have marked modern Russian history from the time of the Tsars to this day, it cannot be said that Intelligence failed or misled the leaders. It was not Intelligence that collapsed, but rather the regimes themselves, regimes that did not know how to deal with the reality they were facing.

The Russians believe they failed politically and practically, in their struggle against the Jewish minority in the country – a minority that served as an important core of intelligence officers immediately following the October Revolution. Despite the fact that up until the Second World War Jews served in key positions in intelligence, they were afterwards treated as potential enemies. However, although the danger presented by the Jews to the Soviet regime had been identified, the authorities did not take the necessary steps to block the campaign for the Jews of Russia that was mounted outside the Soviet Union. Nor did they deal effectively with the expanding circles of proponents of the Zionist ideal inside the Soviet Union.

16

Secret Contacts for Peace: A Lost Opportunity*

ME'IR AMIT

INTRODUCTION

At the end of the War of Independence, the leaders of the Arab countries had no choice but to concede defeat. It was difficult for them to accept, but the reality was inescapable. The great hopes they had entertained had disintegrated into a wasteland that swallowed up all their dreams and expectations. They were deeply disappointed and the open wounds left by their defeat were a never-ending source of vexation and frustration.

King Farouk attempted to learn a lesson from the failure of his expeditionary force, and to correct the distortions and mistakes that had brought it about. In order to do so he enlisted the help of experts who had served in the German Army during the Second World War. Among the most prominent of these were General Fehrmbacher, an artillery officer; Dr Wilhelm Fuss, a former director of the Hermann Goering Munitions Factory during the Third Reich; Rolf Engel, an expert on missiles; and Dr Paul Gorke, whose specialties were radar, electronics and navigation systems.

It is important to point out that Egypt was at that time in the throes of severe internal turmoil. Many army officers refused to accept the outcome of the 1948 war with Israel, and began plotting to topple Farouk from his throne. As these revolutionaries saw it, Farouk bore full responsibility for the military defeat. They also believed that widespread corruption at all levels of Egyptian society had weakened the country and undermined the effectiveness of the army.

Initially the leader of the revolutionaries was General Muhammad Naguib, but it later transpired that he was no more then a puppet placed there by the true leader of the coup: Gamal Abdul Nasser.

---

*Trans. David Zinder.

In Israel there was hope that this group of officers could eventually become a partner for negotiations and constructive cooperation between Israel and Egypt. Several mediators were sent to Egypt through the good offices of the US Government, but all of them returned empty-handed.

The Mossad too opened up a channel of communication: contact was made with an Egyptian diplomat by the name of Abdul Rahman Tzadek who, over a period of three years (from the end of 1952 to the beginning of 1955), served as a conduit for communication with Abdul Nasser.

Through this conduit information and messages were exchanged between the Prime Minister of Israel and the Egyptians. Both sides were highly suspicious of each other, and all the efforts made to bridge this chasm of distrust ended in failure. Several events that occurred in the region during this period, such as the ill-fated Lavon Affair of 1954,[1] did little to reinforce these tenuous and sporadic contacts.

The retaliatory raid by the Israel Defence Forces (IDF) on Gaza in February 1955, following repeated infiltration by Arab terrorists into Israel from the Egyptian-held Gaza Strip, added fuel to the flames, and terminated the 'open conduit' that had been established with the help of Abdul Rahman Tzadek. In April 1955 the Egyptian diplomat notified his Israeli contacts that he was severing the connection.

Ten years after contacts with Tzadek were terminated, the Mossad once again began examining ways of re-establishing contact with the Egyptians, an effort which eventually led to a face-to-face meeting between high-ranking officials from both sides – Egyptian and Israeli. What follows is the fascinating story of that unusual effort.

THE HEROES OF THE PIECE

On 23 July 1962, the Egyptians made a spectacular public relations event of the launching of two long-range missiles, the 'el-Kahara' and the 'el-Za'afar'. These launchings, we must admit, caught Israel very much by surprise. We knew that the Egyptians were toying with ideas for the development of advanced weapons systems, but we had no idea that they would achieve long-range missile-launching capabilities at such an early stage.

It later transpired that the Egyptians' main effort in the field of weapons development was concentrated on a locally built fighter plane. The development of ground-to-ground missiles with non-conventional warheads, and the production of fissionable nuclear material, turned out to be decoys that never approached any real operational level. At that time, however, in mid

1962, alarm bells were sounding loudly throughout the Israeli Intelligence establishment, which proceeded to devote considerable efforts to gathering as much information as possible on Egyptian progress in the field of missile technology.

At the same time as this information-gathering process moved into high gear, operational attempts were undertaken to prevent any further development of Egyptian missile technology, which had been guided primarily by German experts. Key Egyptian figures and their European contacts were, of course, identified and located. There was a deeply ironic twist to the fact that in the end those German scientists – representatives of the Jewish people's most demonic enemies – eventually paved the way for the contacts that led to face-to-face talks on the missile problem. Of course, this only proves that in the intelligence business, everything is possible – even events which are inherently contradictory, and yesterday's total absurdities may turn out to be today's cast-iron logic. This also gives credence to the claim that intelligence is not always a tool to be used 'against' the enemy, but can be a tool put to constructive use as well.

Who then were the main protagonists in this drama?

The first point on the triangle: Mahmoud Khalil

At the very heart of this affair was an Egyptian Air Force officer with the rank of Major-General, one Atzem al-Din Mahmoud Khalil.

Khalil was born in Cairo in 1921 and grew up in an educated, upper-middle-class family of intellectuals. His father was a surgeon and well-known throughout Egypt for his skills. Mahmoud initially considered following in his father's footsteps, and spent much time watching him at work in his clinic. However, as was the case with many of the children of upper-class families in Egypt, he was directed toward a military career, and by 1940, at the age of nineteen, he had graduated from the Military Academy with the rank of second lieutenant. Four years later he received his pilot's wings, and from that time on served in the Air Force, rising through the ranks and filling a number of important positions. In 1952, wearing a captain's insignia, Khalil was sent to the United States to take a course in intelligence, and upon his return was appointed deputy to Ali Sabry, who was at the time head of Egyptian Air Force Intelligence. One year later, in 1954, Khalil was named Chief Intelligence Officer of the Egyptian Air Force.

In this capacity Khalil was exposed to all the infighting and intrigues of the political echelons of the country. And so it transpired that in 1957, when a British-inspired plot was hatched to assassinate Nasser, Khalil was approached to take part.

The ringleaders of the plot, Murtada Almeraji (who had served in the past as Minister of the Interior) and Hussein Khiri (deputy head of Egyptian Military Intelligence), were members of the Egyptian old guard, and maintained close contacts with British Intelligence.

Mahmoud Khalil pretended to go along with them, but in fact informed Nasser of the plot against him, thus preventing the takeover and gaining Nasser's boundless gratitude for his loyalty. In 1959 Khalil was once again promoted to a key position – director of 'Egyptian Army Special Programmes', or, more simply, the programme for development of non-conventional weapons. In this capacity he answered directly to the President's office, and was personally responsible to Egyptian Vice-President Abdul Hakim Amer. In his new position Khalil cultivated extensive contacts throughout Western Europe, particularly in West Germany.

Everyone who knew him, friends and enemies alike, agreed that Khalil was intelligent, shrewd, with a fine sense of humour, and a knack for making friends. At the same time, according to those who knew him, he was also given to extreme mood swings, and suffered from a variety of health problems. He was known to have suffered two nervous breakdowns, one in 1962 and a second in 1965. We also learned that in 1965 he was beset by heart trouble, stomach problems, headaches, toothaches and typhus. He was extremely paranoid, believing that the whole world was after him, and that the hated Israelis had targeted him for assassination. Consequently, he was surrounded by bodyguards at all times, and employed extraordinary security measures to safeguard himself against any possible attacks.

And yet, despite all the above, Khalil was well known for his fondness for the good things in life. He drank regularly, preferably whisky, and was also a heavy smoker and a womanizer (he kept a mistress in Cairo and had a flat in Alexandria where he indulged in sexual orgies). He was an avid collector of the hallmarks of Western consumer culture: transistor radios, cameras, televisions, etc. Khalil was well versed in all the intrigues, machinations and power plays of the Egyptian leadership, and laboured diligently to improve his status within it. It might be said of him that he was among the more important members of secondary-level Egyptian officialdom, enjoying direct access to the *Ra'iss*, President Nasser, and his complete trust.

Mahmoud Khalil was not an extremist. He was a Muslim, but not very devout, a revolutionary but addicted to the good things in life. He was constantly exposed to Western influence, and relished its pleasures. He did not subscribe to any particular doctrine, and from time to time served as an intermediary for contacts between Egyptian officials and officials from Western countries. He felt free to look into any opportunity that came his way, particularly if it could help him enhance his status in the Egyptian establishment.

'Steve' – the 'wheeler and dealer' from Europe

The second point on the triangle of the 'Egyptian Connection' was Steve – a colourful and controversial figure, of mixed Egyptian and European upbringing. While Mahmoud Khalil belonged to the Egyptian military elite, and worked for his country's good, Steve was an international businessman, permanently based in Europe, and concerned primarily with his own personal profits.

From 1930 onwards Steve lived permanently in Europe, with the status of a resident alien in his adopted country. His repeated applications for citizenship in that country were bluntly refused by the Government. In this context it is important to note that Steve's connections came under repeated investigation by the authorities in his country of residence, who were seeking legal grounds to deport him. However, by his own account, no legal reason was ever found to justify his deportation. He was married three times, always to European women, but all three marriages remained shrouded in mystery.

The information we gathered at the time gave us a picture of a highly resourceful man with nerves of steel, obsessed with making money and totally lacking in any ideals. He was involved then, and apparently still is today, in shady deals of various kinds. Steve commanded a 10–15 per cent commission on any business deal he made, and in time became a millionaire, with property holdings around the world.

Through their business contacts, Steve and Mahmoud Khalil developed a strong friendship, leading eventually to the sharing of illegally gained profits and shady dealings. Steve also supervised Mahmoud Khalil's investments and properties in Canada and Europe. He lived in constant fear of the long arm of Israeli Intelligence, and this perhaps explains the contacts that were created with the third point of this triangular connection – an insurance agent named Max.

The third man

Mr Max was an insurance expert who had made a fortune in business in Europe and elsewhere. Free of material worries, he frequently undertook voluntary assignments on behalf of the State of Israel. His connections with Israel, virtually since its establishment in 1948, were mainly in the economic sphere, yet his desire to support the country and help further its peace and security never flagged. This was the basis upon which we built the delicate web of connections we were to weave with him.

I recall a meeting we had in the 1960s at the Sharon Hotel in Herzliya. I was interested in meeting the man our people had named as the driving force behind a variety of operations. When I arrived at the hotel, I was surprised to find an elderly man, sloppily dressed, and looking very much like a character out of Shalom Aleichem's stories of East European Jewry.[2] He was there with his invalid wife whom he looked after. Twice a year, without exception, he treated her to a trip to Israel, once in the spring for Passover, and once in the fall for Rosh Ha-shana, the Jewish new year. During these visits he invariably stayed at the Sharon Hotel.

We had a lively and friendly conversation which was also very interesting. In stark contrast to his appearance, I found him to be an eminently practical man, who was willing to undertake a great deal on Israel's behalf. A man who would not hesitate to take risks in the pursuit of these missions.

Max, for his part, was very excited about meeting one of the heads of the Israeli Intelligence services, and there is no doubt that our conversation strengthened his identification with our cause and his resolve to help us. At that stage we did not discuss any concrete operations. Our meeting served only to allow me to get acquainted with a friend of Israel with a potential for assisting us greatly, someone who could be activated in a time of need.

After a while we learned that, years before, Max had met Steve's second wife. In 1959, on her initiative, Max had met with Steve to examine the possibility of his assuming responsibility for their insurance business. From that time on he saw to the personal insurance affairs of the couple and their family, and served as their business consultant on other financial matters as well.

Max was Steve's confidant, and over the years their business acquaintanceship blossomed into a close personal friendship. It was only natural that Steve should have used Max as a shield against the Israelis, who, he believed, were out to get him, while Max, for his part, tried to find some way of combining his personal friendship with Steve with his strong desire to do whatever he could for Israel's security and well-being. In July 1964 he set out to achieve these aims on his own, without consulting anyone.

FIRST FEELERS

The sources of the contact

In the middle of 1964 Steve found himself in a very complicated situation. His troubles came in clusters and from many different directions at once. On the one hand, his relations with the Egyptian authorities foundered. The 'Development Plans' for advanced and non-conventional weapons were stalled, and, with no visible achievements, their future seemed highly precarious. Steve, as we have said, lived in constant fear of an Israeli attack on his person because of his connections to the Egyptian Development Plan.

In July 1964 he poured his heart out in a private chat with his close friend and personal insurance agent, Max.

Max listened sympathetically to Steve's troubles, and at some point during the conversation, he was struck by an extraordinary idea. 'Why don't you turn the tables, and instead of working against Israel, work for them.' As the idea germinated, he modified his proposal and said to Steve: 'I don't mean that you should actually work for the Israelis, but perhaps you could offer them your services – to act as a mediator between them and the Egyptians.'

At first, Steve was totally taken aback by this startling proposal, and for a short while couldn't say a word. Then he told Max that if he ever suggested such an idea to Nasser, the Egyptians 'would shorten him by a head'. He then went on to say that Nasser would 'go through the roof' and that the timing of the proposal couldn't be worse. At that time, the Israelis and the Egyptians were locked in a bitter debate over the fate of the Palestinian refugees. Discussions had taken place, but the issue was deadlocked.

Max explained to Steve that the idea was entirely his own personal initiative, and that no one in Israel knew anything about it. Taking the bull by the horns, he went on to say that the talks on the refugee issue could be transformed into secret negotiations, with Steve serving as mediator between the two sides. Steve slowly recovered from his initial shock, and began trying to digest the idea.

The net is laid

Steve and Max batted the idea back and forth for over a month, eventually agreeing on the possible nature of the proposed mediation, and deciding that reactions to the idea must be tested on both sides – in Israel and in Egypt. In September 1964 Max travelled to Israel and Steve flew to Eastern Europe. Max tried to find some way of making contact with representatives of the Israeli Intelligence services, and finally, with the help of an Israeli diplomat he knew, he succeeded in arranging a meeting with a Mossad official, and put the idea to him. Toward the end of September, the Mossad decided to try to set up the connection he had suggested.

In the meantime, however, Steve had apparently changed his mind, and decided that the refugee problem was not a substantial enough issue, and could not provide sufficient incentive for contacts between Egypt and Israel. He therefore suggested to Max that they broaden the scope of their proposed mediation, and talk about massive economic aid to Egypt. This was an idea, Steve believed, that would appeal to Nasser. Steve flew to Egypt late in November on his own private business, and promised to bring up the issue with Nasser while he was there. On his return Steve claimed that while he did not have a positive answer, his proposal had not been totally rejected. He agreed to meet with an Israeli representative to discuss matters further.

At the beginning of January 1965 a Mossad official known as 'R' met with Steve at Max's home. Max opened the meeting with a short and emotional speech, in which he expressed his delight at the very fact that such a meeting was taking place, and hoped that it would lead to talks between the two sides, and eventually to the final objective: peace between Egypt and Israel. As the discussion began in earnest, it transpired that the two sides had come to the meeting with very modest goals in mind, and no concrete proposals – save their willingness to listen, to be heard and to discuss the issues at hand.

Steve told his interlocutors that Mahmoud Khalil had cautioned him about a possible Israeli provocation or trap. 'There is no doubt', Khalil had said, 'that the person you will be talking to will be an Israeli Intelligence officer, who will try to recruit you to work for them. You must be very careful and use the opportunity to "milk" the Israeli rather than be "milked" by him.' Khalil had also warned Steve about the possibility that the meeting might be used by the 'Zionists' for propaganda purposes.

In the discussion that followed Max's opening remarks, Steve overstepped the limits of his official brief, and gave a detailed account of Egypt's economic woes. He revealed that because of Israeli pressure on various European countries to refrain from extending loans to Egypt, Nasser, against his better judgement, had no choice but to continue receiving aid from Russia. Steve sounded very pessimistic about the possibility of any real talks between Israel and Egypt. However, at the end of this somewhat inconsequential meeting, arrangements were made for further contacts.

Steve grasps the Israeli straw

'R''s intuition proved correct, and Steve's personal interest in the entire affair surfaced very quickly. Not two weeks after the first meeting, Steve contacted Max and asked him for financial assistance. He needed a $1.5 million mortgage for his properties in Canada, and had been turned down by the local banks. The issue was discussed at Mossad headquarters, and it was decided to use Steve's request as a pretext for arranging another meeting between him and a Mossad official.

During the first half of 1965 (from January to June), no less than seven such meetings took place. Each meeting had its own character and style, but ultimately they were all links in a chain of highly interesting developments, and added a modicum of weight and stability to the emerging connection.

A second meeting with Steve was held in February 1965, once again at Max's home. At this meeting, Steve said that he had recently returned from

Egypt, and could confirm that Vice-President Abdul Hakim Amer and President Nasser himself were fully aware of the existence of these contacts. Nasser had even instructed Steve to carry on with the meetings, though he had not given him any specific tasks.

Two concrete proposals were raised at that meeting: (1) that Israel should help secure the supply of Canadian wheat to Egypt; and (2) that Israel should purchase 100,000 bales of Egyptian cotton. It was implicitly understood that the proceeds from the latter deal (about $25 million) would be credited to Mahmoud Khalil to fund his projects.

Mahmoud Khalil comes to Paris

At the end of September 1965, Mahmoud Khalil came to Paris to prepare Field Marshal Amer's state visit there. The very fact that Mahmoud had been chosen for such a delicate mission was a clear indication of his enhanced status in the Egyptian regime.

Naturally, as soon as he arrived in Paris, he met with our friend Steve, who in turn immediately reported on their meeting in great detail to the Mossad representative. Mahmoud Khalil expressed his disappointment over the fact that Israel had not responded to the Egyptian offer that in return for certain financial arrangements (a loan) for Egypt, Nasser would support the Johnstone Plan.[3] Mahmoud Khalil also agreed to meet with an Israeli representative, but only on condition that the issue of the loan would be settled first.

The Mossad official asked Steve if all these proposals had been approved by Nasser, and to what extent the President was 'in the picture'. Steve, of course, could not answer the question, but replied that in his view, Mahmoud Khalil would have never dared to make such a suggestion without first consulting Nasser.

There was a somewhat bizarre footnote to this entire affair, when Steve, quoting Khalil, passed on warm regards to us from 'Mister Lotz', and in the same breath told us that the Egyptians had known the true identity of this so-called 'German' all along, but that they had played along in order not to create new tensions during our negotiations.[4]

Finally, after talking to Mahmoud Khalil once again, Steve told us that he understood our position but could not set a date for a further meeting at that point, since such a meeting required highly detailed preparations. Our interpretation of this was that Khalil needed Nasser's backing, and that only if the '*Ra'iss*' deigned to give him the go-ahead would he be willing to meet us once again. In the end it was decided that Mahmoud Khalil would look into the possibility of meeting us two to three weeks later, when he was due to return to France together with Marshal Amer for the latter's state visit. Mahmoud Khalil asked Steve to be present at this meeting, should it actually take place.

'Crash landing'

While we were in the process of trying to formulate long-term plans, we learned that Mahmoud Khalil was in Paris. We decided to send a Mossad representative to Paris, to try to contact him directly, without any middle-men, for a face-to-face meeting.

We counted on the positive dynamic that had been created to move events in the right direction, and entrusted the rest to luck. And indeed the Mossad agent contacted Mahmoud at his hotel room, introduced himself as Steve's friend, and told him that he was calling about the European loan they had discussed. He went on to say that before anything could be done about it, there were some details that required further clarification, such as the sums that were involved, who would be responsible for dealing with the details of the loan in the lending country, etc. Mahmoud Khalil, who identified Steve's 'good friend' at the other end of the line, immediately replied that the proposed sum was a very substantial one, and gave the 'friend' the names of the people involved in the transaction.

The Mossad agent replied that this information would enable us to begin looking into the status of the loan. Impatiently jumping to conclusions, Mahmoud asked if he would be able to receive the loan in two weeks' time, when he next returned to Europe. At the end of the conversation, the two men agreed to meet that same afternoon at Khalil's hotel.

After a two-hour discussion, in the course of which Khalil asked for Israeli help in securing the loan, the Egyptian officer asked the Mossad representa-tive for 'something in writing'. Initially he requested that the letter be pre-pared for him by that same evening, but the Mossad agent explained that the issue was a very weighty one, and had to be referred back to Israel for approval. Khalil then requested that the letter be sent to him to Egypt. In the end, however, they agreed to meet elsewhere in Europe at the beginning of October 1965, at which time it was agreed Khalil would be given the letter. Toward the end of the conversation, Khalil mentioned Lotz once again (this time 'from the horse's mouth', as it were), remarking that the Egyptians could have sentenced the Israeli spy to death and executed him, but had decided not to.

Following further feverish consultations at either end of the Middle East, and a number of coordinating moves, the following letter was drawn up in preparation for the October meeting with Khalil. The wording of the letter was approved by the Israeli Prime Minister, who added the section on peace. The letter was written in English and appears here in its entirety:

Strictly Confidential

General Mahmoud Khalil
PERSONAL

Dear General,

This is to confirm our meeting held on my initiative.

I have been instructed by the Prime Minister of Israel to convey, through your good offices to your President, our willingness, prompted by our desire for peace, to proceed with the dialogue, to be kept in absolute secrecy, between yourself or whoever be designated to this effect by your President, and representative of our Prime Minister.

According to your initial proposal and our subsequent suggestions, the following can serve as possible subjects for negotiations:

(1) The establishment of a permanent direct and secret channel of contact between your President and our Prime Minister.

(2) Our willingness to give assistance, if so agreed, towards the obtaining of international credit for the peaceful development of your country.

(3) The undertaking on your part to accept the 1955 Johnstone Plan for the division of water resources between Israel and her neighbors.

(4) The examination of means for the prevention of the unintentional outbreak of hostilities and their escalation and ways to reduce tension in the Middle East.

(5) Any subject of interest to either party.

I look forward to our further contact in Europe after your consultation with your President.

Sincerely yours,
Counselor.

A second meeting

The meeting that had been scheduled for the beginning of October actually took place in the middle of that month. Mahmoud Khalil said that he had

had the opportunity to talk to Nasser about the first meeting in Paris, and that Nasser was waiting for the promised document in writing. Nasser did not respond, either positively or negatively, to the continuation of the contacts. Mahmoud Khalil said that Nasser intended leaving Egypt a few days after Khalil's own return home, but that he would make every effort to meet with Nasser, and even obtain an answer from him prior to the President's departure. Khalil noted that the answer would be transmitted by a courier from a commercial company in Europe, and would include only the time and place of the next meeting.

Addressing the loan request, the Mossad agent said that under existing circumstances, there was no way to talk directly to anyone on this issue without disclosing the contact with Mahmoud Khalil. Nevertheless, we had initiated steps to overcome the obstacles facing the request. Our man in Paris received the impression that Khalil was pleased with the answer. That signalled the end of the meeting, and Khalil hurried back to the reception in Marshal Amer's honour that had already begun.

A month passed, and there was total silence on the other side. Then suddenly, at the beginning of December, Max contacted the Mossad representative, requesting on Steve's behalf that another meeting be set up with a representative of the Mossad.

At the beginning of December a representative of the Mossad met Steve in Paris. Right at the beginning of the meeting, Steve produced a photocopy of a letter he had received from Mahmoud Khalil. Although it was worded as a business letter, it was actually an official reinstatement of Steve to his previous position as principal coordinator of the two-way contacts.

Thinking it through

The lull in the talks gave us the opportunity to examine our options for future action, and a number of points should be emphasized in this respect.

First of all, there was the slight shift that had occurred in the position taken by the Israeli Embassy in the lender country. The Israeli Ambassador there, who had previously voiced strenuous opposition to the creation of any kind of linkage between that country's aid to Egypt and contacts with Israel, had changed his mind, and in a meeting with people from the Mossad suggested that Israel make its aid on the loan issue conditional on the possibility of a renewal of diplomatic relations between Egypt and the country in question.

No one at Mossad headquarters was very enthusiastic about this suggestion, and these reservations were made very clear in the directive dispatched to the Ambassador:

> Let's not lose our sense of proportion. The State of Israel will
> not change its stand on matters of principle just for the sake
> of the Mahmoud Khalil operation, which, in any case, is still no
> more than a gleam in our eye ... We cannot approach any official
> party and tell them that we are in favour of aid to Egypt. If Nasser
> agrees to real contacts with us, then we can re-examine this
> position. I believe that Mahmoud got carried away by his own
> initiatives, and was reprimanded for his excesses. As a result, he
> turned the contact back to its basic starting points, i.e. the loan
> and Steve.

These directives once again highlighted the fundamental conflict of interest
that existed between the two sides: as long as the reliability and good faith
of the connection to Nasser had not been proven *a priori*, Israel viewed with
great disfavour the granting of the loan to Egypt by the European country;
Egypt, for its part, was not at all enthusiastic about creating direct contacts
with Israel until such time as Israel proved its own good faith, first and
foremost through actions.

At a discussion held in my office on 15 December 1965, all the options
relating to this operation were analysed. Mahmoud Khalil's upcoming visit
and the vagueness surrounding our channels of communication with him
(whether they would be conducted through Steve or through a representative
of the commercial firm) prompted the Mossad people to make direct contact
with Mahmoud Khalil in Cairo. Headquarters issued very clear instructions:
'We do indeed want to arrange a meeting with Mahmoud during his
upcoming trip to Europe, but without any grovelling.'

On 31 January 1966 a third meeting took place between Mahmoud Khalil
and the Mossad representative. The meeting was held in a different city in
Europe. It lasted three hours and the greater part of it was held in private.
Steve left the room after a few opening remarks, returning only toward the
end. Mahmoud Khalil stated that the sole purpose of his present trip had
been to participate in this meeting. He told the Mossad representative that
he had taken part in an extensive meeting on the issue in question with Nasser
and Amer. By his account, both Nasser and Amer were highly sceptical about
Israel's sincerity, and even more so in relation to the present issue. They had
expressed profound suspicion that the entire affair was merely a provocation
and an unscrupulous exploitation of the contacts that had been established.

At the end of the meeting, which proved to be very businesslike and to the
point, the Mossad representative suggested to Mahmoud Khalil that he meet
with a high-ranking Israeli official on the following day. In a cable to his
superiors, the Mossad representative suggested that the 'high-ranking Israeli

official' be the head of the Mossad. The very next day, 1 February 1966, I met Mahmoud Khalil for the first time.

The meeting with Mahmoud Khalil

The meeting took place at Steve's home, after appropriate security measures had been taken. Mahmoud showed up in all his glory, a middle-aged man (about forty-five, I thought), with a huge moustache, curly hair, a permanent smile on his face, and oozing goodwill. He was dressed casually in a sweater, a half-opened collar and loosened tie. The first few minutes went without a hitch: a warm handshake, with the perfunctory 'How are you?' and 'How do you do?' He was visibly nervous and uncertain about how to proceed. He smiled continuously, cracking jokes (mostly about liquor), and slapping me on the back. We spent the first quarter of an hour warming up to each other, during which time I learned a few 'important' details about the man, such as the fact that he drank two types of whisky – one in the morning and a different brand in the evening, etc.

After the initial greetings, we got down to work. I began by expressing my extreme pleasure at meeting a man of his stature, and added that we all hoped that this would be the beginning of ongoing contacts, and not an isolated event. I then touched on the issue of mutual distrust, and stressed that we had to make every effort to strike this problem from our agenda before we entered into any kind of discussion or sought any clarification of the issues. At this point, I embarked on the usual litany, that we were both generals, intelligence men and not politicians. We would understand each other better, and could rest assured that whatever was decided would also be honoured in letter and in spirit, and with the appropriate humility. At this point he stopped me and asked a question:

'Why have you decided on a new policy this time?'

'What new policy,' I asked.

'Not to publicize these contacts between us, and not to use them for blackmail.'

'I know of no such policy in the past ...'

'But the fact is that in the past you always made such contacts public.'

'We never made any such contacts public', I stressed. 'Publicity has always been the work of the mediators. And this time, as far as I know, we are working – for the first time – without middle-men. This is a direct contact between high-ranking officials on both sides, and I am convinced that it can be kept secret.'

Mahmoud was not reassured, and reiterated his fear that it would be a 'disaster' if the existence of these meetings were ever leaked. He talked at length about Nasser's suspicious nature, claiming that following any Israeli statement (such as a recent one by Golda Me'ir) regarding Israel's desire for peace, the President immediately expected some act of aggression. It was my impression that these fundamental feelings of suspicion were indeed deeply embedded, and perhaps even had some basis in reality.

Presenting the issues

After summing up the discussion on 'mutual suspicion', I presented the problem from our point of view. I emphasized that this was strictly a bilateral deal, and that in a meeting held earlier that morning in our Prime Minister's office, pressure had been brought to bear on me to ensure a number of things. From our side, we were prepared to make two major concessions.

The first of these was to support in principle the granting of a loan to Egypt, with the following conditions:

(1) The loan would be channelled through a European bank.
(2) It would be granted for a period of seven years (possibly extending to ten).
(3) Interest would be set at 5 per cent (professional bargaining might reduce it to 4.5 per cent).
(4) There would be three instalments (within six to nine months).
(5) The loan would be guaranteed by the Cotton Board (possibly also through Bank Leumi).[5]

The second concession was that we were prepared to suspend any further attempts on our part to 'sabotage' support for Egypt in the United States and in Europe, again with the following conditions:

(1) The Egyptians would show us some more tangible expression of their willingness to stay out of the controversy surrounding the Johnstone Plan (in the form of a letter or written document of some sort).
(2) As a conciliatory gesture, Nasser would allow ships flying foreign flags and carrying goods to Israel to pass through the Suez Canal.
(3) A 'hot line' – an arrangement for continuous contacts in order to deal effectively with potential misunderstandings – was to be established.
(4) Anti-Israeli propaganda in Egypt. would be toned down.
(5) That in the more distant future there might be experts' meetings to find ways of putting an end to the arms race between the two countries.

Mahmoud began by saying that their approach was basically positive, that they would like to open the door to future discussions, and that, if we managed to put an end to the arms race, it would be of great benefit to the starving masses, etc., etc. Here he again put his finger on the main problem: how to overcome the deep-seated mutual suspicion between us. He had to be able to convince his 'boss' of our sincerity, since they were all terrified lest we make all these things public, etc. He asked us to try to understand Egypt's predicament, claiming that if we were to make one gesture 'with no strings attached', this would effectively break the ice. As regards the issues, he then said the following:

(1) The conditions we attached to the loan seemed fair enough to him.
(2) He was very anxious for us to accept guarantees from the Central Bank of Egypt. It was a question of prestige, and after all, he claimed, Egypt always repaid its debts, slowly at times, but debts must be paid!
(3) As regards the Johnstone Plan, he reiterated that they had been taking action to bury the entire issue, and did not agree with my remark that the issue was dying anyway, even without their help. 'Just wait and see how we can bring it back whenever we want', he replied.
(4) Relating to the issue of the passage of ships through the Suez Canal *en route* to Israel, Khalil claimed that it was 'a very reasonable request', but that there were great difficulties involved in its implementation, since the Canal was under the jurisdiction of the Arab Boycott Office, in which other countries were involved. (My response: 'I am certain that if you really wanted to, you could come up with a solution.')
(5) Responding to the issue of the 'hot line', he claimed that it was certainly possible to make arrangements for ongoing communication based on fixed dates for meetings or something along those lines.
(6) As regards the moderation of anti-Israeli propaganda and the possibility of experts' talks, he said that these would come, but at a later stage. Here he asked me to write the words 'PATIENCE, slowly and in stages'! 'And don't overcook the dish', he cautioned. He went on to note that we had never before reached such a stage of negotiation, and that he regarded this in itself as a great achievement that we should take care to safeguard.
(7) He stressed that for the Egyptians it was of the utmost importance that we cease our 'sabotaging' of their relations with the United States and other countries. They were convinced, he said, that we could do virtually anything, and that the positive change in the United States' attitude toward Egypt was a result of the fact that we had stopped interfering. He claimed that only 'the vociferous members of Congress' worried him, and he asked if we could do anything to calm them down .... (I told him that it all depended on their response to our requests.)

Conclusion and plans for the future

Mahmoud Khalil explained that he would now go back to Egypt and report on our meeting to Nasser and his Vice-President. In fact he was supposed to come back with two answers on practical issues: (1) water; and (2) safe passage through the Suez Canal. I told him that if he brought back answers that were satisfactory from our point of view, then, I believed the question of the loan could be resolved. I suggested that he think about additional gestures of goodwill on their part, and I strongly recommended that he come with me to my country and personally reassure my Prime Minister, who kept asking me all the time what we would be getting in return for the $30 million that we would be giving them?

We agreed that Mahmoud would transmit the Egyptian reply to Steve no later than 6 February, and that after they had studied our responses we would meet again on Saturday, 12 February, in Athens to review the situation.

The three-hour meeting that transpired was a fascinating experience, not only because our interlocutor had until recently been one of our prime intelligence targets, and not only because this was perhaps the first opportunity we had had to talk to one of the top officials in the Egyptian Government, in full knowledge of the fact that whatever we discussed would be reported back to Nasser, but also because I believe we found a common language, in a relaxed atmosphere, with occasional jokes at each other's expense and no barriers of any kind between us. Whether or not all this was going to lead to anything, only time could tell.

In my report to the Prime Minister, I appended a personal letter. I sent a copy of this to the Deputy Minister of Defence, Zvi Dinstein, with the following remark: 'Please regard this letter as though it were addressed to you personally, and give us a hand in moving this thing forward.' Here is the text of the letter:

> To Eshkol, many greetings!
> I am sending you under separate cover the report of my meeting with Mahmoud Khalil. The report speaks for itself, but I took the liberty of adding a personal note.
> I left the meeting with the feeling that we had indeed opened up a small crack in the wall that may make negotiations possible, and we should hold on to it for all it's worth and not let go. My interlocutor is one of the top figures in the present regime in Egypt, and I believe this is the first time that we have had the good fortune to find a direct contact such as this. If my impressions are correct, Nasser seems eager to find a way to develop some kind of direct contact or communication.

In my opinion, you must take up this issue wholeheartedly, and it is just possible that you may be able to write a page of history that is unparalleled in our times. I fully recognize the difficulties and the dangers, but I believe that we must make some gesture of goodwill – if only for its historical significance.

The very fact that he has *agreed to accept* a loan from us is of the utmost importance, and is fraught with great dangers for Nasser himself. What is more, I do believe that once we overcome the fears and obstacles of our mutual suspicion, we will be able to make even further progress.

We are now waiting for their answer regarding water rights (the Johnstone Plan) and the Suez Canal. Once these arrive, and before we set up another meeting with Mahmoud Khalil (which has been tentatively set for the end of next week), I may come back home briefly to clarify matters and focus the issues.

I conclude with the hope that we are indeed in accord on all this, and that I have succeeded in conveying to you my impressions and my belief that we are about to make history.

Good health!
Yours,
Me'ir Amit

Mahmoud Khalil returned to Cairo on 5 February 1966, and held an extended meeting with Marshal Amer, the conclusions of which were submitted to Nasser. Their discussion centred around two main themes. The first of these was the loan, the procedures for which they wanted to compartmentalize in such a way that our involvement in it could not be traced. They suggested, therefore, that Steve work through a financial institution which would, in turn, refer him to a certain bank in Europe. As soon as Steve had concluded the major details, representatives of the Central Bank of Egypt would come to sign the loan agreement. The second part of the discussion was concerned with the demands that we had raised on various issues.

Proof of the Egyptians' sincerity

Amer took offence at the very suggestion that proof was required. He even claimed that demands such as these set us back several years in the entire process. Nevertheless, after weighing the matter and considering the fact that Egypt was itself interested in making the contact they agreed to respond to the following demands:

(1) *The prisoners of the 1954 'Lavon Affair'*: The Egyptians agreed to release the prisoners as soon as the loan was secured, and on condition that they be sent to a neutral country and that their release be given no publicity.

(2) *The hot line*: Amer was opposed to Mahmoud Khalil's frequent trips to Europe for these meetings, but he agreed to periodic meetings between Khalil and Amit. Between these meetings contact would be maintained by couriers, and, of course, by the chief courier in this instance, Steve, who was free to travel at will between Egypt and Europe.

(3) *The plans for diverting the waters of the Jordan River*: Amer told Steve that he must persuade Israel that Egypt had already taken steps to put an end to the project. If the Israelis did not believe this, the Egyptians could 'persuade' the Israelis by demonstrating the opposite: showing them that Egypt could, if it so wished, revive the project and turn the diversion plans into a reality.

(4) *The release of Lotz*: Later on in the process the 'Equestrian Spy' could possibly be released in return for a sum of $5 million.

(5) *Flights over the Straits of Tiran:*[6] On the face of it, the Egyptians seemed to tend toward agreeing to remove their prohibition of flights by Israeli aircraft over the straits. They requested that we come to the next meeting with more detailed maps and proposals.

(6) *Miscellaneous*: Egypt would be making additional requests of Israel. In the meantime they mentioned only one – our aid to the monarchists in Yemen. As far as they were concerned, it should be cut off immediately.

(7) *The next meeting – in Cairo and not in Athens*: This was where the bombshell exploded. Amer vehemently opposed my planned meeting with Mahmoud on 12 February 1966 in Athens. He believed that Khalil was a target for all sorts of terrorists, that he had many enemies all over the world, and that his life was danger! A meeting of this nature could not remain secret, would eventually be revealed, and would place in jeopardy not only the budding contact but all those involved in setting it up. As an alternative to Athens, Amer suggested that the meeting take place in Cairo. The date could remain as planned. As he put it, 'Amit and his representative should come to Cairo under assumed identities through a European country.' Amer also agreed to the addition of one Israeli expert to the delegation, if necessary, and assured us that he would be personally responsible for the safety of their guests.

Mahmoud Khalil asked that I be told that this was an invitation based on Arab honour, and added: 'Amit, who speaks Arabic and knows the Arabs well, will appreciate the nature of this invitation.' Amer suggested, too, that we stay at a private home so that – he said jokingly – 'we don't run into any of our own agents in Egypt'. This was the way things stood at that time on the Egyptian side.

At the same time, prior to my return, and based on the reports I had submitted, discussions were held in Israel on the ramifications of my meeting with Mahmoud Khalil.

Discussions back home

Prime Minister Levi Eshkol, Minister of Finance Pinhas Sapir, Foreign Minister Golda Me'ir and Deputy Minister of Defence Zvi Dinstein met to discuss the matter as early as 3 February. Their initial reaction was that they were convinced of the seriousness of the entire affair, yet still felt that it was too good to be true. In their consultations a number of issues were tabled, of which the following two were the most important:

(1) *A sign from the Egyptians as to the sincerity of the contact*: Minister of Finance Pinhas Sapir suggested that the contacts be taken out of the interservices framework and transferred to economic echelons (e.g. meetings at ministerial level between the two sides). Golda Me'ir suggested that the prisoners of the Lavon Affair of 1954 be released prior to any step on our part in the Egyptians' favour.

(2) *A* quid pro quo *for the loan*: On this issue a number of suggestions were raised, among them free passage of goods (not necessarily Israeli goods) to and from through the Suez Canal, the Johnstone Plan, reduction of tensions surrounding the Palestinian refugee problem, reduction of Egyptian involvement in the Arab boycott, suspension of financial support for the PLO and halting the terrorist activities of the Fatah,[7] coordination between El Al Israel Airlines and United Arab Airlines, and the removal of the term 'the destruction of the State of Israel' from propaganda material and from speeches made by Egyptian leaders.

Other points that were discussed touched upon the establishment of a hot line to be manned by wireless operators on both sides, strengthening the budding contact by the addition of another Egyptian official, and an exchange of visits by officials of the two countries.

I later discovered that these discussions on the Israeli side were premature, and totally out of touch with most of the talks I had held with Mahmoud Khalil. Indeed, it was clear right from the beginning that I was not going to have an easy time of it. The inbred suspicion on the Israeli side knew almost no bounds, and the Egyptian side, too, exhibited signs of discomfort and heightened sensitivity.

One of the signs that presaged developments that were to cloud the negotiations was Egyptian nervousness about anything to do with the passage of goods bound for Israel through the Suez Canal. The biggest obstacle, however – the one that caught us completely by surprise – was the cancellation of the meeting in Athens and the proposal to meet in Cairo instead. It was very clear to me that this would be a hard pill for our people to swallow.

On 8 February 1966 I wrote the following entry in my diary:

> All in all I am troubled by developments, and this feeling will not go away. This 'trouble' can be defined in four words: the Jews in Israel. I think the main battle facing me now is how to persuade 'our side'. How to convince them that this is the beginning of an historical process, the direction and form of which we will shape by our own conduct! In the final analysis, the issue here is very clear: for fifteen or seventeen years we have been crying out 'we want to talk', and when at last the 'invitation to Cairo' actually comes, people begin to hesitate, to hem and haw, and pick at minute details.
>
> I am not referring to the loan – which is money we are laying on the line. It is very clear to me today that this is not simply a financial matter, nor a one-shot opportunity. This is the beginning of contacts on a regular basis which can lead to better understanding, perhaps even to greater friction, but nonetheless direct contact! No middle-men, no broken lines of communication, and most importantly – we are dealing here with the 'head', not the 'tail', with the people who matter in the Arab world and not the small fry who, when it comes down to it, don't have the guts to take any real action. And the nagging question is, do our people understand the full magnitude of all this?
>
> After my talks with Mahmoud Khalil, I, for one, have a sense – perhaps more than anyone else – of what is actually happening, and my heart tells me that we are heading for something real. Now comes the other part, the so-called 'technical' aspect – the question of the trip to Cairo. One thing is absolutely clear: the way we handle the first part of this 'baby' will set the tone for a long time to come. Perhaps we can say to them, let's meet once more outside of Egypt, what's the rush? Outside the region everything is more secure. But, if they are willing to take my advice, we mustn't even raise the suggestion. We have to accept their invitation, to take it at face value and hope they won't change

their minds. Because any visit by such a 'delegation' in Egypt has its own intrinsic significance, a significance that no one will be able to erase or cancel.

Finally, two more points: The first point – even if there is a great danger involved, I, myself (personally!), must take the risk. I, who send operatives into the field and give them the order to 'move out!', must be prepared to 'move out!' myself when the opportunity presents itself. This is a cardinal rule of leadership. And the second point – as I see it, there is very little danger. As long as we see to a number of basic security arrangements, there is nothing to worry about.

Finally, at the end of this soul-searching, I cannot help but mention one more thing that is bothering me. I do not know to what extent Isser Harel[8] has been brought into the picture. One thing is for sure, that if he has (or will be in the future), there is no doubt that he will do everything in his power to undermine the whole thing.

In this instance, he has a vested interest – to prove that his nemesis, the man who squared off against him, almost face-to-face, on the issue of the German scientists, is a man who cannot be trusted and should not be talked to.[9]

Armed with a clearly laid-out and concisely worded paper, I came directly from the airport to Levi Eshkol's office, in order to present the issue to him and hold a preliminary consultation. Upon arriving at his office, I found the 'team' already there, including the 'General Adviser', Isser Harel; Deputy Minister of Defence, Zvi Dinstein; and the Political Adviser, Adi Yaffe.

Right from the outset of the meeting, I encountered a hostile, sceptical and hesitant atmosphere. The participants shot down every idea I brought up, and grasped at the slightest pretext to counter my proposals. Heading this wave of negative thinking was, of course, Isser Harel, who terrified everyone within earshot. Here are a number of gems he produced, which I noted in longhand during the meeting:

'Mahmoud Khalil has a blood feud with us.'
'Steve, an international manipulator, a very shady character ...'
'The Egyptians are in dire need of finances.'
'Any strengthening of their economy is directly opposed to our policy concepts.'
'How will we be able to explain our total turnabout?'
'All the CIA needs is a green light, and they will begin pouring money in there.'

'All this without the Egyptians budging an inch from their main purpose – the destruction of Israel.'

'We could lose this money for what will sound like a legitimate reason.'

'They'll just ask for more and continue to complicate matters for us.'

'The *quid pro quo* that they offered us in their last message is negligible. The diversion of the Jordan – that's nothing. In any case they have retreated from their earlier positions under pressure. The passage in the Canal – what they told Amit is nothing. In fact the publicity is the most important thing for them.'

'The release of the prisoners – a very important act from our point of view. From their point of view it is a small sacrifice that is out of proportion to what they're getting.'

'The hot line – what they are suggesting is insufficient.'

'There is no proof that Amer and Nasser in fact know ...'

'Security – Mahmoud has an account to settle with us, and the security guarantees that they are offering are simply not satisfactory.'

'Who knows if Mahmoud Khalil didn't go to Nasser and say 'I'll bring you the Head of Israeli Intelligence', under the cover story of discussions on the loan issue. Until we know more about the security guarantees, in my opinion, no one should go to Cairo, certainly not such high-ranking people: people who, from their point of view, are in possession of all of Israel's most vital secrets.'

At this point in the discussion, Pinhas Sapir, Yisrael Galili, Aryeh Levavi and Zalman ('Ziyama') Aranne joined us.[10] I presented the issue again in great detail, and was followed by Isser Harel, who remained adamantly opposed to the mission to Cairo, and continued in the same vein of doomsday scenarios.

The first speaker from among the newcomers was Sapir. He said, absolutely seriously, that only in Israel was 30 million dollars not regarded as real money. He stressed that in his opinion these contacts should be established via economic channels – 'in the same way that we began our relations with Turkey and Iran' – rather than intelligence channels, and at this point let loose a terrible thought, 'Despite all the pain we feel about the prisoners' plight, they are not worth 30 million dollars.' And he continued: 'Even if the trip to Egypt was less dangerous, I would not agree under any circumstances', and 'Why not meet abroad? We could end up with blackmail and a terrible disaster. What will we discover in Cairo that we can't find out abroad?' These are just examples of the sort of things he said. His thoughts on the matter were absolutely clear, unequivocal and decisive.

The only person who rose slightly above the grim, fatalistic tenor of that meeting was Yisrael Galili, who began by saying:

> This is fantastic. It's hard not to be excited. Their very desire to make the connection is more an indication of their sincerity than a confirmation of their distress. I think the trip to Cairo is very important, but I cannot imagine going there without security arrangements. A secret, top-level delegation to Cairo is in itself very exciting, but only with appropriate guarantees and an understanding that gives the trip political significance. Particularly if there are reliable signs and tokens that indeed this is the case. Examples? If it were possible to be given a sign, before the visit, but after the transfer of a first instalment: the release of the prisoners. Because they cannot be released without Nasser's approval. Some of the items I saw in a negative light are not, after all, all that negative. It is perfectly reasonable to offer assistance within the framework of a desire to establish new relations.

Zvi Dinstein, who was one of the candidates for the delegation to Cairo, said that if he were given the order he would go. Thirty million dollars in cash was a great deal of money. It was hard currency and a large sum. He felt the trip to Cairo was important. His main problem at that point was that there might be some kind of trick behind it all. The question was whether it would be possible to obtain satisfactory guarantees from some internationally known figure.

Then 'Ziyama' Aranne joined in and said:

> Suppose I were sitting where you [the Prime Minister] are, I would not agree to it. I am absolutely clear on this, and I'll tell you why: because of two things. The matter of the guarantee and the matter of the deal itself. You don't have to go to Egypt for that. Things like that can be arranged anywhere in the world in total secrecy. If it were a truly serious proposal, they wouldn't have suggested Cairo, of all places.

At this point I intervened once again and said:

> I don't believe any kind of game is being played here. You have to understand their mentality. I'm not sure they know exactly where

they are headed. You could take the two-hour-old baby and throw it out with the bath water, you can kill this thing right from the outset, and nothing will happen. We must detach ourselves from the question of the dangers involved. We have to put aside the question of the money. I am not saying these things aren't important, but you have to take the bull by the horns.

'The question is', Galili said, 'is it a bull or a goat?' ...

'I think it's a bull', I replied.

At this point Eshkol intervened and began expounding his view of the situation:

First of all, I feel it's as though the groom's family is sitting on one side of the table, getting all worked up and complaining about the match. I can't accept this mood, because the mood and the approach to the issue are both very important. My heart is telling me: what's happening here – have we been defeated, that we have to go to Cairo? David Ben Gurion declared – precisely because we were victorious, he is willing to go anywhere for a meeting, even to Egypt.

Levavi interjected: 'For peace negotiations!'

And Eshkol replied:

To meet the Egyptian leadership! I know that when we say negotiations, we are asked what will be discussed at the negotiations, and we don't know what to say ... For some reason, I can't imagine that the people who go will be in any kind of danger. For the life of me I can't imagine it ... I want, first of all, to support Me'ir [Amit], because this may be the beginning of something – that may also turn out to be nothing ... Ever since we authorized Meir and he went out for those meetings – a week has passed and I haven't heard anything more profound about the things we want. Naturally, we must demand the replacement of the armistice agreement with a peace agreement ... I admit that the meeting in Cairo has special meaning for me, but I have patience.

And in the end he laid down the law:

In the light of the opinion of some of the participants in this discussion, that there should be another meeting outside Egypt – we must propose another meeting which should take place in Europe.

On that same day, I summed up that dismal discussion at the Prime Minister's office as follows:

> A stormy meeting, which lasted for three hours. General opinion is running against sending a delegation to Egypt without cast iron guarantees, such as placing our fate in the hands of de Gaulle or the like. The participants insisted that our demands be stated in the clearest possible manner and in such a way as to ensure that they will not deceive us once we have given them the loan. All in all, it was very difficult.

After hours of deliberation, a summary of the meeting was written up which I later turned into a document. And yet, despite the elegant wording of this paper, it was clear to me that the path we had taken would lead us nowhere.

I made the following entry in my diary:

> I don't know why, but I have a feeling of an ending, a feeling that we are on the brink of losing an historic chance, and the nitpicking treatment we gave the issue, with neither vision nor the slightest measure of faith, will bring us to a dead end. The 'Isserist' approach which says (about everything!) 'We have to look for the crooked side here ...', since it is inconceivable that anyone should have good intentions of any kind. This is something that never crosses that man's mind. The world is saturated with evil intentions, and he revels in it all like a little demon, forever setting off alarm bells to produce primitive but terrifying sounds. This is the picture that haunts me. I simply can't find any peace of mind.

The beginning of the end

We decided that a representative of the Mossad would meet with Steve, and at that point deliver a brief message from me to Mahmoud Khalil. The gist of the message was that Israel regarded the continuation of the contacts very favourably; that I had at my disposal $30 million that would be deposited in the agreed banking institution; and I suggested that we meet with Mahmoud Khalil one more time in Europe in order to set up the next steps in the process. Steve voiced his strong disappointment.

In the meantime, even before my message to Khalil was sent out in the proper channels, a message arrived for Steve, asking him to postpone his planned visit to Cairo with his 'friends', because their host was ill and had been hospitalized. To this day I do not know if this was a 'diplomatic illness' aimed at delaying the entire process, or if it was a response to our message. I believe it was a sort of 'pre-emptive strike' aimed at letting us know that it was they who did not want us to come to Cairo, thus depriving us of the pleasure of saying 'no' first.

On 22 February 1966 a representative of the Mossad met once again with Steve, and delivered Mahmoud Khalil's reply, from which we understood that the entire affair was on its last legs. At the same time, as was his wont, Steve laced the message with a few tantalizing additions, such as a story about Nasser's attempt to resign, which, of course, had been rejected by the Egyptian leadership. Nasser, Steve added, would not last long, and it was in Israel's interest to act wisely and pluck the right strings, so that his 'successor' would be a more amenable person.

In order to prevent the total collapse of the operation we sent Mahmoud Khalil a message in which we told him of our willingness to make 10 per cent of the loan available immediately, in return for the simultaneous release of the four prisoners of the Lavon Affair. We expressed our hope that this would break the deadlock.

One week later, Steve returned from Egypt with his tail between his legs. At a meeting we had with him immediately after his return (on 14 March 1966), he reported that our message had thrown Khalil into a fit of rage. He charged that we had made a fool of him, and that his superiors had been right all along in their belief that every Israeli move was nothing more than a dirty trick. He added that he regarded our reply as a personal affront, and an expression of a total lack of confidence. He also mentioned, surprisingly, that the Egyptians had released Abie Nathan, the 'peace pilot'.[11] According to Khalil, he himself was the one who had given the order to do so, in the hope that Israel would regard this act as a *bone fides* of Egypt's goodwill … .

In his response to us, Khalil also added that he had met with Nasser three times to discuss our communiqué, and following these meetings he wished to inform us that the invitation he had extended to me to come to Egypt was withdrawn, and that he was also cancelling the hot line, which in fact was already operational, after a fashion, through our connection with Steve. Israel had caused the door to be slammed shut.

During their conversation, Mahmoud Khalil dictated the following letter in English to Steve, addressed to Major-General Amit:

Dear General,
H.K. has transmitted to me your words. Believe me, General, I am puzzled at the sudden change which I always receive from you and your country. I could never discuss any offer as it has been submitted to us

(always changes in time of delivery, price, quality – CIF is changed to FOB, and the final result will be not good as I explained in details to H.K.).

Again I would like to advise you that before coming in such a market you have to be ready with a full plan. I am sorry to inform you that the development of the affairs has brought the matter to the zero point. With regard,

M.K.[12]

He elaborated on the message with a few choice phrases, such as that the situation was beyond repair, that if Israel thought that Egypt was in desperate financial straits and was therefore trying to squeeze everything it could out of it then this was a major misconception. The situation in Egypt was not that bad at all.

The dialogue falls apart

Throughout the months of April and May 1966 sporadic contacts were made with Steve and a representative of the commercial company that served as our courier to and from Egypt. But they were of no practical purpose and led nowhere. Their only usefulness was in maintaining a slim line of communication and not severing the connections altogether. The truth is that Mahmoud Khalil also signalled his desire to keep a few options open.

On 22 July 1966 I decided to send another message to Mahmoud Khalil through the director of the commercial company in Europe. In this message I expressed my willingness to meet Khalil anywhere at all, at his discretion. At the beginning of August, I received a verbal reply from Mahmoud, indicating that he was willing to meet with me, but only in Egypt (Arab honour), and adding that 'there is an important reason for us to meet'. When we asked him to send us the message in writing, he refused, claiming that we would soon understand why he was not willing to write anything down.

For my own part, I notified Mahmoud that I was too bogged down at work to leave the country at that time, but I would be very grateful to him if he could send me some more details about the 'important issues' he had mentioned in his message. Naturally, I received no response to the request, and the trail petered out once again.

In September of that year I happened to be in Europe, and I decided to give Mahmoud a call. The conversation took place on 9 September from a Paris hotel. It was totally futile. Despite a few more phone calls in a similar vein, it seemed as though the contact was being terminated.

At the beginning of 1967 we began receiving information that Mahmoud

Khalil was leaking the story of his contacts with Israel. We knew of at least two journalists, one German and one French, who had heard him talk about his contacts with Israel. From these journalists we learned that Mahmoud was giving a distorted account and doctoring the picture for his own purposes. It was patently clear that by leaking these stories he was trying to create a safety-net for himself in case the true story of his contacts with us ever leaked out from other sources.

A last attempt

My last contact with Mahmoud Khalil was in May 1967, during the days of 'The Waiting Period' (when most of the Israeli Army was mobilized but was on hold before the outbreak of hostilities that turned into the Six-Day War). On 19 May 'R' transmitted a very urgent message from me to Khalil through the head of the same commercial company. I expressed my fears to Khalil about the rapid deterioration of the situation, as troops were being called up on both sides of the border. I proposed immediately setting up a direct line of communication between the two sides, in order to facilitate some form of negotiation and attempt to decrease the military build-up on both sides.

This represented one more attempt to take advantage of the connection that had been set up with Mahmoud Khalil, and to use it to transmit a clear message in the hope that it would be delivered directly to Nasser. The representative from the commercial company took the matter very seriously, and made an appointment to meet Mahmoud Khalil that night in Cairo, but to no avail. Seven days later, Gamal Abdul Nasser declared the blockade on the Straits of Tiran, and the rest, as they say, is history.

CONCLUSIONS

Several decades have passed since these events took place. As a result they can now be examined from a far wider perspective, and perhaps some conclusions can be drawn.

I must admit that at no point during the entire operation did I feel that the contact with Mahmoud Khalil, and even the possible visit and meeting with Amer and Nasser, were a hard and fast guarantee of 'salvation'. There were then – and still are now – fundamental conflicts of interest between Egypt and ourselves, and the road to true peace has remained a long and difficult one. Indeed, it has taken two more wars to convince ourselves and each other that, in spite of everything, it was possible to build some kind of bridge to span the differences that separated us. However, the story I have told here is a classic case of the role of intelligence in a peace process.

It is generally believed that intelligence always works 'against' the enemy: gathering and assessing information, mounting operations aimed at putting an end to terrorism, etc., etc. But this is only part of the picture, and not a very accurate one at that. An important aspect of the intelligence services' duties is positive and constructive; action 'for' and not 'against'. In fact, intelligence serves as a kind of undercover Foreign Ministry. It maintains close contacts with countries with which we have no formal relations; it offers aid to minorities in the Middle East that we have an interest in strengthening, and much more. Furthermore, we might say, somewhat metaphorically, that if you want to swim forward, occasionally, when a storm is raging and the waves are too high, you have to dive under the surface in order to make headway. The road to a different Middle East is, to a great extent, paved by intelligence contacts.

It is no accident that the meeting between Egyptian Foreign Minister Touhami and Israeli Foreign Minister Dayan took place in Morocco under the auspices of the King.[13] We were already well established there and had no problem whatsoever in preparing such a meeting. But at the same time, things must be kept in perspective. These special contacts are not a cure-all for our problems. They are breakthroughs, and create a constructive atmosphere, but they cannot replace direct negotiations, international pressure, and so on.

This is why I find the claims made by the 'new historians' somewhat ludicrous. They insist that Israel threw away a chance for peace with Egypt in the 1950s, when, through our old friend Tzadek, a direct channel of communication to Nasser was opened up, and we did not know how to take advantage of it properly. This is a distorted, limited view of the events and, if I may say so, also somewhat childish.

The contact with Mahmoud Khalil was much more significant than any other contact we had ever had before. Nevertheless, despite the fact that because of the 'Wars of the Jews'[14] the contact was severed, I don't for a moment believe that this contact alone contained the seeds of peace. It certainly could have been one important course of bricks in the edifice of peace, but when all is said and done, it was no more than a channel through which it might have been possible to communicate the substantive issues that can form the basis for true negotiations.

We live in a turbulent region. Nothing in this part of the world resolves itself quietly, and no amount of magic incantation can help. From a historical perspective, we are in the midst of a trying, ongoing process that has its ups and downs. It is a constant uphill battle, requiring a great deal of strength, much creative thinking and boundless patience.

For myself, I am happy that I had the opportunity to be a part of this effort and to do my share to help move the process forward. I learned a great deal from it, and drew many important conclusions. But more than anything else, I was pleased with what I did, and my own sense of satisfaction was my reward.

Despite the fact that in the end this operation did not achieve its objectives, it generated many highly effective byproducts. The very fact that Mahmoud Khalil, our No.1 enemy, sat across the table from us and turned out to be a perfectly normal human being was in itself meaningful. Moreover, it was a prime demonstration of the fact that apart from wars and constant confrontations ways do exist to solve problems between nations. Anyone who is able to lend a hand to these efforts must answer the call. We need much patience, a great deal of openness and courage grounded not in narrow-minded provincialism but rather broad horizons, a belief in the justice of our ways, persistence and total devotion to our objective. If we take this path, we can look ahead to a better and more peaceful future.

NOTES

1. In an attempt to drive a wedge between both the United States and Britain, and Egypt, a dormant Israeli espionage team in Egypt was activated and ordered to sabotage American and British institutions in Cairo to make it look as though it had been the work of Egyptian extremists. The action was bungled and the ring was caught. Two of its members were hanged, and the others sentenced to extended prison terms. No one in the Israeli political establishment took direct responsibility for giving the order to activate the ring, and the question of 'who gave the order' became an explosive issue in Israeli politics, leading to a futile commission of inquiry, the resignation of Defence Minister Pinhas Lavon, and, later, to Prime Minister David Ben Gurion's demonstrative retirement to the Negev kibbutz of Sdeh Boker, and recriminations on all sides of the Israeli political scene well into the 1960s.

2. Shalom Rabinowitz (1859–1916), one of the greatest, if not the greatest, of all Yiddish writers of the nineteenth century, whose descriptions of Jewish life in Eastern Europe are among the great classics of Jewish literature.

3. *Translator's note*: A highly controversial plan, proposed by US State Department water expert Eric Johnstone in 1954, for diverting the waters of the Jordan River in a water-sharing scheme between Israel, Jordan and Syria. Israel refused to accept the equal-parts sharing agreement, and the plan was never implemented.

4. The reference is to Ze'ev Gur Aryeh, a.k.a. Wolfgang Lotz, a German-born Israeli (Jewish mother, Christian father) who came to Palestine in 1933, fought in the Israeli Army during the War of Independence in 1948, then was recruited by Army Intelligence to penetrate Egypt's rocket manufacturing operation. Disguised as 'Wolfgang Lotz', a Nazi sympathizer and wealthy horse-fancier, he set up a breeding ranch for horses, and hobnobbed with Egyptian high society, acquiring important information on the German rocket scientists who had been hired to develop Egyptian ballistic missile capabilities. Known for his lavish spending, the 'Champagne Spy' was uncovered by the Egyptian authorities

in the early 1960s, and tried for spying. Throughout his trial he stuck to his cover story, and was spared a death sentence after doubts were raised about his 'Israeli' identity owing to the fact that he was not circumcised. He was eventually sentenced to life imprisonment and exchanged in the POW exchanges with Egypt in the aftermath of the Six-Day War.

5. One of Israel's leading banking institutions.

6. The narrow mouth where the Gulf of Eilat meets the Red Sea. Control over these straits meant control over all shipping in and out of Eilat. The seizure of the islands, Snapir and Tiran, in the centre of this passage-way by the Egyptians in 1967 was the causus belli that prompted the Six-Day War.

7. The military arm of the PLO.

8. Isser Harel preceded Amit as head of the Mossad. He became famous principally for the operation he headed to locate and kidnap Adolf Eichmann from Argentina and bring him to trial in Israel in 1960.

9. A major campaign was mounted by Harel against the German rocket experts who had begun working in Egypt in the late 1950s in an attempt to develop a locally produced Egyptian ground-to-ground missile.

10. Pinhas Sapir – Minister of Finance; Israel Galili – Minister of Information and long-time ideologue of the Labour Party; Aryeh Levavi – Director-General of the Foreign Ministry; Zalman Aranne – Minister of Education, and member of a small circle of close advisers to the Prime Minister.

11. Abie Nathan, a long-time philanthropist and peace advocate, flew on his own to Cairo in a light plane in 1966 as a provocative act in support of peace between the two countries. He was imprisoned briefly and subsequently released by the Egyptian authorities, and sent back to Israel.

12. The letter is quoted here verbatim, in its original form. The terms CIF and FOB are borrowed from the field of trade and commerce. CIF means the price of a product delivered to the customer's destination. FOB means the price of the product at the port of origin. In this case the terms relate to Israel's response to Egypt's offer for a meeting in Cairo. Israel asked for a change of venue from Cairo to Athens. This, according to General Amit, was a direct insult to the Egyptians. It spurned Egyptian hospitality and was an expression of distrust on the part of Israel. H.K. are the true initials of the person who appears in the article as Steve. His true name cannot be disclosed due to security considerations. M.K. is Mahmoud Khalil.

13. The meeting took place in the summer of 1977, and is generally regarded as the turning point in President Sadat's decision to come to Israel in November of that year, and begin the peace process between the two countries.

14. The reference is to the internecine conflicts that preceded the destruction of the Second Temple, as described by Jewish historian Josephus Flavius (Yoseph Ben Matityahu) in his famous *The Wars of the Jews*. The saying is used by Israelis today to describe self-destructive squabbles and rivalries among Jews.

Index

Allied and Axis Signals Intelligence in World War II

David Alvarez, *Saint Mary's College of California* (Ed)

In the 25 years since the revelation of the so-called 'Ultra Secret', the importance of codebreaking and signals intelligence in the diplomacy and military operations of World War II has become increasingly evident. Studies of wartime signals intelligence, however, have largely focused on Great Britain and the United States and their successes against, respectively, the German Enigma and Japanese Purple cipher machines. Drawing upon newly available sources in Australia, Britain, China, France and the United States, the articles in this volume demonstrate that the codebreaking war was a truly global conflict in which many countries were active and successful. They discuss the work of Australian, Chinese, Finnish, French and Japanese codebreakers, shed new light on the work of their American and British counterparts, and describe the struggle to apply technology to the problems of radio intercept and cryptanalysis. The contributions also reveal that, for the Axis as well as the Allies, success in the signals war often depended upon close collaboration among alliance partners.

Contents: Introduction *David Kahn*. A Limited Partnership: Axis Sigint Collaboration *David Alvarez*. Marvelous Machines, a Bit Too Late: Automating American Cryptanalysis 1930–1945 *Colin Burke*. Signals Intelligence in Australia during the Pacific War, *Frank Cain*. New Evidence on Breaking the Japanese Army Codes *Edward Drea and Joseph Richard*. The 'Usual Source': Signals Intellience and Planning for the 'Crusader' Offensive 1941 *John Ferris*. Cautious Collaborators: The Struggle for Anglo-American Cryptanalytic Cooperation 1940–1943 *Lee A Gladwin*. Searching for Security: The German Investigation into Enigma's Security *Rebecca Ratcliff*. New Intelligence Releases: A British Side to the Story *Bradley Smith*. Intelligence in Defeat: Signals Intelligence and Vichy France 1940–1944 *Martin Thomas*. Chinese Codebreakers 1927–1945, *Maochun Yu*.

224 pages 1999 0 7146 4958 9 cloth   0 7146 8019 2 paper
Studies in Intelligence Series
A Special issue of the journal Intelligence and National Security

FRANK CASS PUBLISHERS
Newbury House, 900 Eastern Avenue, Newbury Park, Ilford, Essex IG2 7HH
Tel: +44 (0)181 599 8866 Fax: +44 (0)181 599 0984 E-mail: info@frankcass.com
NORTH AMERICA
c/o ISBS, 5804 NE Hassalo Street, Portland, OR 97213 3644, USA
Tel: 1 800 944 6190 Fax: 503 280 8832 E-mail cass@isbs.com
Website: www.frankcass.com

Intelligence and the Cuban Missile Crisis

David A Welch, *University of Toronto* and **James G Blight**, *Brown University* (Eds)

Intelligence and the Cuban Missile Crisis examines for the first time the role and performance of all three intelligence communities centrally involved in this the world's closest brush with nuclear war. Authored by a distinguished group of practitioners, two of whom had hands-on experience of the crisis, and scholars with unparalleled access to sources.

The ways in which organizational and personality variables affect the political exploitation of intelligence is assessed followed by an analysis of the psychology of intelligence assessment, showing how common cognitive and motivational pathologies can explain crucial errors of inference and attribution made by all three intelligence communities. In closing, the lessons of the volume as a whole are reflected upon for the theory and practice of intelligence assessment, and for our understanding of the Cuban Missile Crisis.

Contributors: Raymond L Garthoff, Aleksandr Fursenko, Timothy Naftali, Domingo Amuchastegui, James J Wirtz, Beth A Fischer, James G Blight and David A Welch.

248 pages 1998
0 7146 4883 3 cloth 0 7146 4435 8 paper
Studies in Intelligence Series
Special issue of the journal Intelligence and National Security

FRANK CASS PUBLISHERS
Newbury House, 900 Eastern Avenue, Newbury Park, Ilford, Essex IG2 7HH
Tel: +44 (0)181 599 8866 Fax: +44 (0)181 599 0984 E-mail: info@frankcass.com
NORTH AMERICA
c/o ISBS, 5804 NE Hassalo Street, Portland, OR 97213 3644, USA
Tel: 1 800 944 6190 Fax: 503 280 8832 E-mail cass@isbs.com
Website: www.frankcass.com

Reuven Shiloah –
The Man Behind the Mossad
Secret Diplomacy in the Creation of Israel
Haggai Eshed

Translated by David and Leah Zinder

Forewords by Shimon Peres and Haim Herzog,

Afterword by Yoav Gelber

> *'An important contribution to our understanding of the early days of Mossad and the Israeli intelligence apparatus.'*
> **Andrew Rathmell, King's College London**

The story of Reuven Shiloah – the man who established the Mossad, and laid the foundations for the intelligence community of the State of Israel – is told here for the first time. Although he was head of the Mossad for only two years, from its inception in April 1951 until his resignation in March 1953, Shiloah was an institution in himself, and through the organisation that he created, he left his imprint on Israeli intelligence, playing a critical role in the complex and crisis-laden history of the establishment of Israel's formidable intelligence network. Shiloah manoeuvred his way skilfully around the grey world of undercover negotiations for three momentous decades, from his induction at the beginning of the 1930s until his untimely death in 1959 at the age of 49.

This book is the most comprehensive portrayal of one of Israel's most esoteric characters and will enlighten and often surprise even well-versed readers of early Israeli history. It is based on documents from private archives – many of which are published here for the first time – and interviews with people who worked closely with Shiloah both in Israel and abroad.

368 pages, illus 1997
0 7146 4812 4 cloth   0 7146 4361 0 paper

FRANK CASS PUBLISHERS
Newbury House, 900 Eastern Avenue, Newbury Park, Ilford, Essex IG2 7HH
Tel: +44 (0)181 599 8866 Fax: +44 (0)181 599 0984 E-mail: info@frankcass.com
NORTH AMERICA
c/o ISBS, 5804 NE Hassalo Street, Portland, OR 97213 3644, USA
Tel: 1 800 944 6190 Fax: 503 280 8832 E-mail cass@isbs.com
Website: www.frankcass.com

British Military Intelligence in the Crimean War, 1854–1856

Stephen M Harris

This is the first scholarly work to focus purely on British military intelligence operations during the Crimean War. It details the beginnings of the intelligence operations as a result of the British Commander Lord Raglan's need for information on the enemy. Charles Cattley, the recently expelled British Consul at the Crimean port of Kertch, supplied intelligence on Sevastopol's garrison, on Russian strength, dispositions and reinforcements throughout the Crimea. This system of long-range espionage and prisoner interrogation helped to ensure that the Allies were never caught off guard for the remainder of the war, and also directed their blows with some precision, thus paving the way to victory. This work demonstrates that intelligence was a fundamental part of the Crimean War and also that this war forms a significant chapter in the history of British intelligence.

212 pages, illus 1999   0 7146 4671 7 cloth
Studies in Intelligence Series

The Norwegian Intelligence Service 1945–1970

Olav Riste, *Norwegian Institute for Defence Studies, University of Oslo*

This work is the first history of a Western intelligence service in the Cold War written by an independent historian with full access to the archives of the service. This history of the Norwegian Intelligence Service (NIS) during the Cold War is the result of a unique enterprise: for the first time a Western intelligence service has opened its most secret archives from this period to two independent historians. The book describes a service which grew from a handful of specialists in 1946 to a multifaceted organisation with a personnel of about one thousand by the end of the 1960s. The author's assessment is that the NIS was 'Norway's perhaps most significant contribution to the strength and security of the Western alliance in this crucial period of post-war history.'

256 pages 1999 0 7146 4900 7 cloth   0 7146 4455 2 paper
Studies in Intelligence Series

Eternal Vigilance?
50 Years of the CIA

Rhodri Jeffreys-Jones, *University of Edinburgh* and
Christopher Andrew, *University of Cambridge* (Eds)

'Uniformly well informed and thoughtful. Provocative and instructive...'
Choice

'A fascinating book.'
The Washington Times

No single volume can seek to cover all, or even most of the CIA's diverse activities during its first fifty years. *Eternal Vigilance?* seeks to offer reinterpretations of some of the major established themes in CIA history such as its origins, foundations, its treatment of the Soviet threat, the Iranian revolution and the accountability of the agency. The book also opens new areas of research such as foreign liaison, relations with the scientific community, use of scientific and technical research and economic intelligence. The editors have sought to include in this volume articles by both well-known scholars in the field and young researchers at the beginning of their academic careers. Contributors come almost equally from both sides of the Atlantic. All draw, to varying degrees, on recently declassified documents and newly-available archives and, as the final chapter seeks to show, all point the way to future research.

248 pages   1997
0 7146 4807 8 cloth 0 7146 4360 2 paper
Studies in Intelligence Series
Special issue of the journal Intelligence and National Security

FRANK CASS PUBLISHERS
Newbury House, 900 Eastern Avenue, Newbury Park, Ilford, Essex IG2 7HH
Tel: +44 (0)181 599 8866 Fax: +44 (0)181 599 0984 E-mail: info@frankcass.com
NORTH AMERICA
c/o ISBS, 5804 NE Hassalo Street, Portland, OR 97213 3644, USA
Tel: 1 800 944 6190 Fax: 503 280 8832 E-mail cass@isbs.com
Website: www.frankcass.com

British Military Intelligence in the Palestine Campaign 1914–1918

Yigal Sheffy, *Tel Aviv University*

Shortly after the First World War, General Sir George Macdonogh, wartime British Director of Military Intelligence, revealed that Lord Allenby's victory in Palestine had been certain because every one of his opponents' cards was known; Allenby was consequently able to play his own hand with perfect assurance. This book tells for the first time how such an astonishing achievement came about. Drawing on extensive British archival documentation as well as Ottoman and German sources, Yigal Sheffy presents the development, operations and contribution of British military intelligence to the campaign against the Ottoman Empire on the Egyptian and Palestinian front during the war, placing it in regional context and historical perspective.

408 pages, maps 1998 0 7146 4677 6 cloth 0 7146 4208 8 paper
Studies in Intelligence Series

Espionage: Past, Present, Future?

Wesley K Wark, *University of Toronto* (Ed)

'.. *a useful contribution for the historian and political scientist alike. These essays are well researched and documented, and insightful.*'
War in History

'*very interesting and worthwhile collection of essays.*'
Journal of Strategic Studies

Highlights of the volume include pioneering essays on the methodology of intelligence studies by Michael Fry and Miles Hochstein, and the future perils of the surveillance state by James Der Derian. Two leading authorities on the history of Soviet/Russian intelligence, Christopher Andrew and Oleg Gordievsky, contribute essays on the final days of the KGB. Also, the mythology surrounding the life of World War II intelligence chief, Sir William Stephenson, 'The Man Called Intrepid', is penetrated in a persuasive revisionist account by Timothy Naftali. The collection is rounded off by a series of essays devoted to unearthing the history of the Canadian intelligence service.

166 pages 1994
0 7146 4515 X cloth 0 7146 4099 9 paper
Studies in Intelligence Series
A special issue of the journal Intelligence and National Security

The Nili Spies

Anita Engle
With an Introduction by Peter Calvocoressi

'This book is a well-merited tribute to an organisation which in the First World War rendered valuable service in the British cause; in particular it is the record of a gifted and gallant family who initiated and worked that organisation and sacrificed their lives for it.'   **The Observer**

'..outside Zionist circles the story of how a small and valiant group of Jewish settlers in Palestine worked as spies for the British, with decisive results, has never become widely known. The names of Aaron and Sarah Aaronsohn are not household ones. In this book Anita Engle does them belated justice.'   **The Daily Telegraph**

An extraordinary tale, much-neglected by historians, of courage, bravery and eventual tragedy which took place during the First World War in the Middle East. It is the story of a small group of people, of whom Sarah and Aaron Aaronsohn were the core, who were devoted to the Yishuv, the Jewish community in Palestine, and who were convinced that it was in imminent danger of extinction from the Turks.

256 pages   1997   0 7146 4803 5 cloth   0 7146 4293 2 paper

Intelligence Investigations
How Ultra Changed History

Ralph Bennett

'In the distorting and self-referential discourse of academic intelligence studies Bennett's is a compelling if awkward voice of sanity.'   **Intelligence and National Security**

Military intelligence, grossly neglected in the pre-war period, had by mid-1942 proved itself indispensable through its gathering of information from radio messages coded in the supposedly unbreakable German Enigma Cipher. Ralph Bennett, who worked for four years at Bletchley Park as a senior producer of the intelligence ('Ultra') derived from the Enigma decrypts, illustrates in this collection some of the steps by which he and others developed the new type de-crypting system and in the process provides a candid glimpse of the workings of British intelligence both past and present.

216 pages   1996   0 7146 4742 X cloth   0 7146 4300 9 paper
Studies in Intelligence Series

Nothing Sacred
Nazi Espionage Against the Vatican, 1939–1945

David Alvarez, *St Mary's College of California* and
Revd. Robert A Graham, *late historian on Civilita Cattolica*

' .. *a lucid and fascinating analysis of Nazi attempts to understand Vatican
strategies during WWII.*'   **Choice**

'*Written by the leading authorities on Vatican history, David Alvarez and
Robert A. Graham, SJ,* Nothing Sacred: Nazi Espionage Against the
Vatican 1939-1945 *not only provides fascinating reading for those interested
in World War II history, intelligence studies, and the history of the Roman
Catholic Church but contributes to illuminating a 'missing dimension' to the
history of that conflict.*'
                    Military and Bravo Veterans Outlook Magazines

Nothing Sacred is the first book to document the Nazi espionage campaign
against the Vatican in the Second World War. Nazi Germany considered
the Catholic Church to be a serious threat to its domestic security and its
international ambitions. In Germany, Hitler's agents recruited informants
to provide intelligence on Church finances, and on the political views
and activities of bishops, priests and lay Catholics. In Rome, however,
German attempts to penetrate the Papacy were less successful, with the
efforts of the local Gestapo office proving largely futile. For example, a
plan to use a Roman seminary as a secret radio station and cover for
German intelligence officers masquerading as seminarians had to be
abandoned, in part because the first group of officers proved more
interested in women than the cloistered life. The German codebreaking
operation on the other hand was highly successful: the Nazis
systematically intercepted, decoded and read secret communications
between the Pope and his representatives world-wide.

208 pages 1997 0 7146 4744 6 cloth   0 7146 4302 5 paper
Studies in Intelligence Series

FRANK CASS PUBLISHERS
Newbury House, 900 Eastern Avenue, Newbury Park, Ilford, Essex IG2 7HH
Tel: +44 (0)181 599 8866 Fax: +44 (0)181 599 0984 E-mail: info@frankcass.com
NORTH AMERICA
c/o ISBS, 5804 NE Hassalo Street, Portland, OR 97213 3644, USA
Tel: 1 800 944 6190 Fax: 503 280 8832 E-mail cass@isbs.com
Website: www.frankcass.com